People don't buy
what you sell
They buy what you stand for

For a complete list of Management Books 2000 titles,
visit our web-site on http://www.mb2000.com

People don't buy
what you sell
They buy what you stand for

Martin Butler

with *Simon Gravatt*

Launch Edition

2000

First published in 2005 by Management Books 2000 Ltd
Forge House, Limes Road
Kemble, Cirencester
Gloucestershire, GL7 6AD, UK
Tel: 0044 (0) 1285 771441
Fax: 0044 (0) 1285 771055
E-mail: info@mb2000.com
Web: www.mb2000.com
Martin Butler can be contacted at martin.butler05@btinternet.com

Printed and bound in Great Britain by 4edge Ltd of Hockley, Essex.

British Library Cataloguing in Publication Data is available
ISBN 1-85252-497-9

Contents

Foreword from John Dean

For the past four years, Martin Butler has played a pivotal role in formulating and developing both the art and science – for it has the ingredients of both – of marketing and branding in the minds of young retail managers attending the annual Oxford Summer School. Martin lives and breathes his profession as the head of a top London advertising agency and it is his dedication, infectious enthusiasm and passion that captivates and inspires these young retailers to learn more about an essential ingredient of their profession.

The concept of brand development and its marketing appears easy at first glance, but as the subject is examined in more depth, it is evident that there is considerable difficulty in grasping many of the core tenets that define and underpin a successful brand and its development. Martin has identified these challenges as a consequence of his speaking at the Summer School and sets out to clarify some of these issues in this very readable book.

Each chapter takes a key theme in retailing and using a well researched case history, based upon interviews with key leaders within the subject organisation, he demonstrates the importance of branding in retail. He brings the subject to life, focusing on the issues that really count, whilst throwing out challenges to the reader to evaluate their own business using the same benchmarks.

More and more businesses today are becoming brands in their own right, indeed every retail business, large or small, that aspires to being really successful must ask the question 'what am I famous for?' Here is a book that will open the eyes and minds of serious and dedicated practitioners within the retail industry, whilst guiding them through the 'minefield' of brand marketing. It is written in a very readable style and is packed full of pithy observations and challenging comments. The reader will find it full of nuggets of advice and guidance and this makes it a 'must have' on any serious retailer's bookshelf.

John Dean
Chief Executive, British Shops and Stores Association

Foreword from Ian McGarrigle

To my mind, retailing has to be one of the most exciting and dynamic business sectors within the British economy. Whatever is happening with consumer spending, the sector continues to innovate, change and adapt.

It also happens to be one of the most competitive sectors there is. To be a retailer is not for the faint-hearted. Despite that, it is significant that those who enter the world of retailing tend to stay in it. Simply, it becomes their passion.

The challenge is very often about attracting people to the industry in the first place. Which brings me on to this book. When Martin first introduced the idea to us, we had no hesitation in backing it and all that it is seeking to promote. Equally, its links with the BSSA's annual summer school, makes this an even worthier project. Anything that can capture the excitement of the industry, which in turn can make new retailers better retailers, has to be a great initiative.

The other reason this book has our support is in its attempt to give focus to one of the key drivers of success in retailing. Retailing is a curious sector in that so many people will tell you that none of the rules of the game are 'rocket science'. Indeed they are not. The two most often quoted of these rules are: 'location, location, location' and the need to have 'the right product in the right place at the right time'.

But even these are easier said than done. And as retailing grows ever more sophisticated, there is another driver that retailers ignore at their peril. That is an understanding of branding. Retailers have to understand what their brand stands for, what their customers expect from it and how it can deliver to its brand values. As a retail adman, this has always been Martin's mantra as you would expect. But he is right. This book demonstrates this, as do all the case studies of today's successful retail businesses.

Retail competition will only grow fiercer. This book acts as a handbook to retailers seeking to understand how they secure and then maintain that all-important competitive edge.

Ian McGarrigle
Editorial Director, Retail Week

Dedication

To Mum & Dad, who have shown me that every good retailer can learn something from the corner shop. Thank you for everything, I couldn't have written this book without you.

Introduction
The Inspiration of Oxford

It's a fresh August morning. There's a gentle buzz of enthusiasm as the students make their way through the hallowed entrance of Keble College. On days like this, few places in the world compare with Oxford.

I feel a surge of adrenalin as I find myself standing alongside Neil Kennedy, one of the country's foremost retail experts, preparing myself to address future captains of British retail. How on earth did I, the son of a couple of Strawberry Hill shopkeepers, get here? Thirty-five years after skipping a university education to start my career with the Metropolitan Police, I find myself addressing three hundred of retail's brightest prospects on marketing and branding. I've never been paid to work in retail, just fifteen or so years helping out Mum and Dad in their hardware shop and yet here I am lecturing fast track retail graduates on how to do their jobs. What do I know?

One thing I know for sure, having done this for a few years now, is that bright-eyed enthusiasm is about to be replaced by frustration and incomprehension. The Marketing day is sandwiched between Finance and Business Planning. Yesterday they spent a day on Finance. They'd been dreading it and ended up loving it. To their surprise they found it easier than expected. Unlike Marketing, it's based on clear rules and principles. Stay awake, pay attention and you're going to know the answers. Not only that, but it had been well presented by David Meckin, a true expert.

The Marketing day, unlike the Finance Day, had been something they've all been looking forward to from the very moment they were granted a place at BSSA's (British Shops and Stores Association) Oxford Summer School. I watch them take their seats. They've come with clean fingernails (because they're expecting to do some drawing), really sharp pencils and a confidence that they're good at writing headlines. Everyone believes that they're a natural at doing ads. They all know what a good ad looks like, how ads work and how to construct them. Everyone has friends who tell them they're good at puns, and so they're fairly confident that a pretend ad will be a doddle. I know, as I wait for them to settle down, that we're about to disappoint them.

The day they've been looking forward to for a bit of light relief is about to prove considerably more difficult than expected. Stan Kaufman, retailer extraordinaire, Chairman of the Oxford Summer School and some might say its heartbeat, introduces the marketing day. Stan prides himself on already knowing most of the three hundred delegates by name. He's a true people person, genuinely interested in their welfare and development, just as he concerned himself with the well-being of every single one of the many thousands of retail staff he led until his retirement a couple of years ago. Unless you've a few hours to spare, don't ask Stan to explain the purpose of the school (it's 'by the trade for the trade' he would say, only in not so few words. He's passionate about it. Really passionate).

It's only right that Stan should make the introductions on this particular day. He's the personification of the Summer School brand and a major inspiration for this book. Straight after the introduction the delegates are going to get a little bit of theorising from Neil and then, as a real live adman, I'm going to talk them through the Oddbins case study that's featured in this book. After that they're on their own with the challenge to find a differentiated position for a new retail concept. And they have to complete it by the end of the day otherwise they don't get to enjoy the bar that evening.

Why do they find it so difficult? The simple answer is that it is difficult. A group of professional marketers would understand the issues, but would still find it near impossible to come up with a truly differentiated and compelling proposition in an afternoon's work. But it's doubly difficult for these guys. They may manage a region of shops for a national retail chain, head up a large B&Q warehouse or work as a buyer of underwear for M&S. Whatever their job their day-to-day is not about marketing, their day-to-day will tend to be focussed on the merchandise. They've never really had to consider what their company stands for. Marketing, they've always assumed, is all about promoting sales items or helping shift stock. It comes as something of a revelation for them to see their company through a branding perspective and for them to begin to understand the importance of centring a retail organisation around a clearly defined and well-articulated brand idea.

The purpose of my day in Oxford is to explain to them that while merchandising is hugely important, something else is probably a little more important. Anyone who doubts this should take a look at Starbucks. For sixteen years they worried about their coffee. For the next sixteen years they worried about their brand. Product-centric Starbucks grew to six stores. Brand-centric Starbucks grew to more than six thousand.

All I want these students to do is open their minds to branding. Not intellectual, highfalutin branding, but the kind of down-to-earth branding that works for retailers. And that's the purpose of this book. I don't have the answers – branding isn't black and white like finance. I'm just putting across a point of view and some thoughts that I hope will help you look at your world in a slightly different way.

I've included a 'behind-the-scenes' look at some of the most well defined, in branding terms, retailers in the country to help demonstrate how important it is to know what you stand for and to own a distinctive position in your marketplace.

The reason I'm writing this book is that not enough retailers give branding enough credence. To them, it's a dark art practiced by the likes of Unilever and Proctor & Gamble and has no place on the shop floor. Although I've never had a paid job in retail, I know enough about it to realise this is a dangerously Luddite attitude. The twenty-first century differs from its predecessor in that we are now a service rather than a manufacturing economy. Retail will increasingly become a battleground of ideas where basic trading skills alone will not be enough. Retailers need to know what they stand for in order to present a persuasive enough reason for their customers to turn left out of their front door to come to their shop rather than turn right to one of their competitors.

I have made my career from advising and working with retailers. I soon realised the police force wasn't for me and left to become a media buyer in an international advertising agency, a job that allowed me to exercise some of the negotiating skills I had picked up from the shop floor of my parents' hardware store. Not long after that, I made Sir Hugh Fraser of House of Fraser an offer he couldn't refuse and found myself planning and buying all his media whilst still in my mid-twenties. From this start in media, I found myself naturally drawn into the world of marketing and advertising and have been advising retailers ever since. The longer I've been doing it the more certain I've become that, first and foremost, people buy what a retailer stands for. Only after they've bought into the retailer and decided that 'this is my kind of shop', will they be in the right mindset to think about the merchandise.

I hope that by the end of this book you'll agree with me, but even if you don't, I would like to think that my words have given you pause for thought and some ideas that will help improve you as a retailer.

A Few Words of Thanks

To my mother and father for putting retail into my blood and lovingly teaching me first principles. The BSSA, and its Chief Executive John Dean, for giving me the opportunity and encouragement to give something back. Retail Week for their unstinting support and for being the voice of reason for the trade. Everyone - Gennaro Castaldo, Tristia Clark, Tim Danaher, Neill Denny, Helen Dickinson, Jo Farrelly, Philip Green, Terry Green, Richard Hyman, Maureen Johnson, Stan Kaufman, David Roth, Ian McGarrigle, Steven Sharp, Jane Shepherdson, David Simons, John Taylor, Peter Williams, Dan Wilkinson, Andrew Woodward – who have generously given their time and thoughts towards this book. All the retailers I've ever worked with, every one of you has helped me know what I know today.

To Mark Brandis, the Managing Director at my agency who patiently and more importantly politely acted as a great sounding board and to my assistant Shirley for her unstinting help. Thanks also to Patrick from my agency for his fabulous cover designs and innovative page layouts – he is one of the most talented designers I have ever worked with and Will, our studio manager – an absolute wizard on the mac.

To my wife Judy for her enthusiasm and encouragement to do this book and for allowing the light on in bed for proof reading.

And finally to Simon Gravatt – an incredible wordsmith with an unbelievable turn of phrase and enquiring mind. He not only ordered my ramblings but brought sense and clarity where there was only emotion and subjectivity. I would like to think he has made this reference book a light, easy read, yet challenging enough to be informative and worthwhile. I hope you all agree.

1

People Buy What You Stand For

What this chapter covers

- This chapter proposes the case that's at the heart of the book, namely that people don't buy what you sell; they buy what you stand for.

- It will explain why, when choosing to turn right to come to your shop rather than turning left to your competitor's, your customer is making a retail brand choice.

- It will argue that the rules of the retail game are changing, that while the last decade has been about controlling costs and increasing scale, the strategic focus of the next ten years will be on adding value, brand value.

- It will help you understand what the company you work for stands for by posing the six essential questions that every retailer needs to ask.

Make your customers weep

The headline of a local evening paper in Middlesex in 1995 read, *Customers weep as shopkeeper retires.* The story continued,

'Customers broke down in tears this week after a Strawberry Hill shopkeeper announced his retirement, ending 36 years of trading in the village. Jack Butler, aged 70, decided it was time to sell his hardware shop in Wellesley Road, so that he and his wife could enjoy their later years 'relaxing, playing golf and fishing'. But news of Mr Butler's retirement has devastated regular customers – some of whom have been using Butler's Hardware since it opened in 1959 – who describe him as so much more than a shopkeeper, more a friend.'

The relationship a retailer has with his or her customers is special. People who don't work in retail struggle to understand this. Retailers themselves all too often don't get it, assuming it's all about what rather than how they sell.

Retail is a people business. For sure, customers pay their money for whatever it is that you, the retailer, sells to them, but there's so much more to the relationship than this exchange. The transaction is simply the final affirmation that the customer buys into what the retailer stands for.

Jack Butler is my father. When he retired he expressed surprise at the warmth he received,

> *'I was amazed by the reaction of customers to my retirement.*
> *I guess you don't realise how popular you are until a time like this.'*

Retail is so relentless that it can be difficult to see what's really going on. The demands of servicing the daily needs of your customers, of ensuring you've got the right level of stock, of balancing the books, of anticipating what you might need to buy for the future, of keeping your staff happy and motivated, all these and many many more pressures conspire to take your eye off the bigger picture. The bigger picture that involves the relationship that your customers have with your shop and why they choose to come to you than go elsewhere. As my father only really understood when he retired, his customers were, first and foremost, buying into him and what he stood for when they walked through the door of Butler's Hardware in Strawberry Hill. This is why the shop, that continued to sell much the same merchandise but without the charisma that had sustained it for the previous thirty six years, petered out only eighteen months later and now has a Thai restaurant in its place.

If this book achieves anything, it will be to encourage retailers to lift their nose from the grindstone for a minute and realise that their customers buy into what they stand for more than what they sell.

I can't guarantee that your customers will weep when you retire, but an understanding of what's really going on is likely to lead to better, deeper relationships and a more successful business.

! **Key point** *People pay for what you sell, but buy what you stand for. The transaction is simply the final affirmation that your customer buys into what you as a retailer stand for.*

A bear of little brain

'People don't buy what you sell.'
To say such a thing is sacrilege to a retailer.
'Of course they buy what you sell,' he will contend,
'if they don't, then what are they buying?'

As far as many retailers are concerned the merchandise is everything. Without product to sell, they haven't got a business. The product, be it mobile phones at Carphone Warehouse, wine at Oddbins or power drills at B&Q, is what the retailer sells. But it's not necessarily what the customer buys. At least, it's not all that the customer buys.

In a world of plenty, and a land of duplication, the brand is a guiding force that helps people choose. If your customers can buy virtually identical items from many different places, you have to ask why are they going to choose your shop. This is where the retail brand comes in.

At the end of the day, I may only be an adman who could never pretend to know as much about retail as someone working at its coalface. But, in the same way that AA Milne's Pooh, a bear of little brain, was capable of the occasional blinding insight, I do know people choose where to shop much as they choose anything else. Gut reaction, empathy, feelings – call it what you want. It's a decision that's rooted in emotions and heavily influenced by what the retailer stands for.

Perhaps I should say a little more about my credentials. (I know if I leave it that I'm simply an adman, I'm going to have an uphill battle convincing you of anything).

I was brought up over a shop. My formative years revolved around my parents' hardware shop in Strawberry Hill and latterly I've made a good living by providing advertising and marketing services to retailers. I've spent my whole life on the edges of retail, as an outsider looking in. Although I've never been a retailer, I can justly claim to have been involved in it for a good forty-five of my fifty-five years. It's long enough to begin to understand why people shop in the way that they do and what goes on in their head when they become a customer of yours.

It's said to be difficult to see the sea that we swim in: only when you step out of the water and look at something from a distance do you get the whole picture. My vantage point on the surface level of retail gives me a perspective that's not always obvious to those fully immersed in it. There's plenty I don't know about retail. I don't, for example, know much about the intricacies of stock-management systems. I don't have half the talent, the instinct or knowledge of those retailers who are featured in this book. But I have something else. I have a slightly different perspective. It's a perspective that's been informed by a career of helping retailers (of every different hue) attract and keep customers. And also, sadly, from having witnessed the demise of too many retailers who haven't acknowledged the fundamental changes now taking place. Trying to simply trade their way out of their situation rather than cleverly retail their way to success. I've learnt as much from having to work with once great retailers who, to their cost, haven't been prepared to listen (to their customers or to the market) as I have from the success stories.

And, it bears repeating, the one thing I know above all else is that people don't just buy what you sell, they buy what you stand for. Understand this and you have a better chance of success in the brave new world of retail; deny it and you risk getting left behind with manual cash tills and other obsolete retail concepts. It's no longer good enough to be a trader; you have to be a retailer.

Life in a service world

Britain was always said to be a nation of shopkeepers. We were also supposed to rule the waves. But the world has moved on. The Empire is now more readily thought of as a celluloid creation of George Lucas, as memories of a proud imperial age fade away. The notion of 'keeping shop' has become somewhat anachronistic and conjures up images of a time when a grocer's daughter became Prime Minister and Ronnie Barker was open all hours. Nowadays, with the decline in our manufacturing base, we have become a service economy. As far as our GDP is concerned, intangibles count for more than tangibles. Service contributes more than product. Even the term 'Gross Domestic Product' is beginning to show its age.

It's no longer enough to build a better mousetrap and wait for the world to beat a path to your door. You can't just keep shop and let the product sell itself because, before you know it, someone down the road will have a better, cheaper mousetrap with more gizmos on it. They'll be selling it with style, service and guarantees. They'll make the act of executing rodents seem fun and they'll emotionally engage with you, promising a better mouse-free life forever more. You'll need something more to entice the mousetrap buying public to give you their custom. That something more has everything to do with making them feel good about you, the seller, and what you have to offer. You need your customers and potential customers to feel that your store is their kind of store. You need to stand for something that they value and can relate to. You want them to feel at home when they walk through your shop door.

Why is it, when you could turn right out of your front door to buy something from Shop X, that you choose to turn left to buy the very same thing from Shop Y? In a world where you can increasingly buy identical items in different shops, how do you decide where to go? It has to be influenced by more than the product itself because that product will have largely become commoditised.

People who want to buy a bottle of wine, for example, will choose to go to Oddbins rather than their local supermarket, or the Threshers over the road, because they feel it's their kind of place. Whether consciously or not, they're buying into what Oddbins stands for, quirky individualistic wine expertise. A different customer might choose to buy that very same bottle in Tesco for the convenience, value and customer commitment that Tesco stand for. Oddbins and Tesco in this instance are selling exactly the same product, but the customer is choosing between two completely different brand propositions.

To argue that people buy what you sell is like saying we live to breathe air. It's undeniably true, but there's so much more to life.

> **!** **Key question** *Why is it, when your customer can turn left out of the door to buy something from your competitor, that they choose to turn right to buy the very same thing from you? You need to be able to answer this. If you can't, then pretty soon you'll find that your customers begin to turn away from you.*

My good friend David Simons, Chairman of Littlewoods Shop Direct Group and previously Chief Executive of Somerfield, points out that the influence of the retail brand will vary from category to category. A Fat Face or Monsoon shopper, he contends, is more likely to be prepared to travel further to get to their favoured shop than, say, someone buying groceries. But, even in a lower interest category such as food where the majority of shoppers are likely to choose their nearest supermarket, close to one in three shoppers would drive past one supermarket to go to their store of choice. According to David Simons,

'The last piece of research I saw was that 25 to 30% of people would drive past some large supermarkets to get to another large supermarket.'

Thirty percent is a significant chunk of business. It's the difference between success and failure. If that's the power of the brand in a low interest category, just imagine what it is in the higher interest categories.

Maybe I'm labouring the point, but it's important because I'm not convinced that all retailers see it. 'Retail is detail,' they'll say, as they busily stack shelves while the big picture passes them by. Attending to the detail is necessary, you can't operate without it, but you need to see the bigger picture. There's no point in having immaculately presented full shelves and brilliant stock control if your store is empty, because all your potential customers decided to turn right to go to another store rather than left to come to yours.

The meaning of retail

The word retail originates from the fourteenth century French verb, which means 'to cut off'. Retail is all about the margin: the difference between the price you pay for an item and the price you sell it for. This is the raison d'etre of retailing. If you can't make a turn on that item, or, in other less prosaic words, add value to it, then you're not a retailer: you won't have a business, you'll have a charity.

The task of the retailer is to get the most leverage out of the margin. To me, there seem to be four prime ways of doing this.

1. Minimise price bought in

2. Maximise price sold at

3. Maximise sales in store

4. Maximise sales by increasing stores

1. Minimise price bought in

Wal-Mart are masters of squeezing every last little bit of blood out of their suppliers in order to deliver rock-bottom prices to their customers. They leverage their enormous buying power to make the economies of scale work to bring the individual item price down to its lowest possible level. Everything Wal-mart does focuses on price.

2. Maximise price sold at

Harrods are good at this. Situated in the heart of moneyed Knightsbridge, and with a global reputation as one of London's iconic destinations, they're comfortably able to charge a premium for most of their merchandise. Their customers know they're paying more, and in a perverse way, that's part of the attraction. They also know that the huge range gives their customers a greater chance of finding what they want and that their customer service will be superior. The Harrods label has an ostentatious quality that touches a chord in our materialistic society. This involves creating an environment where price is not an issue: Harrods marketing seldom plays on price. Everything Harrods do takes focus away from price.

3. Maximise sales in store

In other words, getting more of the right people in through the doors (footfall) and getting more of them to buy more when they're there (conversion). On-line retailer Amazon effectively uses technology (with features such as 'we have recommendations for you' and 'customers who bought items in your shopping cart also bought this') to steer their customers towards additional purchases. Simultaneously, Amazon's 'bricks and mortar' competitors, such as Waterstone's and Borders, are turning their stores into reading zones with comfy sofas and coffee shops to attract more people to spend more time (and money) in their shops.

Every retailer needs to concentrate on the 'look-to-buy' ratio. A furniture retailer may expect his customers to make up to six visits to buy some furniture whereas a burger bar would want a sale from every visit.

4. Maximise sales by increasing stores

Open more stores to repeat the formula. The phenomenal growth of companies like The Carphone Warehouse has been driven by their aggressive store development programme.

The first and the fourth ways tend to concern scale: the first is all about extracting economies of scale and the fourth about increasing scale. The second and third ways are strategies to add value.

The past quarter of a century has seen some spectacular retail growth in this country, but interestingly, as industry analyst Richard Hyman from Verdict observes, most of it has tended to come from increasing scale rather than adding value.

'Until very recently, growth and prosperity for a retail business was determined by the extent to which they had a formula which was scaleable. Because it has been relatively easy to open more stores, most retail growth has been fundamentally driven by physical expansion in the last twenty-five years.'

Hyman went on to speculate that, with reduced opportunities for this kind of growth, retailers will increasingly need to concentrate on adding value.

'I think those days have gone. It doesn't mean that people can't open more shops anymore, it's just that it's much more difficult to do so; the planning laws are much tighter than they were.
The market is reaching a new level of saturation, so the idea of adding value (getting more out of what you've already got) is receiving more attention now. Retailers' understanding of marketing and branding has been poor and really quite primitive. They haven't had to be much good at it. If they were good at property, had a buying team that could drive a hard bargain and had some vague idea of who their customers were, Bob's your Uncle, they've got a growth business. I'm going a bit over the top to make the point but I think that the law of diminishing returns has come in and adding value is going to become much more important.'

This, essentially, is why I'm writing this book. I believe it's critically important for retailers to see beyond the immediate horizon of the product that they sell.

Competitive pressures mean that retailers will increasingly need to get smarter in the way that they position and present themselves; more and more it will become a matter of brain over brawn, because the days of simply being able to muscle competitors out of business will be reduced.

Those retailers who understand that their customers are buying what they stand for as much as what they sell, who think of themselves as a brand rather than a stockist of brands, and who set out to differentiate themselves with a coherent and engaging proposition, are the ones who will win out in the twenty-first century.

Key point *The rules of the retail game are changing. The winners of the future will be those retailers who successfully add value; those who rely too heavily on trading alone will lose out.*

How to know what you stand for?

One of the most popular management trends of the past few years has been for companies to define their mission and values. While I'm a great believer in the principle of a company knowing its purpose and values (it is, after all, at the heart of this book) the problem has been one of poor execution.

In his book *'Smart Retail'*, Richard Hammond bemoans the example of TNT who replaced their 'to deliver every parcel on-time' mission statement with 'service is our only product'.

'What the hell does that mean? Have they given up on delivering parcels, I'm confused?' [1]

A statement of purpose should get to the nub of why that company is in business and where its priorities lie. It should be simple, to the point and true to that company.

These are some of my favourites:

■ To make people happy *(Disney)*

■ To solve unsolved problems innovatively *(3M)*

■ To give ordinary folk the chance to buy the same things as rich people *(Wal-Mart)*

■ To help leading corporations and governments be more successful *(McKinsey)*

All too often management, in their infinite wisdom, try to sum up what their company is about with a load of pretentious and meaningless waffle that has little to do with the reality of their organisation. Not only that, but they do so by using exactly the same words as their competitors, kidding themselves that by putting them in a different order they somehow have a different meaning. The best statements of purpose endure the passage of time and changes of management because they are rooted in the truth of the company. If Christianity has made do with the same Ten Commandments for as long as it has (although arguably it is perhaps finally beginning to look a little tired around the edges), I see no reason why it should be necessary to redefine a company mission, purpose and values every three years or so.

> **❗ Provocation** *Check out your competitors' mission statements on the Internet. If one of them is unique and compelling, go and work for them.*

The secret is to know what you stand for and to express it as simply as possible. I have a short process involving six questions that may help you get to this point with your own company.

Six essential questions that every retailer needs to ask:

1. Where does your company come from?
2. What's it in business for? What's its primary reason for existence?
3. Is there anything that distinguishes it? What makes it special?
4. When it comes down to it, where do its priorities lie?
5. What is the benefit to your customers of buying from you?
6. Can you express it simply?

1. Where does your company come from?

I'm convinced that companies are like mankind in that the template for their character is determined right from the outset. The Jesuit maxim 'Give me a child until he is seven and I will show you the man' can equally be applied, in large measure, to the corporate world. I find the first and often most fruitful place to look in seeking to understand a company is its archives. Find the founding principles and you're halfway there. You'll see from the case histories featured in this book how Ahmed Pochee's (of Oddbins) disrespect of convention, how Gordon Selfridge's flamboyant sense of drama, how John Spedan Lewis's search for a fairer method of capitalism and how David Quayle's (of B&Q) vision all continue to shape and influence their companies even though they themselves are long gone.

To find out what your company stands for, first of all find out where it came from and what the original idea for the business was. More often than not this will contain a clue if not the answer itself.

2. What's your company in business for? What's its primary reason for existence?

Whether the answer is in the archives or not, you need to find out why it's in business in the first place and what is its reason for existence. Neill Denny, former editor of Retail Week, explains this point:

'I don't think a brand can survive indefinitely on looking good or feeling clever. It's got to have something more to it than that. Even a brand like Harrods, which is tarnished at the moment because it's become too trashy and too touristy, still has a place, because it's super luxury and there's a place for super luxury brands. There's still a need for Harrods, so it's got spine to it. Even though it's had a bad ten or fifteen years, it's still there and could easily become the world's pre-eminent super premium brand again. That could happen, with a different management and a new style, because the underlying reason for Harrods to exist is still there.'

Harrods used to overtly play to this positioning with its old slogan such as 'for more than money can buy' or before that, 'enter a different world'.

3. Is there anything that distinguishes your company? What makes it different or special?

IKEA have built a business by changing the rules of furniture retailing. Their idea of selling flat-pack furniture through a system of self-service and self-assembly is radically different from anything else in furniture retailing. It underpins what they stand for; and while I'd struggle to say what MFI stand for, I know that IKEA stand for bringing design and style to the masses by making it affordable and accessible (the democratisation of design). The way they set their stores up and serve their customers all stems from what they stand for.

The issue of differentiation is explored in greater depth later on, but suffice it to say that there are precious few examples of differentiation as obvious as IKEA. Often it's a question of tone and style. HMV, for example, subtly re-enforce their well-defined authority in the music-retailing marketplace with a colour scheme of greys and pinks that denotes a more serious tone than the bright and energetic reds and yellows you'll find in a Virgin store.

4. When it comes down to it, where do your company's priorities lie?

Good branding is all about consistency and coherence. The bedrock of Tesco's success can be seen in their mission and values statement.

Tesco mission statement:
To create value for our customers, to earn their lifetime loyalty.

Tesco values:
- No one tries harder for customers.
- Understand customers better than anyone.
- Be energetic, be innovative and be first for customers.
- Use our strengths to deliver unbeatable value to our customers.
- Look after our people so they can look after our customers.

I'm left in no doubt as to where Tesco's priorities lie and that they stand for 'absolute customer commitment'. While it's a no-brainer for a retailer to put their customers at the centre of everything they do, Tesco have done so with such ruthless rigour and commitment as to be breath-taking. They deserve their success for this alone (although need to be wary of the fair trade issue that is gaining traction and could undermine them. Ironically the very people who they put at the centre of their business could turn around and bite them).

5. What is the benefit to your customers of buying from you?

Your customers don't buy what you sell (the merchandise); they buy what you stand for (your brand). You need to first know what you stand for (answering the previous four questions may help clarify this), but then you need to be able to think about it from your customer's perspective.

Charles Revson of Revlon Cosmetics once said, *'In the factory we make cosmetics, but in the store we sell hope'.* Advertising man David Ogilvy explained, *'a brand is the consumers idea of a product'.* In the case of John Lewis, the benefit to their customers of their unique partnership structure is an integrity that their customers can depend on. It also has the halo effect of helping their customers feel good about themselves because they can reassure themselves that they are making a sensible purchase.

6. Can you express it simply?

As with most things in life, brevity seems harder to come by than complexity. Blaise Pascal famously wrote in 1657, *'I have made this letter longer than usual, only because I have not had time to make it shorter'*[2], a sentiment that management would do well to observe today. Tim Danaher, editor of Retail Week, says,

> *'The best brands don't need to make a song and dance about it – it's not about manuals 60 pages in length. It's about culture and how you run your business.'*

John Sculley, former chairman of Apple Computer, observed, *'I think that more and more people are learning that you have to simplify not complicate. That is a very Asian idea – that simplicity is the ultimate sophistication'*[3]. Nowhere does this apply more than in retail where so many people are involved on so many different levels and dimensions. I like to try and get the essence of what any retailer stands for down to two words.

My favourite example, suggested to me by Mark Taylor, the Planning and Strategy Director at my agency, is covered in the Oddbins case history following this chapter. Everything that matters about Oddbins is expressed in the two words 'unstuffy expertise'.To get it down to two words can require a considerable amount of time and effort. As with a swan gliding over the surface of a pond, you don't see the work that's gone on underneath. You will probably need to write it out longhand first.

For example, 'unstuffy expertise' comes from the sentence 'Oddbins bring together a deep professional knowledge about wine with an informality unusual in a sector that normally prides itself on pomp and ceremony'. This in turn comes from answering the five preceding questions of my process.

In sum

Many retailers have been able to grow their businesses without really having to think about branding their business. This is changing as the retail marketplace reaches saturation. Retailers with shelves full of almost identical products will increasingly need to sell themselves, and therefore their products, on the basis of what they stand for. Anyone working in retail will need to know what their company stands for. Answering the six fundamental questions posed in this chapter will help provide the answer. Any retailer who fails to take his or her brand into their own hands risks losing control of their own destiny. Brand or be branded.

> *If you only remember one thing from this chapter:*
> ———————
> *People pay for what you sell,*
> *but they buy what you stand for.*

References:

1. Richard Hammond, *'Smart Retail. How to turn your store into a sales phenomenon'* Pearson Education Ltd 2003

2. Blaise Pascal, *Lettres Provinciales* (1657)

3. John Sculley, quoted from, *The Power of Simplicity: A Management Guide to Cutting Through the Nonsense and Doing Things Right*, Jack Trout

2

Oddbins: Brand in a Nutshell

The case histories draw from an interview with Dan Wilkinson, former brand manager at Oddbins.

What this case study teaches us

■ This is a story of how a wine entrepreneur indirectly set me on my course in life.

■ This case study illustrates the power of individuality and character. Oddbins is a wonderfully quirky retailer that has survived for so long by doing things in its own way.

■ Oddbins has become a text-book branding case by following its instinct and remaining true to the principles it has always stood for.

■ The primary lesson of Oddbins is one of single-mindedness and how the strongest retail brands tend to be the simplest.

I bought my first bottle of wine some thirty years ago in Oddbins, on the junction between the Kings Road and Oakley Street. While I can't remember why I particularly needed wine at that point, the experience of buying it has had a profound impact on me.

My encounter with Oddbins, at a time in my life when I was training for an entirely inappropriate career with the local constabulary, offered a glimpse into an altogether more sexy and interesting world. I'm sure it's no co-incidence but, not long afterwards, I resigned from the force to join an advertising agency, where I was able to earn a living by working on retail brands like Oddbins (although sadly not Oddbins itself).

I was twenty years old and knew nothing about wine. This was the early 1970s when the height of alcoholic sophistication was a can of Party Seven. Wine was considered a poncey foreign drink. The prospect of having to go into a shop and choose a bottle was intimidating to say the least. I felt sure that all my social inadequacies would be horribly exposed. In fact it proved to be a triumphant experience and I emerged confidently clutching a litre and a half of Valpolicella and having discovered a new life-long obsession. Thirty years later I'm designing my new house around the wine cellar.

Not only are Oddbins responsible in some way for my career in media and my fascination with the fermented grape, but they're also the catalyst for this book. I've been lecturing for some years at BSSA's Oxford University Summer School on retail advertising and use Oddbins as one of the best examples of a well-defined retail brand. The success of applying it as a teaching tool for students of retailing in Oxford has led to my wanting to make it available to a wider audience through this book.

So everything (my career, my hobby and this book) can be traced back to that first encounter with Oddbins.

At the time of my visit, Oddbins had been in business for seven years, having started life in 1963 through entrepreneur Ahmed Pochee flogging bin-end wines off a London barrow. Most of his stock came from speculatively calling recently bereaved widows, whose names he had found by scouring the obituary columns, to generously (and sympathetically) offer to dispose of their late husband's wine cellar.

The origins of any company often cast a die from which its future character and style is determined. The quirky irreverence of Oddbins appears to have been there right from the start.

> **Learning Tip:** *To better understand the company you work for, find out its history. In the fast-moving world of retail, the origins of the brand are often lost in the mists of time. A little bit of archaeological study can reap rich insights.*

Ahmed Pochee sold the business after a few years to Dennis Ing and Nick Baile. While these two astute businessmen were the primary architects of Oddbins success, it should not be forgotten that Mr Pochee bequeathed the brand its two greatest assets: its character and its name.

An oddly effective name

I can't think of a better name for a company. Even today, some forty years after its conception, Oddbins is distinctive, memorable, fun, timeless and slightly, well, odd. It's a great name. Consider what else was on the high street in the Sixties – Hepworths, Waring & Gillow, Lord John. That the

Oddbins name was dreamt up in 1963 – a time when men all wore bowler hats to work; when the height of rebelliousness was to grow collar-length hair and when the orthodoxy was to give your shop the family name and hope one day to suffix it with '& sons' – beggars belief.

The strength of the name is that it perfectly describes the brand. 'Bin' is a technical term in the wine trade for quantities of wine, with 'bin ends' being the wine that is sold at a discounted price. The word Oddbins very succinctly sums up what is being sold: originally it referred to the odds and sods that Pochee had in his barrow; today it describes wine that is out of the ordinary. The promise is something a little different, a little less conventional.

While it's impossible to determine the value of a name, I would be willing to wager that a large part of Oddbins longevity has been down to their nomenclature. Had the company been called Pochee & Partners it is unlikely to have survived, let alone be the subject of a case study in a book on branding.

It's always worth considering what clues to the personality and character of a company lie in its name. John Lewis sounds very straight; Morrisons is suggestive of that company's northern roots and knowing that Tesco was named after Tessa Cohen, the founder's wife, gives a bit more flavour to the company by revealing both its Jewish trading origins and its strong sense of family. It has alternatively been suggested that Tesco's name came from the initials of his business partner, T. E. Stockwell. I prefer to think of his wife as the inspiration.

Part of the problem with the recent fashion for re-naming organisations (most famously the Royal Mail to Consignia) is that it can cut the company from the roots that help define it.

! **Points to consider:** *What does your company's name say about the company? Does it contain any unexploited clues about the personality of the organisation? Is the tone and style of communication consistent with the name?*

I'd love to know how long it took to come up with the name Oddbins. I suspect it was an instinctive decision that felt right at the time. A few years ago, a mobile phone company ran an advertising campaign that asked people to nominate which historical figure they would like to have a one-to-one conversation with. I would be tempted to choose Ahmed Pochee simply to find out how closely he resembled the character and style of the company he spawned.

The essence of Oddbins

I imagine he must have been a bit of a chancer who held little stock in convention or the etiquette of the day. One thing's for sure though: he would have known his wine. It's these two attributes – irreverence and knowledge – that define the company. Oddbins bring together a deep professional knowledge about wine with an informality unusual in a sector that normally prides itself on pomp and ceremony. It's a potent combination.

When looking at a retailer from a branding perspective, it helps to ascertain the essence of the brand. What's the core idea at the heart of that company? What is it that makes it different from its competitors? What defines, distinguishes and drives it? This will be the essence of the brand.

The essence of Oddbins lies in that sentence – *'Oddbins bring together a deep professional knowledge about wine with an informality unusual in a sector that normally prides itself on pomp and ceremony'.*

This can be shorthanded to 'unstuffy expertise'. Everything about Oddbins conforms to the idea of unstuffy expertise.

They don't use flowery wine trade descriptors such *'buttersnaps and toast'* or *'petulant gooseberries'* to describe the flavour of a wine, preferring instead to say that it has a *'stinging fizz'*. They certainly wouldn't use the kind of pretentious language that recently appeared in a Wall Street Journal wine column to describe a simple bottle of Burgundy: *'Rich fruit. Some oak. Nutmeg. Crème brûlée! Toast, carambola, caramel, pineapple, lychee... a fruit bowl inside a soulful wine with weight. Egg custard. Flan.'*

Their shops have a rough and ready wooden feel to them, which is so much less pretentious than the hushed library tones of a typically reverential wine merchant.

The Oddbins staff are all intelligent and articulate about wine. They really do know their stuff, but are never patronising or condescending.

They will tend to be young (although not always), outward, warm and accommodating. In London they've often employed Aussies who are travelling the world and seem to embody the relaxed informal style of Oddbins.

At times it might feel as if you are tripping over wine cases to reach a member of staff, but the reward for doing so will be an intelligent conversation about wine.

! **Key point:** *A brand essence is the core idea that defines, distinguishes and drives a company. The brand essence of Oddbins is, I believe, 'unstuffy expertise'.*

There's a strong sense of accessibility and fun in everything they do. Every point of contact the customer has with Oddbins re-enforces the notion of unstuffy expertise. The graphics, the store designs, the labelling, the logo, the name of the company, the people, everything feeds and perpetuates a virtuous circle.

No rulebook

Interestingly, Oddbins haven't written down or articulated their brand in any way. At the time of this interview, they didn't have a manual or a set of guidelines that prescribes how they should behave, a template of how their shops should look or even how their marketing literature should be written. The knowledge just exists within the culture of the place. Those who get it fit in and stay, those who don't, move on.

I find it quite amazing that a company that has presented itself and gone about its business in such a consistent and coherent way for so long should have done so without any set standards or template. This is very unusual in the world of branding, where high-powered executives can agonise over the fine detail of how a brand should be positioned for months on end before spending millions on turning their words of wisdom into glossy tablets of stone, otherwise known as the brand manual. Somewhat refreshingly, Oddbins have none of this, as their former brand manager, Dan Wilkinson, explains.

'The Oddbins brand has been remarkably consistent, but that is more to do with every member of staff knowing exactly what Oddbins is all about, rather than any kind of centralised plan management. I was the first brand manager that Oddbins has ever had, which is a bit weird if you think about it, but our culture is such that once you start working here you know exactly what it is all about. We didn't need a brand manager, because it was so absolutely crystal clear.'

Oddbins is a textbook branding case study that defies the rules. I suppose this should come as no surprise; Oddbins ignored wine trade conventions, why should it follow marketing conventions?

There is also, I think, a point to be made here about the difference between retail brands and consumer goods (often referred to as FMCG, Fast Moving Consumer Goods) brands. The way we think about brands comes in the main from consumer goods. When we think of the word 'brand' we tend to think in terms of soap powders, baked beans or those products that are frequently advertised on TV. When asked about branding, retailers will tend to think first of the branded products that they are selling before thinking of themselves as a brand. Consumer goods companies like Unilever or Heinz will have battalions of brand managers; retailers might have a marketing manager. Consumer goods companies will intellectualise about their brands; retailers more often than not won't give it a second thought. Consumer goods companies are obsessed about controlling their brand (thus the brand manuals); retailers tend to be much more instinctive and intuitive about it. Because of all this, the branding rulebook has been written by consumer goods companies and is based on an orthodoxy that isn't wholly relevant for retailers.

The lesson of the Oddbins case study is a lesson in retail branding. It doesn't conform to the rules partly because Oddbins tend not to follow rules, but also because the rules aren't necessarily the right rules for retailers.

Strong retail brands have soul, because retail is a people business. I think this is why classically trained FMCG marketers often struggle when they make the move into retail. They don't seem to have quite the same soul that someone brought up on retail has.

Odd graphics

The carrier bag – something that isn't even a consideration for consumer goods brand managers – is one of the most important brand symbols for the retailer. As Dan Wilkinson acknowledges, it promotes the relationship between the customer and the retailer in a very public way.

> *'What really turns people on to buying wine from Oddbins is purely and simply the brand. It's the fact that people will happily take an Oddbins carrier bag with some bottles in it round to someone's house, whereas if the wine had been bought in Tesco, the bag would be in the bottom of the bin.'*

This is not to say that an Oddbins bag is better than a Tesco bag. The very same person who wouldn't be prepared to take their wine to a friend's house in a Tesco bag would have no qualms about being seen by their neighbour unloading the blue and white striped bags out of their car.

'What they're saying to their hosts is – "I've been to a wine merchants to get this wine, I have not just picked it up in Tesco."'

Ask your customers what they feel your carrier bag says about them. It will reveal a lot about your brand. A good research technique is to show respondents pictures of people with different carrier bags and ask them to describe what the people in the picture are like. It's surprising how much can be read into a carrier bag.

Points to consider: *What does your company's carrier bag say about your company? What are your customers saying about themselves when they go out with one of your carrier bags?*

The Oddbins carrier bag works for them, both because they've built a reputation as a good quality and slightly quirky wine merchant, and because the graphics, colour and styling of the bag are, in themselves, suggestive of the unstuffy expertise that the brand is all about.

There's coherence to the way that Oddbins present themselves.

The whole point about standing for something is that it helps you make decisions. Not just major strategic growth decisions or buying decisions, but the day-to-day decisions, such as how you articulate signage, labels and leaflets. Standing for unstuffy expertise, as Oddbins do, informs how they write their point of sale (find a retailer who stands for something and you are likely to find a company, like Oddbins, that has its own distinctive vocabulary); how they interact with their customers and it helps them make lots of decisions day-in day-out.

If you're all about refinement and elegance, then you're not going to have day-glow yellow. If you're about fun and approachability then you might have day-glow yellow. The sandy colours; the quirky wood-chip style typeface of the logo with its raised 'd's and splodges of red; the hand-written boards at store; the promotional copy that's written in-house (rather than subcontracted to professional copywriters) are the graphic elements that coalesce to position Oddbins as an unconventional wine merchant.

It was a stroke of genius to commission Ralph Steadman to design the point-of-sale material. His anarchic style, popularised in Pink Floyd's anti-establishment rock opera 'The Wall', visualised everything that Oddbins stands for.

> 'The Ralph Steadman imagery crystallised into something really strong, unique and inimitable.'

Even though Steadman is no longer involved, his legacy lives on.

> 'We haven't worked with Steadman for about ten years now, but people still associate him with our brand.'

This is partly because Oddbins have continued the same feel if not style, employing a couple of designers who used to work at Oddbins. It's also testament to the fact the scrawled typeface, the blotches of dripping ink and the distinctive angular characters that Steadman specialises in are so right for Oddbins. It's difficult to imagine any other wine merchant appropriating such a style for their point of sale material.

A balancing act

Interestingly, the relationship with Steadman ceased when he increasingly wanted to take the imagery into darker, more threatening territory than Oddbins felt was right for them. There's a tension between pushing the boundaries of irreverence that has helped set Oddbins apart and maintaining the good-humoured lightness of touch that is an intrinsic part of the brand character. This tension (between quirkiness and acceptability) has surfaced again in the past two years with the recent change of ownership.

A couple of years ago, Seagram, owners for the previous twenty years, sold Oddbins to Castel Frères. Under Seagram's benevolent but detached parentage, Oddbins was something of an indulged child – seemingly allowed to do what it wanted in its own way. Undoubtedly, being able to operate independently and free from interference suited Oddbins. The flip side, in the view of the current management, is that the company had become lax on certain basic retailing standards and needed to be brought into line to meet the changing expectations of today's customers.

> 'We've smartened up a lot. We've tried to provide basic retail standards in all of our outlets. So gone are the dusty corners, the grime and the gloomy stores – an Aladdin's cave for wine enthusiasts, but potentially nothing more than a dirty little shop to someone who has been weaned on today's supermarkets. We are refitting new stores at a rate of about two per week, cleaning everything up, brightening everything up and making ourselves a twenty-first century retailer that can compete on the high street. There is, though, a fine line to tread between smartening up and being bland, so we are looking very closely at our in store point of sale, the way things are displayed, and are trying to maintain the vibrancy we always had.'

Time will tell if these improvements strengthen Oddbins. Retail history is littered with companies that failed to adapt to the changing marketplace. Equally, a change of ownership can often sound a death-knell; with new management imposing their way of doing things and inadvertently removing the company further from its roots and away from what made it different in the first place.

The challenge for Oddbins is to find a way of becoming an accessible (some might say sanitised) mainstream high street retailer while maintaining its quirky individuality. It sounds easy but it's not. Having sawdust on the floor could, for example, be the very thing that loyal Oddbins customers really love about the place and yet it could also be the barrier for new customers accustomed to pristine hypermarket floors. Removing the sawdust, as Oddbins have done, could alienate their old customers, but keeping it might inhibit its chance of attracting those new customers that will become the lifeblood of the future business.

I have to say that personally I'm disappointed they've dispensed with the sawdust. Sawdust symbolises tradition, wooden cases, casks and oak barrels. Just the smell of it sets me off and evokes a strong sense of wine values and quality. It's almost as if I can taste the wine as soon as I walk through the doors. I just hope that losing the sawdust doesn't signal that Oddbins are moving too close towards the kind of bland, tasteless offerings of our increasingly sterile hypermarkets.

Maybe I'm just getting old and hanging on to symbols of a bygone age. Certainly the early indications are showing positive results from the changed ownership (and cleaned up floors).

> 'Over the last two years we've seen our profit margin go up, our overheads come down, unprofitable stores close and new stores open in profitable areas. It's been a whole process of rationalisation, which is great for us and has helped us stand on our own two feet financially.'

These are significant decisions that the new ownership has had to deal with. They're decisions that are made easier by knowing what your brand stands for.

This knowledge helps answer three critical strategic questions:

1. What's essential that we need to keep?
2. What's getting in the way that we need to drop?
3. What's missing that we need to add?

Consider a range decision that Oddbins took as part of their recent overhaul.

The issue

Over time, Oddbins had, as might be expected from a bunch of wine enthusiasts, built up an enormous stock of different wines. The new management judged this as overstocked and inefficient from a retail viewpoint. The decision was whether or not to rationalise the range and by what degree.

What's essential?

It is clear, from referring to their brand essence ('unstuffy expertise') that a certain depth of range is essential. If Oddbins simply offered a narrow choice of popular mainstream wines, it would go out of business very quickly, because it would lose its credentials as an expert. There would be no reason for anyone to buy their wine there rather than from their local supermarket.

What's getting in the way?

A sprawling range was getting in the way, not only because it resulted in inefficiencies that were beginning to impinge on providing a good service, but also because it was turning Oddbins into a wine boffin. Too much expertise would endanger the unstuffy element of the Oddbins proposition. If Oddbins staff had to know too much about too many wines (most of which are unlikely to interest the majority of their customers) they could very quickly find themselves speaking a different language (the stuffy language of the wine trade that the brand eschews).

What's missing?

The answer to the third question – 'what's missing from the range that we need to add?' – has been to introduce more direction to the range that plays on Oddbins traditional strength as a pioneer for unexpected new wines.

Applying brand criteria to range reconciliation

What do we need to keep?	An interesting range of wines = expertise
What do we need to drop?	Too many irrelevant wines = too stuffy
What do we need to add?	Unexpected new wines = unstuffy experts

---

A pioneer

Marrying true wine knowledge with a healthy disrespect for tradition has imbued Oddbins with a pioneering spirit. While many of the more traditional wine merchants (who would turn their precious noses up at new world wines now, let alone twenty years ago) were concentrating on preserving the old order, Oddbins were making exciting new discoveries.

'Jacob's Creek started life as an Oddbins exclusive. Back in 1988, two of our buyers went over to Australia to see what all this noise was about and found Jacob's Creek. It became an Oddbins exclusive and one of the first Australian wines to be imported. And just look at it now.'

This is an important aspect of the Oddbins brand. A promise of unstuffy expertise needs to offer relevant knowledge about wines if it is to have any value to the Oddbins customer. In other words, Oddbins have to know something about wine that their customers don't know, but would like to learn. This almost mandates that Oddbins push the boundaries of their expertise to new and different places. As they're unlikely to ever better the depth of knowledge of wine connoisseurs or top-notch sommeliers in traditional wines (knowledge which anyway wouldn't be relevant to Oddbins customers), they're obliged to compete in a slightly different way.

> *'Oddbins has changed the way the UK sees wine. Australian wines are now the top-selling country in the UK. When we first brought it in people didn't even know they grow wine out there.'*

After bringing Australian wine to the UK, Oddbins introduced Chilean wine, then Greek wine (at one time they carried forty different Greek wines) and now they're pushing South African wines. Their claim to have changed the way the UK sees wine is not an idle one.

I remember once going on a trip to Bollinger with a Somerfield buyer in the late nineties, at a time when my agency handled that particular supermarket account. I happened to ask our host, Monsieur Montgolfier at Bollinger, who was their biggest customer and was stunned to hear it was Oddbins. From that point, I began to reappraise them as something more significant than my local off-licence.

Getting it right first time

The success Oddbins has experienced in introducing new wines to this country is testament to the strength of the bond they have with their customers. You need to be able to trust the advice of someone who recommends that you try something different. Many customers have, like me, been introduced to wine by Oddbins.

> *'In any one store you might have, say, between a dozen and twenty customers who first came to us completely naive, and who are now buying £12/£15 wines to drink at the weekends.'*

This is a great asset for Oddbins. There's a real advantage in being first. Who ever forgets their first love? It comes because they are so accessible and work to de-mystify the dark art.

> *'If your experience of wine has been your father pulling something out of a cellar and presenting it with great pomp and circumstance at the dinner table, or in restaurants that have deliberately created a rarefied atmosphere around their wine, it must be great, after having been kind of talked down to all these years, to find a wine merchant who speaks directly to you.'*

This reflects my own experience thirty years ago and I guess it would also be my daughter's experience now (other than she is considerably more savvy than I ever was). The benefit for Oddbins of being an entry point into wine is that it presents an opportunity to earn the trust of the customer at a time when, because of their lack of knowledge, they are at their most vulnerable.

I've probably now spent tens of thousands of pounds in my lifetime at Oddbins. If I'd been intimidated on that first occasion in the Kings Road in 1970, I would never have returned. Had that happened, it would have been easy for Oddbins to have dismissed it as nothing more than a lost ten shillings.

! **Key point:** *Your first time customer might be worth much more than you think. Treat them well because first impressions do count. Like a good wine they appreciate being looked after and they deliver over time.*

A special relationship

A brand is a promise of future performance. If every can of Coke tasted different from the last, the brand would have no meaning. Similarly, if their customers had a completely different experience with variable advice every time they went into Oddbins, they would very quickly lose the trust that binds them to the store.

Brands keep their promises or die. Implicitly, Oddbins promises good advice that you can trust. A duff recommendation may shake that trust, but if the relationship is strong enough, it will still hold. A series of poor suggestions, though, will inevitability result in a lost customer, because the promise has been broken and is worth nothing.

To be able to recommend a bottle of wine requires that you know your wine and you know your customer. Many retail operations are started by people who are passionate about the products they are selling and who are at one with their customers. Ahmed Pochee was into wine, Charles Dunston at Carphone Warehouse is naturally interested in mobile phones, Richard Branson has always been into music, and Stephen Marks was in the rag trade when he started French Connection. Great retailers know their customers intimately; more often than not they inhabit the same world.

Dan Wilkinson, an articulate young man with a passion for wine, could equally be an Oddbins customer, serving customers on the shop floor, or their brand manager. When he describes the typical customer he is, in fact, describing himself.

> 'A lot of our customers are in their late twenties and early thirties, with no children. They're probably not married but might be a couple living together. They will spend about £15, usually on bottles of about £5 to £7, as much as three times a week. They're willing to learn, wanting to absorb information that they can regurgitate to their friends and look impressive. They want to know about what they're drinking. You could argue that this sort of person is just that little bit insecure, and needs to find himself or herself by what they take into their life and what they purchase, but that's fine, I'm the same.'

Oddbins aren't simply selling wine; they're selling knowledge. And they're selling it in a very approachable manner. In other words they're selling unstuffy expertise. Personable service is imperative to this.

You can go into an Oddbins store, either as someone who knows absolutely nothing about wine or as an expert, and you can still converse at your chosen level with the same member of staff in a relaxed way. Oddbins really is the only place in the marketplace where you can wander in off the street and strike up a conversation with the person behind the counter who not only knows his stuff, but also won't talk down to you. It feels as if you've just gained a mate really.

Dan illustrated this by explaining how, when he was manager of Oddbins in Altrincham, he would continually experience people greeting him in the street with invitations to join them for a drink. He was very much part of that community. To an extent, this kind of relationship is likely to

2 Oddbins: Brand in a Nutshell

prevail for anyone working in a shop in a friendly Cheshire town, but it's likely to be even more so for someone who works at Oddbins.

I imagine the local pharmacist might have a different experience, selling, as he does, prescriptions from behind a counter with an air of professional formality. Wine is a social lubricant, whereas medical products aren't. Pharmacies are all about delivering quasi-scientific white-coat reassurance, whereas Oddbins is all about reducing barriers between their staff and their customers.

For many years my 'mate' at Oddbins was Kenny, manager of their Fine Wine Unit in Battersea. Fine Wine is a sub-brand within certain Oddbins stores that provides more top-end wines to cater for people like myself who have made a sad hobby of wine drinking.

Kenny, a great wine aficionado (somewhat surprisingly perhaps given that he hails from the land of the grain rather than the grape), embodies the Oddbins brand perfectly. He would let me browse for as long as I liked, chat to me and make me feel as if it didn't matter whether I bought a bottle or not, giving the impression he was just happy to share the time of day with me. He would always be advising me on wines and particularly those I'd never tried before.

I trusted him totally and consequently would, on many Sundays, venture south of the river from my Chelsea home to his store in Battersea. The truth is I probably stayed with Oddbins despite outgrowing them because of Kenny. When he moved on, I found that I also moved on. Although I still shop at Oddbins, I also now buy my wine from different places.

Points to consider: *Relationships depend on trust. To earn the trust of your customers you need to keep your promises. Does your company keep its brand promise? Do its customers trust it?*

The retailer's conundrum

The argument of this book is that people don't buy what you sell; they buy what you stand for. Clearly I buy wine from Oddbins, but it's wine I could get elsewhere if I wanted. What, in fact, I'm buying is their knowledge, expertise and informal style of service.

In other words, I'm buying what Oddbins stands for. Kenny personified this for me so effectively that he bridged the gap between the Oddbins proposition and my changing needs. Maybe it's my age or my increased disposable income, but I've become more selective. I now only really buy Bordeaux wine and, while they cater for that in their Fine Wine Units, it's not quite the same for me now that Kenny isn't there.

Consequently I'm tending to shop more often at my local Majestic, which seems to pick up at the £15 bottle and go through to £200. Their emphasis on cases also suits me. And it just happens to be five times closer than Oddbins and on my side of the river.

The point is you can't be all things to all people. While as a retailer you want to appeal to as broad a section as you possibly can and stretch the brand as far as you can, you do need to decide where your market is. Oddbins is all about accessibility (encapsulated in the idea of 'unstuffy expertise') and is probably most at home catering for thirtysomethings who want to pick up a bottle that costs between £5 and £10 on their way home from work.

If they adjusted their positioning to match my own shifting taste, they would end up compromising their core proposition, because, although I'm loathe to admit it, I would undoubtedly be judged to be relatively stuffy by your average twenty year old.

Many companies fall into the trap of religiously following their customers rather than sticking to their own convictions, only to find their ageing customer base has taken them up a cul-de-sac that's a million miles from the younger market they need to attract into their brand.

The retailers' conundrum is when to follow your customer and when to let go? I think it's probably right that Oddbins should be prepared to let go of me. They would be much better adjusting their sights on my daughters than me.

It would be wholly wrong if they tried to be the authority on top-end speciality wines that I buy as well as the £5 wines that my daughter takes along to parties. But it's a difficult decision because on the face of it, I will be worth so much more to them than a younger buyer because I spend so much more on wine.

A subtle evolution

Refreshing your company so that it continues to be relevant to new audience can be harder than it sounds.

> *'A few years ago, we changed our High Street Kensington store radically to try a space-age shop-fit, all glass and light and fun. I was working in a shop in Cheshire at the time and one of my customers came in brandishing a newspaper and said – "look what they've done to your shop in London, you won't do that here will you?" That was when I realised how personal people get about a brand, about their local shop.'*

In this instance I'm inclined to feel that the customer was right, but they're not always. The trick is to know when to listen to your customers and when not. Sometimes you need to listen between the lines rather than to the lines. If mankind had only ever listened to its customers, it would never have got beyond the horse and cart, let alone to the moon. What Oddbins have managed very successfully is to subtly evolve over time.

> *'Our literature tended to be very copy heavy. Today you can't expect that sort of time investment from a customer. You need to make it easy, digestible and accessible. In the early nineties you could give people a book to read before they bought from you, but nowadays it's a lot faster. So we've cut down the copy in our publications and we've made the illustrations a lot brighter and simpler.'*

This is similar to the way the stores have evolved. It's difficult to know how much has changed, but I wouldn't be at all surprised to find, if I was transported thirty years back, a very different Oddbins. And yet in my mind I tend to think that Oddbins stores have remained more or less unchanged. There used to be a fantastic design museum in Gloucestershire (curated by Roger Opie and now sadly closed) that had packaging going back decades. It was fascinating to see how the household brands such as Marmite, Persil, Cadbury's Drinking Chocolate had changed over time. Put a 1980s pack of Persil against its 1970s predecessor and it can be difficult to spot the changes, but if you compare today's pack with one from fifty years earlier the difference is very noticeable. I think the same must be true of Oddbins as it is of these great consumer brands. There's a lot to be said for consistent fine-tuning rather than radical overhaul.

One of the main challenges for Oddbins is how to continue to deliver the expertise and knowledge that's at the heart of their proposition to customers who increasingly want to be left alone and not hassled by over-zealous sales staff.

> 'We did some customer research a few years ago which showed that for customers today, particularly if they're not wine savvy, the prospect of going into a wine shop is quite daunting. They, and particularly women, hate to be put on the back foot. What they often want is to go into the shop, see something clearly marked, buy it and go home. They really want to interact with the staff only at the till and don't want to be approached or offered help because they feel that makes them look stupid.'

Ten or twenty years ago, service standards demanded an attentiveness from sales staff that encouraged the kind of interaction that Oddbins are naturally good at.

> 'Assuming that everybody wants an encyclopaedic breakdown of wine in store delivered in a quirky way wasn't doing us any favours in terms of attracting new customers. We had to recognise that increasingly people are coming in, not really talking to the staff, and going home. Only when they return at a later date are they ready to ask questions and experiment.'

The changing way people shop has required a modification of style to give customers more time and space.

> 'This led us to look at our in-store proposition and to layer it a bit. Now, when you walk into the store you might see some shelves with one product per bin and a big sign on it saying £5.99. In other words, a simple experience. If customers want to browse or question a member of staff they are at liberty to do so.'

Significantly, a couple of decades ago, fewer women would be buying wine than today. This has ramifications. Being able to show a degree of knowledge about wine is quite a masculine thing, and so Oddbins need to be able to adjust their expertise to meet the needs of their new market. Rather than simply give information for the sake of it, they need to channel it in a way that helps the buying decision.

Questions to consider:

Does your company have strength in its convictions?

Is it prepared, if necessary, to let some customers go in order to stay fresh and relevant to a new customer base?

Is it fully in touch with the changing needs of its marketplace?

In sum

The thing I love about Oddbins is that the company is single-mindedly built on one simple idea. It has evolved over time in accordance with the changing mores of its market, but the basic principle that drives Oddbins is the same today as it was when I first chanced upon them thirty-four years ago and even before then when Ahmed Pochee first sold his second-hand wine from a barrow. Anyone connected with Oddbins from customers to staff to suppliers know precisely what Oddbins is about and what it stands for.

They may use their own words, but ultimately they'll all be remarkably consistent in the way they describe both the company and what it offers.

This is because Oddbins is based on a singular brand idea that is carried through every aspect of the company. In a nutshell, it stands for unstuffy expertise.

3

A Matter of Trust

What this chapter covers

■ This chapter will explain how customers need to feel reassured and confident about their purchases and the place they make them.

■ It will show how branding provides the reassurance that wraps the purchase and gives customers reason to return.

■ It will illustrate how trust, the heart of the relationship between the retailer and his customers, is the benefit of branding.

■ Above all else, this chapter aims to encourage thought about the importance of customer trust and what you can do about it.

Maternal sales instincts

My mother would never describe herself as a saleswoman, and yet one technique in particular betrayed her talent not so much for making the sale, but for preparing the ground for future sales. Quite often, as she rang up an item on the till she would say, 'We sell a lot of these.' Sometimes it would be little more than a reflective murmur to herself, although always audible across the counter; on other occasions she would address it directly to her customer.

I can remember to this day when my curiosity finally got the better of me. It was a grey Saturday afternoon not long after my twelfth birthday and I was helping out in the shop to earn some extra pocket money. My mother had just told a lady who lived in the posh part of Strawberry Hill that she sold a lot of trimming knifes. *'Why did you say that?'* I asked, *'Why do you always tell people you sell a lot of them. They've already decided that they want it; so what that you've sold one before?'*. *'It gives them confidence and reassurance.'* she replied gently, but with a firmness that brokered no further discussion.

It was like a light bulb suddenly illuminating my impressionable mind. With six short words, *'It gives them confidence and reassurance'*, my mother had made the case for branding. Unwittingly she had lit the fuse for my future career.

Just the other day I bought a shirt in Thomas Pink. As the girl was folding it up she said, *'This is a really nice shirt'*. I'd already decided that I liked it enough to part with my money, but this throwaway comment from a sales assistant made me feel even better about my purchase. And even though I knew full well that, had I had hung around to observe her next sale, I would, more likely than not, have heard her say the same thing to her next customer, her little reassurance had an amazing impact.

> **Learning tip** Make it your business to give confidence to your customers. Observe how other people reassure their customers. Ask yourself what you could do to make them feel better about you and their purchase during the whole transaction. You represent the brand first and the merchandise second.

If I hadn't made it my business to deal in these little reassurances and so didn't know it to be part of the human condition, I might have regarded myself to be a shallow, impressionable fool to be influenced in such a way. But because I work in advertising I know that, not only am I a shallow impressionable fool, but also that everyone else is too.

Wrapped with reassurance

People buy things for a whole host of reasons. There is a rational reason for just about every purchase, although I do sometimes wonder what that might be when I hear some of the music that my daughters buy. The rational reasons for buying that shirt in Thomas Pink included a fundamental need to clothe myself, as well as an urgent need to upgrade my wardrobe by replacing some of my older well-worn shirts. But there's also an emotional aspect to every purchase, and it's this that is all too often neglected by busy retailers. If you think your customers are rational creatures who buy on logic alone, then I have to point out that you're being illogical. In the same way as they say that 90% of communication is non-verbal I'm inclined to argue that 90% of purchasing behaviour is non-logical, or rather that's it's governed more by emotion than rational thought.

Even that lady from the posh part of Strawberry Hill buying a knife in a local hardware store would have been motivated by her own self-image. She would have felt a little uneasy about being in a hardware store in the first place. It was quite possibly the first time she had bought such a knife and, so feeling a little uncertain about the task, she might have been unsure whether that knife was what she needed. She would want to feel that she wasn't being ripped off or being made a fool of in any way. She was – as even my untutored twelve-year old eye could tell – someone who took great care over her appearance and so her inner voice would be running some sort of commentary about the impression she was making on my mother. And then there would be all of those deeper hidden feelings and motivations that drive us all and unconsciously influence everything we do. All of this would be going on in her head and her heart, some knowingly, most of it unknowingly, as she went through the process of buying that basic trimming knife back in 1962.

My mother knew this, or at least had an instinct for it, and so was able to reassure her customer that everything was okay, that she'd made a good purchase that reflected well on her and wouldn't let her down. She couldn't quite put it like that though without causing offence, so she said, *'We sell a lot of these'*, which is saying pretty much the same.

In retail, branding is the reassurance that wraps the purchase. It's what gives customers the confidence they need to feel good about the transaction. It's a confidence that will make them feel better about the item they've just bought and more inclined to return to the shop they bought it from.

> **!** **Key point** Branding is the reassurance that wraps the purchase and encourages the customer to return.

A good retail brand is an editor. It selects and reduces choice on behalf of its customers. People don't want vast choice; they want an edited selection. You go to the place you know understands you.

Working with House of Fraser fifteen years ago, we were intrigued to find out why people would buy a Jaeger branded garment from a department store rather than the stand-alone Jaeger store down the road. We discovered that the relationship the customer had with her House of Fraser store was such that, because she felt they understood her and knew exactly what she was after, the edited choice they offered on the fashion floor would be more appropriate to her and save her time. We called it the 'my store' theory: it's my sort of store because they perfectly understand me. That's why I tend to think of retail brands as helping shorthand customer choice.

Brands answer customer needs. To do this they need the trust of their customers.

Trustmarks

It all comes down to trust. My dictionary defines trust as *'belief or confidence in, or reliance on, the truth, goodness, character, power, ability etc of someone or something.'* Trust is the benefit of branding. If your customers believe in what your retail organisation stands for and if they have confidence in its truth, goodness, character, power and ability, then you've got a strong brand that they will continue coming back to.

I like Larry Light's, (VP of Marketing at McDonald's) definition of a brand as a *trustmark*. Howard Schultz at Starbucks talks about earning the trust of customers in an uncertain world.

'Across all channels of American society and culture, there is such fracturing of values. There are no heroes. There is little trust in a number of public institutions. I am not saying Starbucks is going to save the world, because we can't. What we've done is provide a safe harbour for people to go. I think the brand equity of the name Starbucks has supplied a level of trust and confidence, not only in the product, in the trademark, but in the experience of what Starbucks is about. At a time when there are very few things that people have faith in. It's a very fragile thing. You can't take it for granted. It's something that has to be respected and continually built upon.'[1]

And because of this, Starbucks are able to charge 1,000% mark-up for their coffee and still have people queuing through the store for it and averaging eighteen visits a month! Interestingly, Howard Schultz also said that they didn't initially think about building a brand.

> *'We never set out to build a brand. Our goal was to build a great company, one that stood for something, one that valued the authenticity of its product and the passion of its people. In the early days, we were so busy selling coffee, one cup at a time, opening stores and educating people about dark-roasted coffee that we never thought much about brand strategy.'*[1]

I have to say I think to argue you're 'not building a brand, but building a company that stood for something' is a contradiction in terms. By my book a corporate brand is a company that stands for something and a retailer that stands for something is a retail brand. But his point about unconsciously building their brand is, I'm sure, how most strong retail brands come about. Trust is the reward for doing things properly. It's the reward for good branding.

In writing this, I hope I don't come across as wistfully looking back to a bygone golden era, glossing up something that never really existed as the good old days. But I really do believe that retail branding is often a matter of returning to, and applying, the standards of the corner shop (and this won't be the only time you hear me bang on about corner shops). I was pleased to read design guru, Wally Olins, expressing the same thought in his book *'On Brand'*.

> *'Banks were created around the idea of individual relationships with the customer. Retail banks long ago established a network of branches, each with its own manager. The bank manager, a pillar of society, the very personification of integrity and good sense, established the closest relationship with his local community, and in that way the bank became part of it. All this represented everything the very best service brands aspire to. Until the middle of the twentieth century banks didn't of course, think of themselves as brands; the idea would have horrified them. They hardly thought of themselves as wholly commercial entities. They didn't compete with each other for business, not overtly anyway, or as a senior banker said to me in the early 1970s, "I don't like my people touting for business. It's vulgar". Their products were, as indeed they still are, more or less commoditized; their branches were designed to be imposing and conservative; their communications were ponderous and patronising; but they were also amicable without being intimate. The real*

> *strength of banks lay in the behaviour of their people – especially those rocks of probity, their branch managers. Branch managers carried out the marketing policy of the organisation. They were respected, cautious, careful, helpful, accurate. Banks were, without knowing it, classic service brands of a particular type.'*

Trust to dust

Wally Olins uses the term 'service brand' for retail brand, arguing (as I am with this book) that they are so much more complex and harder to manage than simple product brands, because as he puts it *'product brands are about products. Service brands are about people'*. He goes on to explain how banks ceased to be paragons of customer trust from the moment they began to regard their customers as numbers rather than people.

> *'Now banks are no longer respected; indeed, in many countries they are hugely distrusted … customers became, in the language of so many so-called service companies, Revenue Earning Units. This is a telling and dismissive phrase. It characterises a contemptuous attitude to customers and almost deliberately encourages uncaring and thoughtless behaviour amongst staff. The impact of all this on retail customers was appalling. When there was no personal relationship, nobody to talk to, no single individual to deal with, trust between the bank and its customers turned to dust.'[2]*

Trust to dust, I love that.

I find one of the best ways to create dust from trust is with an automated phone system. Making customers interact with a machine rather than a real person, forcing them to sit through a long range of options (none of which exactly matches what they want) while on many occasions charging them premium phone rates. Why do companies do this? It can only be motivated by a desire to give really bad service, but not having the time to do it personally. It's indicative of the contemptuous attitude to customers that Wally Olins talks about, which is the consequence of detached management syndrome. Philip Green illustrates this point when talking about Marks & Spencer.

> 'Old Lord Marks died walking down the aisle of Marks & Spencer, checking out the store. He was engaged, immersed in every detail of the business, always trying to make something better. Now we've got big businesses with boards of directors and some of them have never been in a shop in their lives. There's no engagement. They're just corporate animals and it's these people in charge that kill them off. The brands just die out without personal engagement and motivation. Mediocrity ticks over and ticking over isn't good enough. Then failure breeds failure.'[3]

In fact, the ladies' tailoring department quite literally gave Lord Marks a heart attack. Hurling clothing to the floor and yelling, *'You are trying to ruin my business'*, was his final dramatic demonstration of how much he cared about the business. He was seventy-six years old at the time. The legacy of his passion was a company that continued to maintain his meticulous standards and utmost respect for his customers for a further thirty years after his death. Consequently it held the mantle of Britain's most trusted company.

In the nineties, things started to go wrong for Marks & Spencer. Maybe even earlier, for the seeds of its decline were probably sewn in the eighties when the reins of the business were handed from its founding family to the kind of businessmen that Philip Green contemptuously dismisses. There had been a subtle shift in focus at Marks & Spencer from the shop-floor where Lord Marks eventually met his Maker to the boardroom where his successors felt more comfortable spending most of their time. And eventually it began to show in slipping standards.

> 'I first knew M&S was going into problems when I stuck my finger through the side of my underpants when I was putting them on. I thought, hang on, that hasn't happened before.'[4]

Maggie Taylor, Research Director at my agency, points out how, during M&S's glory days, if something shrunk in the wash people would wonder what they had done wrong in the washing process, such was their faith and trust in Marks & Spencer. Nowadays if something shrinks, people will see it as further evidence that M&S isn't what it used to be.

The interesting thing about this kind of experience is that previously the customer would be inclined to think that they themselves had done something wrong rather than that the item itself might be substandard. Such was the strength of the Marks & Spencer brand. Their famous 'no questions asked' returns policy (unique at the time with its underlying message of confidence in their product and respect for their customers), their overall integrity and the exacting standards they were known to impose on their suppliers, all added up to give an impression of righteousness. Their customers trusted them because they had earned trust through decades of obsessive dedication (so well demonstrated by Lord Marks in his final moments) to meeting their needs. As soon as they started taking that trust for granted and selling underpants with holes in them, they began to lose that trust. And as Howard Schultz said, customer trust is a fragile thing. There is no room for complacency.

Retail expert, Maureen Johnson, Chief Executive of The Store, describes a similar story at Sainsbury's.

'Sainsbury's had a reputation for fresh high quality products, produce in particular, and occupied a higher ground of quality before Tesco did. Then they lost their way. Their new chief executive or whatever he is now, was quoted as saying that Sainsbury's was letting the customer down particularly on stocks, that the whole of the central distribution process had failed miserably, that the staff aren't unloading stuff at the back of the store and getting it onto the shelves fast enough so stuff is deteriorating at the back end. And of course, as a shopper, you notice these things. Retail brands are more vulnerable than manufacturer brands because they have more touch points. You expect Sainsbury's to have it in stock. The whole point of a 'One Stop Shop' is that it is a 'One Stop Shop'. If you then find you've got to do two other calls to get what you should have been able to get from Sainsbury's that's terrible, they've let you down.'

! **Key point** *Let standards slip, take your eye off giving your customers what they want and need, and pretty soon their trust will turn to dust.*

We used to work with Somerfield supermarkets during what, I like to think, was their halcyon period. We found (and I know I'm oversimplifying here) that if they happened to run out of bananas at 4.00pm on a Saturday, it wasn't just a case of non-availability of merchandise, it was a question of losing the customer's trust. Letting people down who had planned their weekly shop on the assumption that the merchandise would be there is a sure-fire way of losing trust, particularly if you do it more than once. Just think of the logistics that are involved in buying green bananas from some hot clime in sufficient quantities to ensure that the local store in Kings Lynn and every other corner of the country has enough, but not too many, perfectly ripe bananas every Saturday afternoon. It just shows how difficult it is to earn trust and how easy it is to lose it.

Another supermarket example concerns that bête noire, queuing. I was fascinated to find that, provided all tills are manned, customers are inclined to be much more forgiving; it's the lethal combination of queues and unmanned tills that really irritates them. Such are our heightened expectations in today's service society, that if customers see evidence that their shop isn't doing everything possible to serve them, they'll question its ability to meet their needs.

The example of Marks & Spencer, Sainsbury's and Somerfield show just how hard retailers need to work to maintain their customers' confidence and trust. Retail customers extract a high price for their trust. A supermarket with unmanned checkouts risks suffering a loss of trust from any customer waiting impatiently in a long queue to pay.

Building a powerful retail brand is not that easy. Not only do you have to earn the trust in the first place by doing what you do exceptionally well, but then, as a bare minimum, you need to be able to keep it up day after day delivering what you're promising through the hundreds of different members of staff who represent your organisation. Good retailing is infinitely harder to keep up than it is to manage a simple manufacturer brand.

This is why a retail brand needs to be built on rock solid beliefs and principles. It's why it has to stand for something. You, and everyone who works for your organisation, need to believe in it, to have certainty and conviction that it really is in your customers' best interests to come to your store. If you're half-hearted about it, if you don't keep your promise, then pretty soon your customers will stop trusting you.

Someone once said to me that retail is the business of being chosen. With high streets and shopping malls bursting with different retail options, this rings true and emphasises that all retailers must do everything they possibly can, not only to get noticed and chosen in the first place, not only to earn trust, but to continue to deserve that trust so their customers continue to choose to shop at their store.

Julian Richer of Richer Sounds talks about the importance of integrity.

> *'You are selling integrity as well as a product. If you show integrity, the customer will trust you and buy from you again. If you do not have integrity, the customer will soon find out.'* [5]

And Howard Schultz about the emotional dimension …

> *'In this ever-changing society, the most powerful and enduring brands are built from the heart. They are real and sustainable. Their foundations are stronger because they are built with the strength of the human spirit, not an ad campaign. The companies that are lasting are those that are authentic.'* [1]

These two quotes capture what it's all about. If you take nothing else from this chapter please read and re-read these quotes and remember them forever. These two guys have hit the nail on the head. Both Richer and Schultz are saying that you must believe in what you say. There is no room in today's competitive retail world for hollow promises or superficial puffery.

> **Key point** *You, and everyone who works for your organisation, need to believe in it and what it stands for. You need to be convinced that it really is in your customer's best interests to come to your store. If you're half-hearted about it, if you don't keep your promise, then pretty soon your customers will stop trusting you.*

Would you buy from your store regardless of any staff discount? I'm sure that The Carphone Warehouse employees would buy from The Carphone

Warehouse as indeed would the staff of any of the companies featured in this book.

The little man

I'm often asked, by ambitious managers, how can they assess the principles and values of their company and if there is anything they can do if they happen to find themselves working for a retailer of shaky conviction and loose morals.

To such questions I always say, study your company. Does it have a set of espoused values? Most do nowadays, and unfortunately many don't live by them, but your first step is to find out what your company thinks it stands for. If it's not written down anywhere, then talk and listen to as many different people as you can find to ascertain what they think it stands for.

Unfortunately, I must say that, in my experience, value statements tend to be the biggest single piece of puffery that any company produces. Look at your own company's stated values and see, by trawling through their websites, how many of the same words are used by your competitors. You'll probably need to go beyond the rhetoric to determine what your company really stands for.

As part of my research for this book I asked the following questions in my interviews with those companies featured as case studies:

- What would you say that your company stands for?

- How would you describe your company's brand? Do you have a standard expression or articulation of the brand?

- Why do you feel that your customers choose to shop with you rather than at your competitors? What are their motivations for choosing to buy from you? Do you have any evidence to support this?

Read the case studies in this book and learn how some of the best retail brands in the country define themselves and ask yourself how well your company stacks up against them.

If you have an advertising agency, ask them what your company stands for. After all it's their business to know. And if they can't tell you, go straight to your Marketing Director and suggest he or she find another agency that can.

This process of interrogation will help give a better idea of what your company says it stands for. The next, and most important, thing is to determine what it *really* stands for. Is its behaviour consistent with its positioning? Does it do what it says it's going to do? Are its espoused values the same as its actual values? Does it keep the promises it makes to its customers? Has it got integrity? Does everyone in the company from cashier to Chairman know and live by its values?

Ask these questions, even if they haven't been asked before. Get your colleagues thinking about them. If nothing else, you will show yourself to be someone who is interested in the company that you're working for. And if that isn't valued, I suggest you think about dusting down your CV and finding a company where it is valued.

In response to the question of what you personally can do, I would advise that once you've understood what your brand stands for, then work to make it true.

Because retail is a people business (as Wally Olins puts it, *'service brands are about people'*) it stands to reason that the very people who make up the brand can affect the brand.

In the same way it is said poor service from a disgruntled and de-motivated cashier can undermine all the good work that everyone else in the company has done in building the brand. The opposite also applies. A customer who receives exemplary service, in a manner fitting to whatever it is that your company stands for, is more likely become a customer that trusts your company and talks well of you than a customer who receives average service.

'One busy lunchtime I called in to my local Pret à Manger for a coffee. As usual, the place was packed and the staff very busy. Nevertheless the service was prompt and friendly. When I came to pay, the young lady said: 'the coffee is on the house sir'. When I asked why, she told me that she felt I had waited longer than she thought I should. That in itself created a branded customer experience and has reinforced my already positive experience of this exceptional company. Do you think Pret will cover the cost of that free coffee in purchases from me in the future? Of course – I have been converted from a consumer into a 'brand advocate'.'[6]

A well-developed retail organisation where everyone from cashier to Chairman knows and understands what the company stands for, will tend to live the brand without thinking about it. It will be instinctive rather than considered, and it will be something that they all do even when no one else is looking.

The Carphone Warehouse encourage every sales assistant to imagine they have the whole company sitting on their shoulder whenever they engage in a conversation with a customer. This is because they believe that the company really does depend on those conversations. What a brilliant way of short-handing a whole company ethos. I read it as these conversations are really important and not that the company is checking up on you!

As my colleagues would sometimes testify, I'm no expert in interpersonal skills, but small things such as a smile, rather than a frown, can be infectious and help change the atmosphere of a store (unless of course you work for a teenage brand that makes a virtue out of its surly attitude, when a frown may be more appropriate than a smile). I'm much more likely to buy something if I like the sales assistant.

Even if you happen to work in the back room away from customer contact, you can still make it your mission to live out the values of your company's brand in everything you do and say. It will make a difference, I promise you. If nothing else it will help you to feel more engaged with your work. Incidentally if you do work in the backroom, I would urge you to do everything you can to get experience of serving your customers. If, for example, you work in the accounts department and hear there's a staff shortage problem on the sales floor, volunteer to help out. No one has ever risen to the top of a successful retail organisation without interacting with customers.

Great retailers thrive on action and interaction. As Philip Green says,

> 'Life is about taking a view, backing yourself. Taking the risk. I always say, look, there are six chairs round this table. Say there are six people sitting in them. Normally three of those can't make a decision, two will say nothing and one will say I'll do it.'[3]

You want to be one of the fifteen percent that say 'I'll do it'. Because if not, you will diminish your company's brand and reduce its chances of gaining the trust of its customers and the sales success that naturally flows.

In sum

Good retail branding is the reassurance that wraps the purchase. It makes customers feel good about their shopping experience and leads to them trusting the retailer. Trust is the benefit of branding. Branding is all about setting standards and delivering it consistently. It helps customers to know what to expect (and decide whether it's their kind of shop). It conditions the experience they'll receive. In return, customers will reward the retailer with their trust (as long as and until they let them down). The complexity of retail, with the sheer number of people involved, demands that retail brands are built on rock solid principles and beliefs so that everyone connected with it understands it and believes in it. Everyone needs to be pointed in the same direction.

The late Mark McCormack said,

> *'In normal circumstances, most people prefer to buy from a friend. In abnormal circumstances, most people still prefer to buy from a friend.'*

In other words, people prefer to buy from those they know and trust.

If you only remember one thing from this chapter:

---

*You're selling integrity as well as product.
If you show integrity, the customer will trust you
and buy from you again.*

References:

1   Howard Schultz, *'The Best Way to Build a brand'*, 1997, appearing in *'The Book of Entrepreneurs' Wisdom'* by Peter Krass, published by John Wiley & Sons Inc, 1999

2   Wally Olins, *'On Brand'* published by Thames & Hudson, 2003

3   Interview with Philip Green, *The Guardian Weekend*, October 23 2004

4   Jan Moulton interviewed in *'Real Business'* by Amanda Hall, June 2001

5   Julian Richer, *'The Richer Way'*, published by Richer Publishing, 2001

6   *'Experiencing the brand and branding the experience'* by Shaun Smith, Admap article reprinted from WARC

4

John Lewis: A Cultured Company

This case study draws from an interview with Andrew Woodward, Marketing Director and Helen Dickinson, Head of PR, at John Lewis.

What this case study teaches us

- This is a story where the tortoise beats the rabbit and shows us how the best things can indeed come to those who wait.

- John Lewis exemplifies how a retail brand is the sum of what makes that retailer different and special.

- John Lewis is a retail conviction brand that illustrates the power of principles.

- John Lewis affirm that if you set out your store in a distinctive and clearly defined way, the right kind of customer (one who empathises with your values and standards) will naturally be drawn towards you.

- The primary lesson of John Lewis is to demonstrate how running the business for the benefit of your staff will be to the ultimate benefit of your customers.

The tortoise and the hare

Whenever I think of John Lewis, I'm reminded of the fable of the tortoise and the hare.

It took thirty-nine years from opening their first shop in Oxford Street in 1864 before they added a second with the purchase of Chelsea's Peter Jones shop in the Kings Road. By comparison, today's young retail whippersnappers, The Carphone Warehouse, had over two hundred outlets in less than ten years.

When the ban on Sunday trading was dropped in 1994, most retailers gave their employees three months notice that they were going to change to seven-day a week trading. With their process of consulting all employees at all levels, it took John Lewis almost four times as long.

Only in the last few years have John Lewis started accepting credit cards, thereby giving their rivals the best part of a ten-year head start.

And they're on only their fourth Chairman since establishing their Partnership structure in 1929. With an average tenure of nineteen years, and the current incumbent Sir Stuart Hampson having held the position since 1993, it's probably as close to a job for life as you could find.

No one could ever accuse John Lewis of being over-hasty.

But, like the tortoise, they are formidable competitors. For John Lewis is now, well over a century after first opening its doors for business, the UK's largest department store group.

On the high street, where the chill winds of faddish fashion blow and only the quick are supposed to survive, John Lewis are a bit of an anomaly. How is it that they've managed to achieve their current position of pre-eminence despite not moving as fast as their competitors? How have they been able to ride the storms of change and emerge even more strongly in the same shape that they've always been? One might as well ask how is it that the tortoise beat the hare?

Neill Denny, former editor at *Retail Week*, feels the answer lies in their consistency.

> *'They have a consistency at the root of what they do. They offer pretty good value, pretty good ranges, pretty consistently. They get 80% of it right, 80% of the time. They never make major mistakes, they don't undertake disastrous foreign expansions like some retailers and they don't throw away huge amounts of money on speculative brand extensions or dodgy takeovers. They just play it safe, look to the long term and pay their staff well.'*

John Lewis stick to what they know. Not for nothing was a 2002 feature on the company in Forbes magazine entitled *'No follower of fashion'*. The recent makeover at Peter Jones is in itself an example of the benefits of the company keeping its eye firmly on the long-term. *'Not many companies would be prepared to wait ten years for a payback on their investment'*[1] says

Beverley Aspinall, the store's former Managing Director. And judging from its many plaudits, it's been worth the wait.

Architectural correspondent at The Guardian, Jonathan Glancey observed:

'Its success lies in its ability to be modern yet old fashioned: entrepreneurial and well-mannered at one and the same time.'[2]

A thought to consider In a retail world that lauds speed, quick reactions and responsiveness, might the lesson of John Lewis be that, sometimes, good things come to those who take their time? Just occasionally, could it be worth pausing for thought?

A principled place

John Lewis is a series of paradoxes. It is, as Mr Glancey says, both old-fashioned and modern; both a laggard and a pioneer; both a conformist and a radical. What would perhaps surprise people the most about John Lewis, as they walk through its ordered and conservative interior, is the knowledge that it's one of the most progressive and different companies in the world. Behind the rows of crisp folded white sheets and the deferential sales floor demeanour lie a solid set of corporate principles like no other.

The eponymous founder of John Lewis rose from a background of poverty to open his Oxford Street draper's shop in 1864. By choosing to set up in Oxford Street, which in the late nineteenth-century was yet to become the shopping heartland it has grown into today, the first John Lewis was paving the way for a successful enterprise. But a more significant factor in shaping the future company came from his contrary management style and short temper. According to his son,

'The conditions of his early life had so overdeveloped in him a passion for accumulating money and a dread of losing it that, where money was concerned, he was like a man driven by a demon.'[3]

This drive, translated into a determination to guarantee his customers the finest quality stock at the most competitive prices, ensured that the little draper's shop had grown into a large department store by 1905. It also had a profound impact on his son, John Spedan Lewis, who was well aware of his father's shortcomings.

> *'The perversity of some of his notions and the arbitrariness of his temper made the strain of working with him considerable.'*[3]

The partnership structure that sets John Lewis apart from all of its competitors came, in part, as a filial reaction to a stereotypical entrepreneur.

John Spedan Lewis is deservedly credited as the extraordinary inspiration behind this unique department store, but some recognition should be accorded to his father who bequeathed the hard commercial nous that has enabled John Lewis to succeed where other collaborative ventures have tended to fold.

His father's success also meant that John Spedan Lewis started his business life on a firm financial footing. When he was only twenty years old, he walked into the then ailing Sloane Street store and produced twenty £1,000 notes to buy Peter Jones outright.

John Spedan Lewis, jaundiced by his father's robust management style and alarmed by the spread of communism, felt that the world needed a better form of capitalism. His simple idea was that the real advantages of ownership should go to those who give their time and labour to the business rather than those who supply the capital. It's a philosophy that underpins the organisation today and resulted in John Spedan Lewis being voted Britain's greatest business figure in a 2002 BBC poll.

In 1914, when his father ceded full control of the Peter Jones shop to him, John Spedan Lewis launched his first experiment in staff participation – the Committee for Communication re-named all employees 'Partners' and promised that when the store returned to profit they would all share in that profit. He was able to honour that promise five years later when every single partner received the equivalent of five weeks' pay. Ten years later he created a trust to take over the assets of the company and run it as a Partnership before, in 1950, relinquishing his controlling interest in the much-expanded business.

You may at this stage be beginning to question what relevance all this historical background has in a book about twenty-first century retail brands. The answer is that it's highly relevant. The die of any company is often cast during its formative years. A retail brand is the sum of what makes that retailer different and special. Branding is all about finding, defining and articulating the essential truth of a company. It pinpoints the reason why its customers choose to shop there rather than elsewhere. More often than not this can be traced back to the company's early days even if it's not immediately apparent or, as is all too often the case, the management of the company try to deny its past. John Lewis is one of the few organisations that live by its (now ninety-year old) principles. It would be fair to say that they've stood the test of time.

> **Key point** *The art of branding is all about finding, defining and articulating the essential truth of a company. A retail brand is the sum of what makes that retailer different and special. It is, then, the culture, the way people act instinctively, that is important because it cannot be manufactured ... it has to be felt by all concerned.*

The essence of John Lewis

Strong brands have a sense of purpose. They know why they exist and what they're in business to do. The fundamental purpose of John Lewis, set out in its constitution, is to create happiness for its partners. In other words the Partnership is run first and foremost for the benefit of everyone who works there.

'The Partnership's ultimate purpose is the happiness of all its members, through their worthwhile and satisfying employment in a successful business. Because the Partnership is owned in trust for its members, they share the responsibilities of ownership as well as its rewards – profit, knowledge and power.'[4]

In itself, such a statement of purpose, although way ahead of its time, is not unusual. Many companies today proclaim that their staff come first. The difference is that John Lewis really mean it. The partnership structure ensures the company is owned by its employees (or at least held in trust for the benefit of employees), saving it from the capriciousness of outside investors looking for short-term returns or the whims of a self-interested despotic owner.

The benefit, for John Lewis's customers, of its co-operative partnership structure is a better quality of service from more committed staff. They're committed because they co-own it. And, because they own it, they're more likely to be in it for the long-term. Even for the most junior sales assistant or delivery boy, it's more than just a job. Andy Street, John Lewis's Supply Chain Director, illustrates this with an example of staff turnover in Northampton, where many national chains have their warehouses.

'One of the big problems is labour turnover. It's not unusual for it to be well over 50%. We're running distribution centres there with a turnover rate of no more than 12%.'[5]

John Lewis believe that running their business for the benefit of their staff will be to the ultimate benefit of their customers, because it becomes the interest of those staff to cultivate long-term relationships with their customers by serving them to the best of their ability.

'For customers, it is the only remaining department store which hasn't descended into a depressing shabbiness, and which employs staff you can rely on to know what they are talking about.'[6]

This, I believe, is the defining statement of the John Lewis brand – John Lewis believe that running their business for the benefit of their staff will be to the ultimate benefit of their customers, because it becomes the interest of those staff to cultivate long-term relationships with their customers by serving them to the best of their ability. It's a statement of philosophy, because John Lewis is a brand based on a philosophy (the Partnership even describes itself as 'an experiment in industrial democracy'). It's not a set of words they themselves use, but it's how I, as an outside brand advisor, can best sum up what their business stands for.

> **!**
>
> **The defining philosophy** *John Lewis believe that running their business for the benefit of their staff will be to the ultimate benefit of their customers, because it becomes the interest of those staff to cultivate the 'long-term'.*

The practice of articulating what a brand stands for is a process of reduction. In scientific terms, an essence is what is left when everything else has been boiled away. A brand essence, therefore, is what's left at the core of the company when everything else has been stripped away.

The rationale for attempting to define and describe it as succinctly as possible is that doing so gives a much better understanding of what makes that company tick. In turn, this understanding can lead to more effective management and better performance. It's like the practice of medicine. In the days when only a rudimentary understanding of how the body worked existed, medical care was much more of a hit and miss affair. Life expectancy was shorter and illness more debilitating. Nowadays, medical science can make a real difference to the human condition and performance.

Similarly retailers have tended to get by with only a rudimentary understanding of what their brand is all about. They'll have an instinct for it, but are unlikely to be able to properly diagnose its essence, let alone communicate it to others. I'm fairly sure that this skill will become increasingly important, which is one of the reasons why I'm writing this book. And an important aspect of this skill is the ability to distil everything that a company stands for down to its base element: *to the essence of the brand.* In John Lewis's case, the essence (which comes from the philosophy) is best encapsulated, I believe, in one word – *integrity.*

People trust John Lewis. They know they're not going to get ripped off. They know they'll be treated decently and receive a polite informed service. They'll also be confident that, if they have a problem with anything they've bought from John Lewis, they'll be entitled to fair recourse.

John Lewis is one of the most trusted names on the high street. It may not be the sexiest or the fastest moving company around, but it has integrity. And in the brutal cutthroat world that is the UK retailing scene such integrity is in short supply.

Trust and integrity are two of the most over-used words in marketing. If ever someone says *'Trust me,'* my reaction tends to be exactly the opposite. My line of work involves helping retailers define the benefits they offer to their customers, and I've lost count of the number of marketing directors who will argue with complete conviction that a key quality of their company is its trustworthiness. They will conveniently ignore the way that their sales staff happily give their customers inappropriate advice to get better commission or feel their high staff turnover is irrelevant. They will also 'forget' the occasions when they themselves put merchandise on the sales floor at an unrealistically high price with the sole intention of being able to subsequently show 'huge' discounts during promotional periods. I found that marketing tends to be the biggest violator of trust. By my book, trust is earned, not claimed, and John Lewis is one of the very few companies in the world that earns it.

There's a real solidity to John Lewis. It's not in business to make a quick buck. It's there to create a virtuous circle of supporting its employees by enabling them to give valued customers superior service. It's a proposition that engenders a high degree of trust from its customers because they know they can rely on the retailer to meet their needs. Andrew Woodward, Marketing Director at John Lewis, explains,

> *'The bedrock, and what makes this business different to others, is the partnership structure. This gives us four key attributes: co-ownership, independence, the ability to look long-term and mutual responsibility within the business.'*

John Lewis is a conviction brand. It has a view of the world and has designed its business around that view. In following its convictions rather than following the market, it has an inner strength. A mission in life drives the most powerful brands. Wal-Mart, for example, have grown to become the biggest company in the world by striving *'to give ordinary folk the chance to buy the same things as rich people'.* John Lewis's simple single-minded pursuit of maximising the happiness of its entire staff is a big idea that resonates through everything that the company does and is the source of its whole identity. As such it's a brand idea.

Key point *The John Lewis brand is rooted in a set of beliefs. Its strength lies in its convictions. This gives it substance and integrity.*

Iron fist in a silk glove

What is generally considered to have separated John Lewis from the many other well meaning but ultimately failed or failing co-operative ventures is the way that it aligns its egalitarian instinct with commercial focus. Its constitution decrees,

> 'While the partnership's ultimate aim shall be the happiness of its members, business efficiency will be a necessary factor in attaining this aim.'[4]

It's a happy fusion of the compassion and vision of John Spedan Lewis with the determination of his commercially hard-nosed father to provide the best service at the most competitive prices.

It was John Spedan Lewis who coined a motto in 1925, *'Never knowingly undersold'*, that is still in currency today, making it one of advertising's most enduring slogans (another example of longevity at John Lewis). It's a peculiar expression, very English, from a bygone age and quite difficult to understand. My mother, who shops at John Lewis, doesn't really know what it means, other than it represents some sort of price reassurance. I think that's probably why it's survived so long; its very quirkiness finds a different way to make the kind of boast about low prices that every other retailer is shouting about on the High Street every day. Because it uses a slightly different language to say the same thing, it cuts through the clutter and sticks in the memory. Its familiarity also helps. The fact they've been saying the same thing in exactly the same way for eighty years, until recently even featuring it on all their carrier bags, means it's an integral part of the brand and commands a high degree of awareness amongst customers.

As Andrew Woodward says,

> 'People trust our price positioning. They believe we offer value for money because of 'Never knowingly undersold'. Emotionally and functionally it's key.'

It's a considerable asset when a retailer can command such trust over a price promise. And, while this should be primarily attributed to their proven track record in delivering the pledge rather than just the words themselves, the clumsily worded slogan has undoubtedly played its part. It's in keeping with the straight-laced, upright, middle-class Britishness of John Lewis (in that it cleverly circumnavigates talking directly about that rather grubby issue of price). Hence it subtly re-enforces a distinctive brand character for the retailer while simultaneously making a potent price claim. You might expect me as an advertising man to argue that it's not just what you say, it's how you say it that matters. 'Never knowingly undersold' provides compelling evidence for such a point of view. Softly spoken words, loudly heard.

Points to consider *Are your company's price messages as creative and distinctive as that penned by John Spedan Lewis all those years ago? Do they get the message across in a way that is noticed, remembered and believed? Do they also add to the character and personality of your brand? Or are they like the million other vacuous price claims that clutter up our high streets?*

Interestingly, John Lewis's sister company – Waitrose – have developed a similar tone of voice with their *'Quality food, honestly priced'* slogan. I really like this; it embraces all that is good about the John Lewis Partnership in a more modern expression.

The combination of genuine integrity and ruthless pricing makes John Lewis a formidable competitor. Much of the merchandise they sell can be bought elsewhere and yet they tend to be the preferred retailer. This is because they have built a brand that stands for integrity, an integrity that includes offering its customers the best possible value at the lowest possible prices.

A great creative thinker and friend, Steven Sharp, Marketing Director of Marks & Spencer talks admiringly of his competitor and with, perhaps, a touch of envy at their freedom from the pressures of the City.

'I think integrity is a great watch-word for them. John Lewis is in a unique and almost unrepeatable position because they don't have shareholders, they have partners instead. They don't have the pressure of the City and they can decide what they want to do with their business

> *and investment without any outside pressure. Their caution has served them well and continues to serve them well. Of late, with the refurbishment of Peter Jones in Sloane Square, with their current advertising and with the way Waitrose is performing, you have to say that the tortoise seems to have found a bit of a turbo charge.'*

Recruiting to type

John Lewis attracts a particular type of person. In a gently mocking Channel 4 documentary a few years ago, the staff came across as, well, just a little strange. There was a hint of the brotherhood and a slight air of smugness that comes from being part of an exclusive club. It does take a certain kind of individual who will happily subordinate their own individuality for the cause.

They themselves will admit, as Andrew Woodward did, that they take great care to recruit people who will conform to the culture.

> *'It doesn't work if a partner comes in expecting to behave in a different way. It's all about behaviours and cultures and getting that right.'*

Andrew went on to explain how, in recently recruiting someone to his department, he had involved someone from another completely unrelated department as part of the interview process in order to get an independent assessment of the applicant's character and personality (free from the distraction of appraising skill levels).

It's a rigorous process that's applied to all levels of recruitment and contrasts significantly from the common high street practice of taking on all applicants and immediately putting them on the shop floor. Unsurprisingly John Lewis boast much lower staff turnover figures as a result.

Getting the right people on the bus is one of the most critical skills of any business. One of the best proponents of this are the Walt Disney Company who religiously recruit to type. With *'no cynicism'* as one of their core values they adhere to strict tightness-of-fit hiring guidelines.

'They present a rather standardised appearance. The girls are generally blonde, blue-eyed and self-effacing, all looking as if they stepped out of an ad for California sportswear and are heading for suburban motherhood. The boys…are outdoorsy, all-American types, the kind of vacuously pleasant lad your mother was always telling you to imitate.'[7]

Neither Richard Schickel, the author of this observation, nor myself would come anywhere near getting through a Disney interview. We're far too cynical. But that doesn't stop me admiring them for knowing the type of person they want to represent the company and then making sure that they only recruit those who fit. John Lewis, while perhaps not quite so extreme, are similarly disciplined. It's a good example of the business efficiency demanded by their constitution. John Lewis do everything they can to avoid the waste of employing the wrong people. So many retailers forget that their staff are more important than their customers; John Lewis don't.

! **Points to consider** Good retail recruitment is much more than finding someone to do the job; it's all about finding the right person who will personify the company in the right way. Does your company recruit to fit?

The soft-sell

Think of a John Lewis customer and an image of middle-England will pop into mind.

Although they haven't consciously gone out to target any particular customer segment, they've ended up with one of the most middle-class and clearly defined customer franchises of all the department stores.

Until recently, John Lewis didn't advertise, regarding such self-promotion as perhaps just a little too grubby and out-of-character. They undoubtedly sympathised with the socialist sentiments of George Orwell who once described advertising as 'the rattle of the stick inside a swill bucket'. It grieves me as an advertising man to admit it, but I must say that not advertising probably helped them enormously. (Although they've had the good fortune of being able to succeed without advertising in part because of a lack of serious competition. Had John Lewis been up against a department store as good as them, they may have needed to turn to advertising earlier than they did).

John Lewis have built their business through customers coming to them (and, once arrived, finding a store that fits their sensibilities). The whole style and demeanour of John Lewis draws like-minded customers. The policy of not advertising reflected an English reserve and modesty that their customers empathised with. Even now, with a change in that policy, they are very careful to maintain an understated tone to all their communication. A recent summer sale, for example, was announced in store windows with low-key, copy-only posters in muted colours that explained what they meant by an end-of-season sale. The impression is of a kindly vicar politely asking if you might like to try one of his parishioner's butterfly cakes at his Church fete. I find it as hard to imagine John Lewis ever resorting to day-glow colours and brash self-promotion as I do my mother sporting a Mohican. It just wouldn't happen. Andrew Woodward confirms that the relationship between John Lewis and its customers is:

'A very British relationship: personal, but at the same time not too familiar.'

The reason it works is that their customers can identify themselves in the manner and behaviour of John Lewis. They feel an affinity; they really do consider it 'my shop'. Everything about the way that John Lewis presents itself is designed to form a bond with its customers by making them feel safe, comfortable and at home. As Andrew Woodward explains,

'You've got nice wide aisles and can actually get through the shop. In some other stores you can find yourself having to fight your way past clutter and shop assistants who are trying to accost you. By contrast, we work to maintain simplicity in the retail environment and simplicity to the way we communicate. When we have a ticket it clearly tells you what the product is made of and what its benefits are. It's very simple language, down to earth, straightforward.'

John Lewis are a surprisingly open company. It comes with the territory of sharing information and decision-making throughout with the whole company rather than keeping it behind closed management doors. Entrusting such information leads to staff expertise, which is arguably one of John Lewis's primary competitive benefits.

The one thing, though, that John Lewis are very secretive about is their customer profile information.

> 'We've moved from a social demographic profile of our target customer towards a needs-based one and built it on research. We're actually very guarded about it and don't share it with anyone. We have a clear idea of the needs of our customers and define them accordingly. Regardless of whether they're male, female, C1, AB, or whatever, we focus on their needs.'

In this, Andrew Woodward hints at one of the reasons why John Lewis is so successful. Rather than target customers on the basis of who they are, they concentrate on understanding what they need and want.

It means they are, in effect, at one with their customers. They're effectively cutting wasteful targeting; concentrating only on communicating with those people within their franchise and not worrying about those outside their middle-aged, middle-class market. Trying to be all things to all people is a recipe for retail disaster. John Lewis flourish by having a well-defined customer base.

> **!** **Points to ponder** *The example of John Lewis shows that marketing doesn't necessarily have to be all about hunting down your customers; sometimes it can be more effective to let them come to you.*

John Lewis are confident that if a potential customer has got as far as walking through their door, that they will be able to meet their needs. It explains why, at a time when a number of its high profile competitors – such as Selfridges, Harrods and Harvey Nichols – are all increasingly dropping low-margin business in a shift towards high-margin fashion, John Lewis continues to position itself as the only store where you can still find everything from buttons to refrigerators. It's the mentality of an organisation that truly believes it can best meet its own needs by meeting the needs of its customers. This is something that many companies claim but very few actually mean, because their true priority is to maximise shareholder value (which tends to mean maximise immediate shareholder value).

A question that springs to mind is, 'how do John Lewis get new customers if they're not courting them as aggressively as some of their competitors?' I believe the answer lies in a combination of factors. First, and most importantly, is their longevity, aligned with their consistency. People know John Lewis, they know what to expect, and they know that they are dependable and have integrity. In short, they already know what they stand for. If their mother didn't shop there, their friends almost certainly will. This is the advantage of the tortoise: they are known and trusted and have proved that they can stay the distance. They've built up a stock of goodwill that's worth more than any million pound advertising campaign. Although, as Marks and Spencer have shown, reputations are not always enough.

The second reason why they are able to attract new customers is, I believe, because they're very much in tune with the needs of middle-England (arguably in way that Marks and Spencer lost sight of) and have been able to evolve to continue to meet those needs in a competitive way.

The third reason is their ability to continue to provide superior service, which not only persuade customers to come back again and again, but also increases the chances of them referring John Lewis to a friend. And, although true service costs more, it's one of the best ways of keeping competitors away because it increases the cost of entering the market by raising the bar on the standards that customers expect.

If you are their type of customer, eventually you will discover them and appreciate them. In a sense you come to them, they never appear to come to you - so perfectly defined is their brand.

The way we do things around here

I think the triumph of John Lewis has ultimately been to create a unique culture. Corporate culture is one of today's business buzz concepts and has thus tended to become a flabby word; taken to mean anything to do with the way a company behaves. The trouble is that without anything distinctive in their behaviour, values or ideas, the term becomes meaningless. John Lewis have a clearly defined culture in the truest sense of the world. They've established a set of conditions and grown as a result of those conditions into something that is clearly different from anywhere else.

What is a retail brand if not a distinctive culture? In retail, the brand is an amalgamation of space, people and ideas. It's a living organism. Can there be a purer example of a corporate organism that determines its own growth than John Lewis? As Helen Dickinson points out,

'I don't think any other company would let staff themselves decide a change of hours. The management of most businesses would come in and say, "Okay, you're going on to do seven-day trading". Here it can take up to a year to get a local branch council to debate, to decide, to bring everybody on board and either say 'yes' or 'no'. Here they can say 'no' and they know they can say 'no'; while they don't make all the decisions about business, they do make those decisions where it touches their lives.'

Andrew Woodward told us of an occasion when he had spent half a day with somebody who was conducting a review which would do away with his own job.

'He was perfectly happy doing that because, being a partnership, he knew he would be looked after whether he had a job in the business or ended up being made redundant. He was therefore able to look at this thing with a completely level head. That was an interesting example of a tough decision that had to be made, and where the business case came first.'

Acting in the best interests of the business is well entrenched at John Lewis and evidence that all staff do, as set out in their constitution, share the responsibilities of ownership as well as the rewards.

An example of this is that the Partnership, unlike many of its competitors, have chosen not to incentivise sales staff with a commission reward scheme. This means there's no particular benefit to be had by selling a customer one model over another. This has resulted in numerous occasions where customers have been sold a cheaper product than they had come into buy simply because the shop-floor assistant could see that it met their needs just as effectively as the more expensive version.

In these incidences the customer has been able to depend on the integrity of John Lewis to act in her own best interests.

The same emphasis on making the right decisions for the business apply throughout the company, as Andrew Woodward explains,

> *'The management at John Lewis are always very conscious of the fact that they need to explain why they're making a decision. It doesn't mean because we're a partnership we avoid tough decisions, it means we handle them in a different way.'*

The issue of accountability to the rest of the business is the hand brake against making unsound decisions. Management are called to account. Not only are they obliged to respond to the open letters in the disarmingly frank in-house magazine, *The Gazette*, but also they can, as Beverly Aspinall, ex-Managing Director of Peter Jones, found to her cost, find their behaviour closely and critically scrutinised. When Ms Aspinall was spotted shopping at one of Waitroses's rivals (John Lewis owns Waitrose), an eagle-eyed partner wrote to say that she was undermining the company by not shopping at Waitrose. Ms Aspinall had to explain that she had been pressed for time and was hungry and so had nipped into Safeway for an apple.

It's peculiarities such as these that give a company a distinctive culture. *'The way we do things around here'* often gives a good insight into an organisation. Richard Branson, for example, by apparently personally responding to every letter that is written to him, is demonstrating his personal involvement and interest in the Virgin business. Consequently the Virgin brand is inextricably linked with his own larger-than-life personality. The Carphone Warehouse, by insisting on training their staff for two weeks before letting them loose on customers, reveal themselves to be a very different company from the norm of their market, where wet-behind-the-ears sales staff may find themselves serving customers on the shop floor almost immediately on their first day. As a result, The Carphone Warehouse has been built on the quality of their service. The concept of accountability – personal responsibility and collective reward – is a differentiating principle for John Lewis. It is evidence of doing things in a different way.

❗ Points to consider *What peculiarities of behaviour help to define your company? What is the way you do things around there? Is it unique and does it make a difference?*

It's when your rivals copy your idiosyncrasies that you know there must be something in them, even though the copy is invariably inferior to the original. Sam Walton the founder and driving force behind Wal-Mart took inspiration from John Lewis. After visiting London he returned home to re-designate all his staff 'associates' having been much taken with the John Lewis notion that all their staff were partners.

He stopped short, though, of sharing ownership, although he did also introduce two other initiatives that he may have picked up from the English retailer – profit sharing and greater openness about company finances. It is said that imitation is the best form of flattery, but it would be wrong to present Wal-Mart as an imitator. Sam Walton like all good entrepreneurs was simply picking and choosing the best ideas from all over the world and adopting them into his own business - something to be heartily encouraged.

Wal-Mart, in fact, provide one of my favourite 'the way we do things around here' examples. Apparently the current Chief Executive, the top man at the biggest company in the world, drives as his company car a simple Volkswagen and whenever the senior management of the company travel on business they all stay in cheap budget motels, doubling up on rooms wherever possible.

This practice (alien as it is to an advertising man like myself, who has become accustomed to certain executive comforts like my own room) says everything about the company's religious approach to getting rock-bottom prices. Wal-Mart is a company driven to get the lowest prices in order to realise their mission of *'giving ordinary folk the chance to buy the same things as rich people'.*

Wal-Mart, of course, are famously tough negotiators. The owner of one of their advertising agencies recently told me that, *'they start agency fee negotiations at free and then work down'.*

John Lewis is a very different company from Wal-Mart, but they both share, and have profited from, a dedication to a core principle. Wal-Mart's priority is lowest prices; John Lewis's is the well-being of its partners.

As Beverly Aspinall put it when describing her role as Managing Director of Peter Jones,

'Making money and profits are not my prime purposes – we are here to look after the partners.'[8]

In sum

John Lewis exemplify what this book is all about. They are one of the few companies in the world, let alone retailers in the UK, that genuinely stand for something. By following their conviction that there is an alternative, better and more compassionate way to structure a business, they have been able to deliver superior service to a highly loyal base of customers.

Companies tend to adopt a variety of different means to achieve the end of maximising profit; some even concentrate on staff motivation as their primary means towards their end profit goal. John Lewis reverse the equation by using profitability as a means to maximise their end goal of the happiness of their staff. This makes them different from their competitors, which is no bad thing given that differentiation is one of the primary objectives of branding. It has also given them the zealous sense of mission that has helped drive their company on and on, like the Energiser bunny, while others fall by the wayside. And it has imbued John Lewis with an integrity that anyone connected with the company can depend on.

Partners don't just join John Lewis for a job, they subscribe to a whole set of beliefs. And people aren't just shopping at John Lewis for the products they sell; they are buying (sometimes at an unconscious level) into everything that the partnership stands for.

The brand idea of John Lewis is an idea about the culture of a company; as such it determines and informs everything that the company does and doesn't do. Buy a light-bulb from John Lewis and you will have done so in an uncluttered understated environment, you will have been served by a co-owner of the business and you will have the reassurance that the price is as good as you can get anywhere. You'll also know if it doesn't work, or you subsequently decide it isn't quite what you wanted, that they'd change it without asking any questions. These factors all stem directly from the convictions and integrity of what is a very cultured company.

References

1 Quoted in Forbes.com, *'No follower of fashion'* (25.11.02)

2 *The Guardian*, 14.06.04

3 John Spedan Lewis, quoted in *The New Statesman*, *'Not knowingly undersold – employee partnership in business'* (15.11.99)

4 The Constitution of the John Lewis partnership, ninth edition reprinted April 2004, original version 1929

5 Andrew Street, John Lewis Supply-Chain Director, quoted in Forbes.com, *'No follower of fashion'* (25.11.02)

6 Paul Barker, in *The New Statesman* (15.11.99)

7 Richard Schickel, *The Disney Version*, Simon & Schuster, 1968

8 Quoted in BBC News, '*A woman's touch for Peter Jones*', Emma Clark (29.08.04)

5

Walk a Mile in
Your Customer's Moccasins

What this chapter covers

- This chapter will highlight the importance of closing the gap between the retailer and its customers.

- It will tell the story of how Starbucks grew to become a customer responsive brand en route to conquering the world. The unlikely tale of how a bunch of coffee nuts became a pre-eminent retail organisation.

- It will explain how every retailer worth his salt is close to his customer, understanding what he or she wants almost to the point of it being instinctive.

- It will show how this empathy arises in part from an interest in people and an interest in shopping, and it will offer some simple suggestions to help you see the world through your customer's eyes. Something that no good retailer can afford not to do.

Get yourself a coffee, make yourself comfortable and read this brand fable

If any story endorses my belief that people buy the brand rather than the product, it's the Starbucks story. It's compellingly told by John Simmons in his book *'My Sister's a Barista'*, and it neatly illustrates the difference between a company that prioritises product and one that prioritises brand.

For its first sixteen years, from 1971 to 1987, Starbucks was a product-centred company. For its next sixteen years and beyond, it became a brand-centred company.

By 1987, the product-centric Starbucks had grown to six stores in and around Seattle and was valued at $4m. Sixteen years later the brand-centric

Starbucks had 7,500 stores in 34 countries and was valued at $14bn.

I acknowledge the comparison is not entirely fair, because brand-centric Starbucks was built on product-centric Starbucks, which has given it rock solid foundations. However it still provides a persuasive example, because in the mid-eighties the orientation of the company very definitely hung in the balance between the two approaches.

Howard Schultz's 1987 purchase of Starbucks from its founders, Jerry Baldwin and Gordon Bowker, signalled a clear change in focus. In fact, the debate between Schultz's vision of a brand built around the coffee shop experience and Baldwin's obsessive commitment to product purity had been raging for four years.

> 'The opportunity he (Schultz) saw was to unlock the romance of coffee in American coffee bars: to liberate the idea of high-quality coffee from its location in the home, where Starbucks had always seen it. Experiencing Italian expresso bars had shown him coffee's social power. Starbucks sold produce; it did not sell what Howard believed was the heart and soul of coffee, something that had existed for centuries in Europe. He attached words like 'community' and 'romance' to his vision of Starbucks potential as a great experience, not just a retail store.'[1]

On the other hand,

> 'Jerry Baldwin insisted, "we're coffee roasters, we'll lose our coffee roots."'[1]

At first it seemed as if the product purists had won when, in 1985, Schultz accepted that he couldn't change his colleagues' minds and amicably agreed to leave the company he had joined in 1981 to set up a new coffee company – Il Gionale – that was more akin to his vision.

It was only when Baldwin and Bowker decided to sell the business in 1987 that Schultz returned to the fold by buying it and implementing his brand-centric approach.

John Simmons writes,

'So the product – the taste, colour, aroma of the coffee – matters,
but arguably everything else matters a bit more. This was the possibility
that Howard saw.'[1]

I couldn't have put it better myself.

> **❗ Key learning** The product matters, but everything else matters a bit
> more. Ask yourself if everything else beyond the product that you sell
> matters enough. Or are you, like product-centric Starbucks were,
> holding yourself back by confining your attention (and your horizons) to
> your product?

John Simmons goes on to illustrate how focussing too obsessively on the
product can blind retailers to the bigger picture.

'Retail is detail is a popular saying, but it is hard for shopkeepers to live
up to it every minute. Of course there will be times when the detail is not
100% right, and in a contemporary Starbucks, maintaining the brand is
about maintaining lots and lots of details. Paradoxically, it would have
been easier for Starbucks to get all the details right in its early days
when it was focused on the product. Achieving the perfect roasted
coffee bean in an obsessive way gives you license to focus less on
other details generally covered by the word 'service'.

If Howard Schultz had a serious criticism of Starbucks in 1984, it was
that its service was poor, mainly because its certainty about its own
product quality led to arrogance and the unintentional belittling of
customers whose appreciation of coffee fell short of the Starbucks mark.'[1]

There are a number of pivotal moments in Starbuck's history and some
key people who have shaped it to become what it is today, which is one of

the top hundred most valuable brands in the world. Firstly, there were the three founders, Jerry Baldwin, Gordon Bowker and Zev Siegl. These were the guys for whom product was king and who lay the foundations. Then, of course, there was Howard Schultz, the man with the inspirational 'coffee shop' brand vision. There were two others – Howard Behar (who championed a customer focus) and Scott Bedbury (who introduced a brand framework).

I will discuss Scott Bedbury in a later chapter, but the difference Howard Behar made is relevant here and now.

A double tall skinny hazelnut decaff latte

Howard Behar's arrival represented a further step away from Starbuck's product obsession. Howard Schultz may have broken the umbilical cord with his coffee-house vision, but when Behar joined in 1989 the culture of the company was still rooted in product quality. Behar felt this was to the detriment of the customer and so he set about giving the company more of a customer orientation.

'More than anything else it was his (Behar's) focus on customer service that made a difference. His arrival at Starbucks marked a virtual cultural revolution. Chairman Mao-like, he changed everything and everyone, especially Howard Schultz. Obsession with coffee quality has always been endemic to the exclusion of everything else. Why? He asked. What if a customer does not agree with your judgement of what constitutes the best coffee? What if the customer wants coffee with skimmed milk? As he was to prove, some customers did indeed want coffee with skimmed milk. His philosophy was 'Say yes to customers,' and made it a mantra with partners. It has led to the wilder concoctions that customers ask for in a language that is unique to Starbucks: 'A double tall skinny hazelnut decaff latte.' Whatever; it's the customer's drink. Starbucks will provide the best possible version of that drink.' Howard Behar insisted, 'We're not filling bellies, we're filling souls.' Be less obsessed with absolute product purity if that means a narrow range of customer choice. But be as obsessed as you can be with giving the customer a drink that will meet her desires. Think more about people, less about product.'[1]

This was significant because when he arrived, the new semi-brand-centric Starbucks was in its third loss-making year. If Behar hadn't put the customer higher up the Starbuck's agenda, it's quite possible that Shultz's grand coffee-house vision would never have got off the ground.

Behar helped Starbucks evolve into a customer-responsive organisation. It was the third stage of evolution, following as it did the 'product is king' phase that got the company off the ground and the 're-framing the brand' phase that opened up bold new horizons. Although it hadn't been pre-ordained to grow in this way, it is difficult with the benefit of hindsight to improve on such an evolutionary sequence. It meant that, by the time the organisation shifted towards becoming more customer responsive, it already had a pretty clear idea of what it stood for and where it was headed. With such belief the company was sufficiently confident in itself to be able to listen to its customers and respond to their needs without being blown off course.

Try this *Say 'yes' to your customers and see where it takes you. (It helps here if you and your customers know what you stand for, what's on- and off-brand).*

People people

Retail is a people business. The best retailers are people people.

By nature, retailers are salespeople. To make a sale you have to be able to frame what it is that you're selling in such a way that the person you are selling to perceives it as meeting his or her needs. To do this you need to know what their needs are. And to know what their needs are you need to be able to put yourself in their shoes.

An old Native American ('Indian') wisdom cautions, *'before judging a man, let me first walk a mile in his moccasins.'* With its updated, more prosaic version – 'put yourselves in their shoes' – this sentiment has always struck me as one that retailers would do well to heed.

Almost all retail businesses start life in a product area that is close to its founder's heart. The genesis of Starbucks came from the shared passion for good coffee of three college buddies; Oddbins from Ahmed Pochee's interest in wine; The Carphone Warehouse from Charles Dunstone's experience of flogging phones for NEC. This means, more often than not, that the entrepreneur is both the customer and the retailer. He doesn't need to think about putting himself in his customer's shoes because he's already wearing them. The instinct of the entrepreneurial retailer and his ability to understand the customer often comes down to the simple fact that he's selling to himself. Incidentally, as an aside, I wonder if some of the travails suffered by Marks & Spencer can be attributed to the fact that in the past few years they have had people at the helm who haven't had their core business running through their veins. As Neill Denny, former editor of *Retail Week*, put it, Marks & Spencer hadn't, until Stuart Rose took over, had a fashion man in charge.

> *'You wouldn't have someone tone deaf running a music company,*
> *and they haven't had someone who really understands fashion running*
> *the business.'*

Interestingly, Stuart Rose served his early years at M&S on the food side before eventually going on to run Booker, a food wholesaling operation. In between and after these two companies he has held too many fashion positions to mention. So not only does fashion run through his veins, but he's also had a great grounding in food. He's uniquely qualified to be Chief Executive of Marks & Spencer.

As a business grows, it's all too easy to become distanced from the customer. The founder may have been catapulted into a completely different financial and social strata by the riches of his or her business and the people who have been brought in to run the business have probably been recruited for their business skills more than their natural interest in the product.

The challenge, therefore, for anyone in retail is to always put themselves in their customer's moccasins. As Our Price Records founder Garry Nesbitt said, of his investment in the health and beauty centre, Ragdale Hall,

> *'People who have come out of business schools and what-have-you are*
> *all saying "this is what the text book is telling us we should be doing."*
> *I say to hell with the text book, I'm telling you that I've been walking*
> *around here for two days talking to customers and you think you're*
> *getting it right, but I'm here to tell you that you ain't because I've*
> *actually seen it, I've experienced it.'[2]*

> **!** **Key point** *You can learn more about your business from your customers than from any business book, except, of course, this one!*

Giving customers the respect they deserve

I once heard Terry Leahy of Tesco describe customers as holy cows to worship rather than milk. Tesco are, as Neill Denny points out, one the few big businesses to successfully institutionalise customer orientation.

> *They're probably the only retailer I know that I would say is really about customer focus. They're obsessed with customers to an almost unhealthy degree. They really do care what customers think and feel and they act on it.*

Maureen Johnson of The Store endorses the view that Tesco set the standards in looking at the business through the eyes of their customers.

> *'I think retail should be about what Tesco is about, customer centricity. Before they do anything, any retailer should ask the question, 'how is this going to benefit the customer?' This, first and foremost, is why Tesco has been so successful.'*

One of the marketing world's bad habits that has always irritated me is the tendency to call customers 'consumers'. What does this mean? 'Consume' is quite a derogatory word (as well as meaning to eat or drink, it can also mean to destroy or to devour/overcome completely). I know that it has become an accepted part of the vernacular in today's 'consumer society' to the extent that my dictionary defines a consumer as *someone who buys goods and services for personal use or need'*, but I still think it's inherently disrespectful. To refer to your customer as a consumer depersonalises her, conjuring up, as it does for me, an image of a greedy creature hoovering up all that comes before her. I think language like this creates distance between you and your customer; it's a bit like describing a houseguest as a hospitality vulture.

I don't like it as marketing terminology, but I hate it even more when retailers lapse into it. Usually it's a sure sign of someone who has come to retail from the manufacturer's side of the fence. When you describe someone as a customer it puts you in mind of what's needed to service them, what's needed to get their custom. In rewriting the rules of branding to the language of retailers, I would start by insisting that retailers have customers not consumers.

> **!** **The first rule of retail branding** *Customers, not consumers - in other words, real live people. Retail is about contact and humanity.*

The love of shops

Putting yourself in your customers' moccasins means imagining that you are them. Whenever I'm in a meeting or we're talking about marketing strategy, I always ask myself, 'would my mum believe this?' In other words, will she understand it or is it so full of jargon and subtleties that it'll pass over her head? And, is it sufficiently persuasive for her to consider parting with her money (because, like much of the population, she isn't easily parted from her money)? It's an exercise that helps me because it takes me out of myself, out of my ivory tower, and enables me to judge a concept or a strategy from the customer's perspective.

I tend to believe that anyone who works in retail should love shopping. It needs to be in the blood, as it clearly is for Pret à Manger founder, Julian Metcalfe.

> 'While his mates might be kicking a ball around in a park, Julian Metcalfe could be found down at Camden Market. "I was genuinely interested in shops. As a young boy, I was always in shops. I used to love being in markets. Every Saturday and Sunday I used to go to Camden Market."'[2]

In her profile of BHS owner Philip Green, journalist Sally Vincent reveals a similar passion in her subject (although clearly not one that she herself shares).

> *'You don't know where Green's heart is, or get the full alpha-male effect of him, until you walk with him down the street he loves. Oxford Street on a Tuesday afternoon is not peak time, but it is jam-packed with women. We turned smartly into Topshop and descended into what, to me, a shopaphobic, are three levels of hell and to him seem to be the closest thing to heaven.'*[3]

If you don't like shopping, how can you possibly imagine what it must be like to be one of your customers? I once heard or read someone give the following advice – *'forget you are advertisers; remain consumers. Stick with what makes sense to you as an ordinary MBA-less homo sapiens.'* I'll forgive him the consumer reference for the sense of his sentiment.

At its best, the classic local corner shop that knew all its customers by name, and was probably the meeting place for all village gossip, provided the standards that I believe today's retailers would do well to aspire to. In those halcyon days, customers would be warmly greeted from behind the counter and without even having to ask for it, the shopkeeper would know what they wanted. He might also say something like:

> *'I knew that your son was back from university so I've got just the thing for you, some veggie burgers. I made them up specially last night because I know that Jonathan is a vegetarian.'*

This might be an exceptional example, but I know it to be true and representative of the very best service that a local shop could provide. The customer would be flattered and feel very special. This is what Customer Relationship Management is trying to do nowadays with technology (and, I have to say, often with a lot less success). The closest most major retailers get is knowing you as a good customer only once you've identified yourself by paying for something. Wouldn't it be great if in the future they could identify you whilst browsing, if it's not too Orwellian, through something like eye scans?

From my own experience, a good example of a company that effectively uses technology to achieve this level of personal service is a direct wine selling organisation called Bibendum, with whom I have a flourishing e-mail affair. They only send me information on what I'm interested in – claret, and never waste my time on Australian wine or anything I'm not interested in. Whenever I spot an e-mail from them I dig straight into it because I'm interested in it. I look forward to opening their missives nearly as much as their bottles.

Contrast this with the finding of the 2000 Yankelovich Monitor Study that most Americans agree with the statement:

> *'Most of the time, the service people I deal with for the products and services I buy don't care much about me or my needs.'*

I fear what the equivalent figure might be in the UK. As Richard Hyman from Verdict, pithily and rather depressingly, put it:

> *'Customer service is probably one of the things a lot of hot air is talked about, but where the reality is that it is something that retailers need to get much better at but can't really afford to. It's as simple as that.'*

Question to consider *Does everyone in your organisation genuinely care about their organisation and what it stands for or do they simply pay lip service to the idea?*

Retailers in the UK are currently experiencing negative price inflation, which means increased pressures on margins.

This is a climate that doesn't favour good service, because as much as anything else, good customer service is about getting a high calibre of staff, paying them more and training them properly. All of this costs money that many retailers are not prepared to pay at a time when they are under pressure to reduce overheads in order to remain competitive on price.

The next chapter deals with how to motivate your staff to deliver exceptional service, but the basic point that this chapter is trying to make concerns something that doesn't necessarily cost anything. And that is to always see things from your customer's point of view.

I'm conscious that it's all too easy in a book like this to present examples of excellence as standard. It's a nice idea to send your staff around the world to help them understand the subtle nuances of the product they're selling as some of the wine merchants might do, but for many retailers who are running a tight ship, such investment is just not possible.

However, there's no excuse for any retailer not to embed a certain standard of service within the DNA of the organisation. If you know what your company stands for, you don't have to be given a script of how to act. If you know your company stands for *'every little helps'*, like Tesco does, then the home delivery van driver will know that he needs to be able to do that little bit extra for the customer without having to be told exactly how to do it.

Charles Dunstone talks about the art of fantastic service, where staff are empowered to sort things out there and then. An extreme example of this comes from Ritz-Carlton where every single employee, be they the kitchen porter or the room cleaning maid, at any Ritz-Carlton Hotel anywhere in the world is allowed to give an on-the-spot $2,000 refund to a customer if they feel the circumstances merits it. Very few ever give it out because they take their responsibility very seriously.

But where it really can make a difference is through those everyday service initiatives that make life easy, such as opening the door or picking up a spilled bag.

These kinds of gestures need to be second nature to any retail organisation worth its salt, so that even the part-time staff pick it up immediately. A retailer that has clearly defined what they stand for will tend to find such standards easier to maintain.

Mark Twain once wrote that the advantage of telling the truth is that it means you don't need to think about what you do. If you build your brand on a truth about your company, the service that brings the brand to life comes so much more naturally.

The notion of *'working smarter, not harder'* has, I feel, particular resonance for retailers. Hard work comes naturally to retailers, they're used to working when others don't.

Even the expression 24/7, that has grown to mean a society that never stops, comes from retail. But hard work can become an addiction. And when that happens, it's hard to cut corners and think of smarter ways to do things. Increasingly, retailers have to become smarter. One of the ways of becoming smarter is to instil an instinct within the organisation for taking the customer's perspective. As Neill Denny observes:

> *'Charles Dunstone of The Carphone Warehouse is a bit like Terry Leahy (of Tesco) in that he's very interested in what his customers are up to and thinking. He sees the company as an expression of their desires. He doesn't impose a solution on his customers. Instead his customers are tweaking the tail of the company all the time and the company reacts to that. They're constantly thinking, "what could we do now to make life better for our customers?"'*

Practice customer responsiveness, not customer slavery

I would, however, like to add a word of caution by pointing out that there's a difference between walking in customer's moccasins and slavishly following their every whim and wish. The former seeks to understand them in order to best meet their needs; the latter abdicates responsibility.

Without wishing to denigrate your average retail customer, they are not especially good with abstract concepts. Shopping is a *'here and now'* activity. A lot of it is spontaneous; customers often only really know what they want when they see it.

It's almost impossible to properly recreate the shopping experience for research purposes. I would therefore always urge any retailer to use research to seek to understand their customers and to get inside their heads, but not necessarily to do everything they say.

It's a thin line though, because in the example I used at the beginning of this chapter, Starbucks benefited hugely from quite literally giving their customers whatever extraordinary coffee permutation they asked for.

I suppose the difference is that Starbucks are responding to their customers in the here and now rather than in an artificial research setting. They are also practicing the kind of customer responsiveness that retailers will increasingly need to savvy up to.

'Choice is also fragmenting. Consumers no longer solely want lots of choice; they want offers that are tailored exactly for them. In addition, availability has become much more important, which means that the penalties of poor availability are now much greater than they used to be. Sales are lost forever if you cannot have your product in the stores when customers want to buy it. They will simply go to the shop next door. The whole issue of choice has become more complex. The key factor here is that what people really want is 'edited choice'. They want the retailer to make certain kinds of decision for them. The old 'sea of merchandise' approach is not going to work anymore, and editing choice is the way retailers can build loyal customer bases.'[4]

By my way of thinking, customers don't want choice, they want what they want. They want edited choice. The reason I like Bibendum so much is that they make my choice easier by filtering out what I'm not interested in and helping focus my attention on what I want.

Learning tip Listen with intelligence to your customers. Don't become a lap dog that unthinkingly does everything they say, but do be sure that you're fully meeting their needs in your own individual way.

The Research Director at my agency, Maggie Taylor, has a nice way of putting it. She says that you need to listen between the lines. Very often you won't get the answer straight out. You need to think about what's been said and what's not been said to really understand what's going on. Next time you receive a complaint from one of your customers, try listening between the lines of what they're saying about the brand and what you might be able to do.

Addressing complaints properly can enter a restorative chain of events that converts complainants into fans. It's easier said than done, but well worth the effort and always a pillar of great brand building.

Philip Green, owner of too many fashion brands to mention and retail entrepreneur extraordinaire, still makes time to do this.

> 'It's amazing when you contact these people how you can turn a negative into a positive because they don't believe they're going to hear from you. When I read "I doubt this letter will get to you", I will call them from my desk at six in the evening and say "I got your letter this morning". Some man wrote to me yesterday saying, "I've been in your store, you don't normally carry my size, I loved the suit, I tried the jacket which was great, but the trousers were too short." I phoned our supplier and asked him to make this man a pair of trousers. Obviously you can't do that every day with 2,300 shops, but odd things like that, spreading some goodwill, make the difference.'

If Philip Green is able to find time while running a multi-billion pound empire to do this and still believes that it's sufficiently important, there's surely no excuse for the rest of us. He added:

> 'These little things matter. I encourage my people not to waste ten minutes of their day talking to their mates and to phone these four customers instead. They could end up touching forty customers, because the four they phoned will say 'guess who I got a call from today?''

Some simple tips towards a pair of moccasins

The advice I would give any student of retail who wants to get closer to his or her customers and truly start to see the world through their eyes is simple.

1. **Be a customer.** When you're out shopping, try to have an 'out of body' experience and be up there looking down on what's going on and thinking about how it relates to the brand and what you think that company stands for. You would be surprised how many good ideas are hidden in places you wouldn't normally look. Just being out on the High Street or browsing through shopping malls will throw up

numerous possibilities for how you can bring alive 'what your business stands for'. There's nothing new in retail, so shamelessly nick great ideas (and add your own personal touch to them). Whatever you don't usually shop for, volunteer to do it. Not only will you get brownie points at home, but I promise you (if you do it with your eyes wide open as to how that particular retailer conveys what his brand stands for) you'll gain free exposure to fantastic thoughts and ideas that will help your career.

I personally love grocery shopping and spotting how different retailers have addressed different issues. I find myself drawn to corners of stores without realising it: how did they entice me to the shampoo section? Why was I interested in an eight foot tall teddy bear? Become conscious of the unconscious.

Also read Paco Underhill's excellent book, *How People Shop*, about the issues of the physicality of shopping and how that impacts on branding. In Manchester train station the other day, I was confronted by a huge pile of wooden crates right in the middle of the concourse. There were enormous baskets of fresh vegetables and vivid peppers overflowing everywhere, lots of sawdust and bright enthusiastic staff handing out little paper bags with jars of sauce in them. Okay so this was a giveaway stunt to encourage trial, but wow did they make it feel a special event. I defy anyone not to be tempted.

I was, and I was also predisposed to believe that the sauce was going to taste great. Contrast this with someone trying to stand in your way and force something you don't want into your hand. I will remember this and use the learning. Great retailers are great shoppers.

Interestingly, Philip Green said to me:

'Most of us in whatever walk of life are creatures of habit, we go to the same restaurants, we go to the same shops. Take me down three streets you go down pretty regularly over the last year and I'll point out to you three things in that street you haven't even noticed because you've got a pattern of how you walk down those streets.'

Sir Stanley Kalms used to spend a day a week in Dixon's stores; David Ross will still help out on the shop floor at The Carphone Warehouse despite the fact his business has gone stratospheric and his behind-the-scenes role as the hard-nosed money man driving the business on; Lord Marks was still pacing the aisles right up to the moment he died in his seventy-seventh year. As an agency man, I always respect clients who ask agency staff to spend time helping out on the shop floor. As Robert Duvall said in Apocalypse Now, *'I love the smell of napalm in the morning'*. Only when you're in the heart of the action can you really sense what is going on.

2. **Talk and listen to customers.** Go into each customer conversation with the mindset that this conversation in going to change the company in some way. This will help you really listen, it's called deep listening, by opening your mind to any possibilities that it throws up. Be interested in what your customers have to say and look to their feedback as the gold dust that will help you improve your business. It's not always easy so choose your moments carefully, particularly if you're sitting on the check-out trying to process an increasingly long queue of increasingly irritable customers. But the trick is to become more conscious of the brand you represent and just how important each and every customer is to that brand. Set yourself a task each day of doing something that exemplifies what the company stands for and you'll soon be walking in moccasins before you know it. Don't forget that people who work on the manufacturing side have to book an appointment to listen to what their customers have to say. You've got your customers beating a path to your door. Be sure to use it.

3. **Buy a pair of moccasins.** Take them to work. They will be an icon to remind you that there are times when you might need to change shoes.

In sum

I haven't met a great retailer who hasn't been a great shopper. Being a great shopper gives you an unfair advantage over your competitors because it enables you to identify what your customers need and want before anyone else. The biggest of the many advantages that retailers have over manufacturers is proximity to their customers. Where manufacturers have to go to great lengths for dialogue with their customers, retailers come into contact with them every day. Any retailer who fails to use this advantage to properly understand where his or her customers are coming from and what they really want, probably doesn't deserve to be in business.

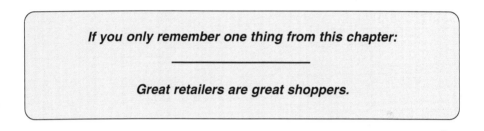

If you only remember one thing from this chapter:

Great retailers are great shoppers.

References

1. John Simmons, *'My Sister's a Barista'*, published by Cyan Communications, 2004

2. Simon Gravatt and Jane Morgan, *'Forever Young. Immortalising the Entrepreneurial Instinct'* Simon Gravatt, 2001

3. Sally Vincent, *'How I Did It'*, The *Guardian Weekend*, 23.10.04

4. Richard Hyman, *'The Retail roller-coaster: Message from the high street'*, Market Leader, Summer 2002

6

Topshop: No Place for Men in Suits

This case study draws from an interview with Jane Shepherdson, Brand Director, and Jo Farrelly, Marketing Director of Topshop.

What this case study teaches us

- This is a story about a business that re-energised and transformed itself from a somewhat dreary middle-of-the-road teen store to become a magnet for the fashion conscious from all over the world.

- Topshop teach us the importance of putting yourself in your customer's shoes and, if it comes to it, being prepared to prioritise the needs of your customers over the needs of your business.

- Topshop also provides an object lesson on the importance of getting real and avoiding getting caught up in theories. Common sense rules in retail.

- This case study shows the obvious importance of getting the product right, of really understanding and empathising with your customers, of having a bold vision for your retail brand and taking strong steps to realise it. You can only get it right if you know what right looks like; by knowing what your brand stands for.

- The primary lesson of this case study is the value of being at one with your customers.

I had just settled down and, having brushed a small speck of dust off the sleeve of my suit, was preparing for a theoretical discussion on the principles of retailing.

> '*I have a thing about about men in suits you know, people who drone on about the principles of retail. What bollocks. There aren't any principles of retailing.*'

This was Jane Shepherdson's opening gambit. All of a sudden I started to feel a little overdressed and a little pompous. She continued.

> '*We're anti-marketing and anti-brand...*'

I began to wonder if my being there was a sensible idea. To be frank, it made me aware how uncomfortable it must be for women having to cope with the male machismo of the business world. Now the boot was very much on the other foot.

> '*We're not one those businesses that are run according to textbook brand philosophies.*'

I was about to get defensive and argue that I wasn't writing a textbook, but then I realised that she was absolutely right. Not so much about this being a textbook (not unless the definition of textbook is taken to be 'exemplary' rather than 'standard'), but about the whole notion of retail businesses being mismanaged by people (invariably, it is true, men in suits) who slavishly follow rules without questioning whether they make sense.

Real retailers don't do business with cardboard cut-outs

Retail is a live organic thing that changes from day to day. It's full of real live people having real live conversations, real live negotiations and real live transactions. It's a people business. The best retailers are interested in people and like to get involved. They get off on the humanity of the whole thing. Those who seek to reduce it to figures, balance sheets and a list of do's and don'ts are not real retailers. They're men in suits.

And the same applies to branding. Good retail branding is not, and should never be, a set of irrefutable rules. If it is taken (as it unfortunately is all too often) to be a dry theory, rather than a way of thinking about and organising a business, then yes I too confess to being anti-brand. I hate it when someone says they've re-branded their business when all they've done is change the logo. What kind of re-branding can that be when customers are subjected to the same old dismal service, when the window displays remain as dreary as they ever were and when the merchandising continues to look as if it was designed by a colour-blind accountant.

Jane (I think I should refer to her as Jane, to use her full name seems too formal for Topshop), in describing the prevailing wisdom at Topshop when she took over only six years ago, illustrates how common sense can be lost behind the macho posturing that is all too common in boardrooms.

> *'At the time when I took over, they thought in-store merchandising was blocked departments. Literally. You'd see these guys who'd sit there saying, "you don't understand, Jane – if you want to sell volume, you have to have blocked departments." I was like, "Are you serious? You cannot really be serious." But of course they were. The reality though is something that those kind of people can never understand, which is that the only way to excite people about your clothes is to show them how they can be worn, to make the stores look exciting, to make the stores look creative, to have colour, to have something that is interesting and visual to look at.'*

! **Provocation** *In retail, always choose to get your hands dirty on the shop floor over pontificating behind a desk. Never forget that your customer is a real person rather than some amorphous anthropological footnote to a marketing plan. Observe and ask rather than assume. Apply common sense, not business nonsense.*

My only disagreement with Jane, then, concerns the brush that she is tarring branding with. I would argue that she is describing bad branding, not branding per se. Good branding, as I hope this book brings out, concerns exactly the kind of stuff that she believes in and has practiced with spectacular success for the past five or six years since she took over the reins of the business in 1999.

Topshop was a product of the swinging sixties, starting life in 1964 as a concession in a small department store in Sheffield. The current management play down its achievement in surviving for its first thirty-five years in the fiercely competitive fashion market by saying that it was nothing more than a cheap and cheerful, somewhat naff, high-street retailer. But it must have done something right simply to last so long. I suspect it was down to the fact that it has always been a well-targeted business. Even although it wasn't particularly profitable, Topshop has, since it first opened its doors, been a place for teenage girls. The very fact that the business has survived without being particularly well managed hints at the advantage of having a clearly defined market. Jane and her team have simply leveraged this market to great effect by servicing it properly, by really delivering what its customers want and by taking a more expansive view of their target market.

The genius of Topshop has been to break out of the confines of a rigidly defined market. Jane argues for a more embracing approach.

'That's a manager's textbook view, to say your target market has to be fifteen-year olds. The only people we don't target are people who aren't interested in fashion. It's all about attitudes; it's about having a fashion attitude rather than age.'

However the reason she is able to make such an assertion is that Topshop has such a strong centre of gravity.

'Our core target is 18 to 30 year olds, opinionated, cutting edge, fashion cognoscenti. However our market stretches from 12 to 45 years old.'

Not only are they very clear on whom their customers are, but they know them inside out. And they know them inside out because they put themselves firmly in the shoes of those customers. As Jane says:

'I don't think I could do the same for a brand such as Evans because we just don't get it. Here we simply buy what we like. It's the easiest buying job you could have because you're buying for yourself.'

> **!**
>
> **Key observation** *Good retailers understand their customers; great retailers are at one with them.*

Good retailers understand their customers; great retailers are at one with them. Jane considers doing the right thing for her customers as her main priority. Meeting the needs of her customers is more important to her than seeing to the needs of the business. Mostly these will be aligned, but not always, as Jane remembers when she first took charge.

> 'I would go into meetings and say, "yes, I know that's selling and it's selling two thousand units but I don't care, it's awful and we're not going to buy awful things anymore regardless of whether or not they will sell". If you're going to earn people's trust, you have to set a standard. That set the standard; all the buyers now know that, and all the buyers now stand by every single thing in their range. Compare this to ten or twenty years ago when some buyers would sit there saying, "have you seen this, isn't it horrible? Guess how many we sold last week... isn't that great?" I thought that was outrageous. How could they do that? It's not right, there's no integrity.'

I wonder how many retailers can claim to have withdrawn an item that is selling well simply because they don't like it? Have you ever done so? It requires the confidence that comes from knowing your customers intimately and a clear sense of what's right for your brand. The lazy position would be to argue that because an item is selling well it must be something that customers want. But to take such a position can be an abdication of leadership. The sentiment that the customer is always right shouldn't be interpreted to mean that you can sell poor quality merchandise to them just because they are prepared to pay for it. Gerald Ratner found this to his cost, when he foolishly admitted that the products he was selling were 'crap'. A good retailer has a responsibility to its customers because they will look to it for leadership, particularly in fashion. This is what Jane means when she talks about integrity. And, by raising the standard of the clothing that they sell, Topshop has succeeded in transforming their brand.

'Once a dull, teen-focused clothing store, Topshop, which attracts 180,000 visitors each week, is now a fashion source for designers, stylists and celebrities, including Madonna, Kate Moss, Liv Tyler and Cher.'[1]

The lesson from Topshop is that your customers aren't simply a socio-economic group on a page of the marketing plan, they're real people. Advertising man David Ogilvy was once famously quoted as saying *'your customer isn't a moron, she's your wife.'*

If you think of your customers as an impersonal homogeneous grouping, you might be better off selling to cardboard cutouts. Champion your customer as if your business depended on it, rather than championing your business as if your customers depended on it.

> **Key point** *Champion your customer as if your business depended on it, rather than championing your business as if your customers depended on it.*

Chickens and eggs

Topshop, in fact, provides a strong challenge to the fundamental precept of this book. At the start of my meeting, Jane and her Marketing Director, Jo Farrelly, were keen to disagree with my assertion that people don't buy what you sell, they buy what you stand for. They argued that since the first step in transforming Topshop had been to get the product right, the product must be more important than the brand.

'The first thing we had to do was to get the clothes right or there would have been no point in doing anything at all. No point in trying to make it a brand or trying to market it or anything. We didn't advertise at all for years until we felt comfortable that the product was at a stage where we wouldn't disappoint.'

I would contend that although Topshop may not have advertised for years, it was still a brand. In fact you don't have to advertise to be a brand at all: just look at Bodyshop, one of the all time great retail brands in its day. Topshop may have been a brand in transition: from being dull and teen-focused to one with fashion credentials *('We all have one singular vision, which is to be the fashion authority')*, but nevertheless it was still a brand. And, furthermore, I would add that the brand vision to re-establish Topshop's fashion credentials came first and the products that would deliver such a brand vision followed. But perhaps that's like trying to argue that the chicken came before the egg.

Jo makes the case against my argument by pointing to her previous employer, Levi's, an example she argued, of what can happen when brand takes precedence over product.

> *'Topshop do things the right way round, that's why we disagree with your assertion. While Levi's had a fantastic core product and an amazing heritage, they just lost sight of their product. They just got too wrapped up in branding in a vacuum, so you'd have this amazing advert that cost the earth and then walk into a store and the product wouldn't live up to it, and the store would disappoint as well. Their whole business model felt wrong.'*

Superficially, it's difficult to argue these two points, but digging a little deeper you realise that the decision to become a 'fashion statement' retailer and ruthlessly pursuing that direction is in fact branding in action. It's a brand positioning: its success or failure depends on the ability of the management team to deliver that positioning more effectively than its competitors.

Like all good ideas, Topshop's brand positioning seems blindingly obvious with the benefit of hindsight. The offer of leading-edge fashion at incredible prices is hardly something that the market is going to reject. The skill here is in giving it to them even before they know they want it. As with a great advertising headline, it always looks easy when someone else has come up with it in the first place.

I don't believe that any retailer has an option between optimising the product that is sold and the brand that is created. Both are important, but I would place the big idea, the brand, slightly ahead of the merchandise. A good retail brand can't sustain poor products indefinitely any more than good products can sustain a weak retail brand. But, in most cases, people can buy what you're selling elsewhere.

I believe passionately, and will continue to argue until the cows come home, that people are first and foremost buying what you as a retailer stand for. Young women who are into fashion are drawn to Topshop because it has the right fashion credentials. Once there, they're given the reassurance that the item of clothing they like the look of comes with the blessing of a trusted fashion confidant, i.e. Topshop. Without Topshop they probably wouldn't have found the item in the first place let alone have had the confidence to buy it. And, of course, this creates a virtuous circle in that manufacturers and designers now beat a path to Topshop in order to supply unique fashions, further strengthening the brand's authority.

Even before Jane had made Topshop sexy, it was a brand that stood for something. She was able to concentrate on the product precisely because she knew she had a customer base and a reputation (of sorts) as a place for teenage girls' clothing.

Similarly people are prepared to pay a premium for Levi's jeans because they are buying into a brand. Levi's is a brand that's a composite of its hundred and thirty year history, its track-record of good quality jeans, its battery of memorable and evocative advertising images, and a whole host of other impressions. If what Jo is saying though is true and product quality is being neglected (or that the design has failed to move with the times), then the brand will soon suffer. As it would, incidentally, if either they stopped advertising or started churning out poor quality advertising: for the brand is the totality of all these different elements.

If Topshop lost its touch and started selling poor quality clothes or, even worse, unfashionable clothes, then its brand would begin to lose its meaning. It would lose its aura and its reputation as a place for fashion, creativity and excitement. It's that aura (otherwise known as the brand) that its customers are ultimately buying.

> **Point to consider** An aura is defined as a distinctive character or quality around a person or in a place. Branding can be thought of as an aura. Is there an aura about your store?

I wouldn't want anyone to take out from this book that the product isn't important. Product is critical. With nothing to sell, there would be no business. But the message I'm seeking to get across is that people don't buy that product in isolation because in many situations they can buy a similar (if not identical) product elsewhere. In this case they buy an item of clothing that is wrapped up in the Topshop brand. The two – product and retail brand – are indivisible. To argue the customer buys only the product and that the retail brand it comes from is not a factor would be like trying to argue that I'm writing this book on some circuit boards and moulded plastic rather than on an Apple computer.

The Anti-Brand Director

A retailer who thinks only of her raw materials (the products that she is selling) misunderstands the buying mentality of her customers. No one, however, could accuse Jane or Jo of not knowing their customers.

Jane, somewhat ironically given that she described herself as 'anti-brand', has the job title 'Brand Director'. I wonder if someone at Arcadia (Topshop's parent company) is having a joke. Fashion retailers are notoriously funny about what they perceive as the hierarchy of job titles, which often leads to anomalies like we have here, because by any standard definition, Jane's title would be Managing Director.

But in actual fact I believe the title of Brand Director is spot on for the top position at any retail organisation. To me, Managing Director says that your responsibility is to manage the directors. This is archaic. It's a 'men in suits' expression that implies distance between the top guy and the shop floor that is wholly unsuitable for a twenty-first century retailer. Chief Executive Officer is much the same, it says... well, I'm not sure what it says other than being a pompous statement of status. But Brand Director is perfect. Jane's job is to direct the Topshop brand. And it's a job that she performs fantastically well.

It interests me that Jane was a buyer before her elevation to run the show. In part, this explains the importance that she places on getting the product right. But I've always felt the buying department tends to be a neglected nerve centre of any retailing operation. As explained in the Selfridges case study, Peter Williams, like Jane, identified the overhaul of the buying department as being a key step in the revitalisation of Selfridges. Buyers need to know and understand what the retailer they are buying for, stands for. They need to know this because it gives a necessary context to their buying decision. To illustrate with an extreme example, the Topshop buyer will know that a frumpy knitted jumper would be inappropriate. Not only would it be unlikely to sell, but it would also send out the wrong signals about what kind of place Topshop is.

I recommend that anyone starting out in a new retail job should seek out the buyers and get their views on the company. If they can't articulate the brand, how can they buy for it? It can be a quick and effective way to get the pulse on the culture of the place. And if you happen to find that the buyers are not aligned with the Management or the shop floor staff, it can be a sure sign of underlying weakness in a retail operation.

As an aside, buying is different from marketing. Whereas buying is a distinct department with specialist skills, I tend to believe that marketing should be an ethos (rather than a department) that pervades every facet of a business. I get nervous whenever I meet a new client who tells me that they have a strong marketing department, because, more often than not, this means that marketing is disembodied from the rest of the organisation.

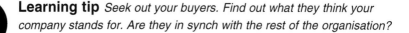

Learning tip *Seek out your buyers. Find out what they think your company stands for. Are they in synch with the rest of the organisation?*

This is probably even more so at Topshop than anywhere else because they've made speed of merchandising a central platform of their business. As Jane explains,

> *'We have three hundred lines a week in our Oxford Circus store so it's virtually re-merchandised every couple of days. And things sell out a lot of the time. Our stock cover is so fast that probably a third of our stock at any one time is on one week's cover. That means it's gone after a week and you've got to put something else in there.'*

To help meet this demand, the buyers at Topshop get daily sales figures. They are completely on top of the business because they have to be.

> *'When US fashion editors come to London, they all head to Topshop. It has broken away from the high-street tendency to play to the bland middle market. Clothes are cut to fit, the styles are right on the (Edwardian detail)*

button and turnover is flickeringly quick. And the way we shop has changed accordingly. Instead of three or four sluggish collections a year, Topshop's rails change roughly every three weeks, encouraging consumers to pop in more often, and so to spend more money.'[2]

Even The New York Times recognised the 'genius' of Topshop's emphasis on speed.

'Shepherdson's high demand for faster deliveries along with the coolest looks have helped name her 'genius' in the art of retailing. The Oxford Street store gets two deliveries a day and 7,000 looks a season. Items turn over so quickly that shoppers become consumed with buying before stock runs out, creating a 'dynamic of desperation'. As all retailers know, there is no recipe for success in the world of retailing. The ability to change and work innovatively with the times, and be able to meet the demands of a changing market is key. Of the 28,000 visitors per day in Oxford Circus, 14,000 leave with a purchase. Now that is successful retailing.'[3]

So what, I wonder, might be the words that a Topshop buyer would use to describe their brand. By definition, each one would be personal but then again each would share an attitude.

My guess is for sure 'fashion' would be one, others might be 'young', 'exciting', 'creative', 'accessible', 'cat walk', 'funky', 'clever', 'smart', 'now', and 'uncompromising'.

Fashion leader

Fashion, because that's the business Topshop are in, although quite possibly those men in suits who used to be at the helm didn't think of it that way, let alone understand it. It has been a stunning achievement by Jane and her team to turn an unexciting and unexcited run-of-the-mill high street retailer into a destination store for fashion vultures, writers and cognoscenti from all over Europe.

*'We're very English. The way we approach fashion is very English.
Fortunately for us, English style has now apparently become the most
popular in the world. French people come over on Eurostar every
weekend to shop at Topshop because the English now are seen to be
the most stylish. How fantastic is that?'*

Quite frankly, it's pretty incredible. Ten or fifteen years ago it would have
been utterly implausible, to have said as much would be sufficient to have
been certified as insane. Prone to wild and fantastical delusions, they would
have said. I love stories where businesses and brands turn perceptions on
their head and successfully become something that was previously
unimaginable.

Fashion is fickle and easy to get wrong. It's fearsomely difficult to
maintain. Something that becomes popular on the basis of being
fashionable can very soon find itself unfashionable simply by virtue of its
popularity. This is one of the reasons why speed of turnover is so important
to Topshop.

By continually having new things and new ideas they are staying ahead
of the game, and what's fashion if not being ahead of the game?

Fashion is also perception. It can swing on the opinions of a few. Jane
cited how bringing a leading and respected designer in as part of her team
helped change the perceptions of opinion-forming fashion journalists.

*'Bringing Ronnie Cooke-Newhouse in was important because it allowed
that core of people, the fashion journalists, to reappraise us. She doesn't
work with the high street, and her clients include Comme des Garçons.
Just the fact that she agreed to work with us was a sign that we must
be doing something different or that we want to take some chances.'*

Getting written about and talked about is essential if you want to be seen
as fashionable.

Topshop don't buy stories, they try to inspire them.

> *'We would never do paid-for editorials ever. The product speaks for itself so we have that, but also it's about continually coming up with new ideas so that we can just get the stories out there and be the most talked about brand.'*

This means that fashion journalists tend to come to Topshop for stories instead of, as is the relationship between most retailers and the press, going cap (or rather, press release) in hand to plead with the journalist for coverage.

In truth journalists like someone else to do their work for them and that's exactly what Topshop does; it sources new and exciting trends and presents them altogether in an accessible way.

Questions to consider *Do you try to buy stories or inspire them? Do you work hard enough to get talked about and written about? What do people say about your company behind your back? Do they say anything at all? Or are you just not talked about?*

A creative culture

Inspiring stories is easier said than done. I sometimes wonder how many man-hours are wasted by suited executives labouring through 'brainstorming' sessions in artificially-lit rooms and coming up with exactly the same long flip chart list of so called ideas that every other similar session generates.

This is no way to come up with ideas.

Much better is the way that Topshop do it, which is to make creativity a core value and to readily put ideas into action even when (probably especially when) cold rational business logic would dismiss those ideas. It's all about being open to opportunity and seeing what's going on in the world. Nothing illustrates this more than one of Topshop's ideas that literally came from the streets.

> 'Five years ago everybody was talking about the markets, people were going to Portobello every weekend. Every magazine was talking about market couture, so we thought right, okay, let's go and get them in. If that's what people want then that's what we have to somehow give to them. We tasked one of our teams to go out and talk to these people and ask if they would like to trade in Top Shop by saying 'this is our commission rate, but you'll be guaranteed two hundred thousand customers coming past every Saturday and it won't be as cold and wet!' It was a huge success.'

This would have been such an easy idea to dismiss out of hand. Those brainstorming executives in their grey suits looking blankly at each other over cheap office furniture would not have had the gumption to think of asking market stall holders to come and sell hand-made items in their precious, pristine, sterile shops.

And even if they had, they would have known the idea would have been quashed by their boss who would have told them to stop being so stupid and be more professional. They would have missed a golden opportunity that Topshop grasped with both hands.

> 'We're a creative business and therefore should be run by a creative person. You have to have somebody with some kind of creative vision of where it's going. Otherwise it's just going to be the same as everywhere else, running on nothing more than a set of principles. You can't do that. This is a very emotional business. People get very passionate about it.'

Jane goes on to say,

> 'I care passionately about the business, but my primary motive is not whether or not it makes or loses money. I care about creating something that's fantastic and amazing that everyone else wants to copy. That's all I care about. The fact that it makes a huge profit as well is an added extra.'

Their spirit of creativity gives Topshop energy and buzz. New things are happening all the time, giving all the more reason to pay a visit.

Bold, unexpected ideas are fun and exciting and keep it at the forefront of people's minds.

'It's about creativity, it's about creating something, if you can create something that's exciting enough, then people will buy it. If you can excite your customer and do something that they think is absolutely wonderful, then of course they'll keep buying from you.'

The high street theme park

In researching this book, I came across a travel piece in The Observer about an adventure holiday in Egypt that involved a camel ride in the desert, sleeping aboard a felucca in the Nile and seeing the pyramids.

The piece was entitled 'Even better than Topshop' because that was the point of reference for the writer's teenage daughters and was intended as high praise (albeit with a hint of irony).

'It's our duty. Nowadays we shop in our leisure time. Shops are the equivalent of your theme park or whatever and so they've got to be as exciting, as fun.'

Topshop is exciting and attracting, as it does, four times as many visitors as The Tower of London and drawing people from all over Europe, it can legitimately claim to vie with the major tourist attractions for its fair share of mind.

Topshop is all about helping their customers to make an impression, to look good and to feel good. This comes both from the clothing and from the whole atmosphere of the place.

The value equation, to use marketing terminology, is weighted in favour of the customer.

> *'They get the most incredible value for money. The clothes are exciting, they're really well made, they're designed beautifully, and the fabrics we use are better than other people use. For what you pay, you get more in Top Shop. The choice as well – the choice is huge – the whole theatre and experience, the atmosphere.'*

To buy from Topshop is a smart choice. Leading stylist Bay Garnett has been quoted as saying:

> *'I think people are as label-conscious as ever, just more discreet. People will still happily pay a lot for cashmere, but feel like a mug spending hundreds on a cotton Balenciaga sweater when the cheaper Topshop equivalent is, ironically, cooler.'*[4]

Topshop are totally committed to doing everything they possibly can on behalf of their customers. Their stores have a buzzing club-like atmosphere.

They stage fashion events.

They offer a free personal shopping service and VIP dressing rooms. They've just launched a made-to-measure atelier service, *'a ludicrous idea'*, smiles Jane *'that will never make us any money because we hand-make these dresses, sew them and pattern them.'* They offer Topshop To Go, where a style advisor will come to your house with a van full of fashion options.

They even hold student lock-ins every six months (basically a party for students with free beer. Hardly surprising that they were mobbed with four thousand students on the first occasion and now experience queues all the way down the road whenever they host one of these events).

Their aim is to indulge their customers.

> *'Indulgence of our customers is the spirit and that's what we get excited about. Obviously we get excited by the product, but there's nothing better than thinking your customers are amazing and giving them a lovely bag to walk away with and all kinds of treats.'*

In return they've been rewarded with not only the loyalty of those customers, but have also become a defining part of their lives.

> 'Girls have been identified by names that define their styles throughout the years. Mods, Dollies, Heathfields, Punks, Sloane Rangers. Today it is difficult to find one word to accurately define the look girls are after. Though if there were one, it would be Topshop girl.'[3]

In sum

Putting customers first can mean putting your business second. Are you brave enough to do this? Does your business do it?

In other words does your business sacrifice a little of today for a lot tomorrow?

You can't be all things to all people and that is the key to retail branding. Decide what you want to stand for and don't let anything stand in your way. The art is to make sure what you stand for is not only differentiated, but compelling. That's why so few retail brands become icons of our time, and then, and only then, go on to make the big bucks.

The brand at Topshop is well articulated, not by a brand manual, not by long theoretical marketing speeches, but by Jane and her teams' every action and it is these actions that inform every part of the business. They are all brand managers.

Topshop put their customers at the heart of their business. They are at one with the young (and not so young) girls and women that covet what they sell and love what they stand for. And, because Topshop sees the world through their customers' eyes, they not only give those customers exactly what they want, but also have enormous fun doing so. To a stuffy old sod like myself, it may look as if the lunatics are running the asylum, but there's undeniably method in their madness. And although they may disagree with this – after all what do I know, I'm a man in a suit pontificating about marketing theory – Topshop is a textbook branding story.

References

1. *'Topshop's lofty status',* Ellen Burney, WWD (Feb 2003) article from Thomson Gale

2. *'Riding the retail revolution',* Hadley Freeman, *The Guardian Weekend* (October 23 2004)

3. *'She's a Topshop Girl',* Cathryn Horyn, *New York Times.* July 11 2004

4. Bay Garnett quoted in *'Catering to the masses'* by Samantha Conti & Ellen Burney, WWD (Jan 2004) article from Thomson Gale

7

Your Most Important Customers Are on Your Payroll

What this chapter covers

- This chapter seeks to show just how important the staff are to any retail organisation, because they embody the retail brand and turn that brand into reality.

- It will emphasise the need to respect, nurture and involve staff, to the degree of prioritising their needs over the needs of the customer.

- It will explain how, as retail is first and foremost a people business, the staff have a pivotal role to play in retail branding. Without staff a retail brand is nothing.

- It will offer some simple suggestions towards encouraging your company to take its staff more seriously than it may otherwise be inclined to do.

- Fundamentally, it's a chapter about the human dimension of the retail brand.

Lessons from Beijing, New York, Acton and an airline from San Antonio

One of my colleagues tells the story of a shopping experience in China in the mid-eighties, when the country was only just beginning to open up. He spotted a shirt in the shop window that he liked and pointed it out to the shop assistant. She went to get one from the back of the shop and returned with the identical shirt other than the stitching, which had come undone down one side. My colleague pointed this out and the assistant, a little grumpily, went back to find another shirt. This one had a small tear. At this point the assistant flatly refused to get any more shirts. She told my colleague, that if he didn't want either of the two shirts she had got for him, he could go without. China, after decades of repression, didn't have a service culture. One of the problems the Chinese had at the time was the tendency of shop assistants to get into fights with customers, because they felt they weren't being treated with proper respect. The authorities responded by docking the pay of any shop assistant who fought a customer, which had the unfortunate outcome of shop assistants doing everything they could to avoid customers. You can't dispute the logic that decides the best way of not getting into fights with customers is to keep your distance from them, but it tends not to lead to great service.

The same colleague recently had the opposite experience in New York. He had bought a pair of soccer boots in Niketown having tried them for size. Unfortunately he found, after playing in them, that they were too tight after all and he ended the game with a couple of blisters. Being English, he had no expectation of being able to return the now muddied and scuffed boots, but as he was passing the store he decided to give it go. They changed them with no questions asked.

America is a service culture. Unlike the Chinese in the eighties, and, I have to say, at times, the English in the twenty-first century, Americans don't have any hang-ups about serving customers. It's part of their cultural DNA. On the other hand, I feel the British still harbour some deep-rooted prejudices against service. It's strange in a once-great trading nation, one that was even dismissed by Napoleon as being a nation of shopkeepers, that being a shop assistant is often looked down on.

Steven Sharp, Marketing Director at Marks and Spencer, made the following observation.

'I remember standing in a queue at Disney World with an Englishman behind me and an American in front of me. After a while the American started talking to me and told me he was a bartender. He said he was the best bartender in his town and that was really important to him; he enjoyed serving drinks and making people happy. After a while I turned to the Englishman behind me and found that he too worked in a bar. He told me that it was filling in the time for him while he waited for something better to do. It summed up the different cultural attitude to service: the pride of the American for his job against English apologist.'

I feel this denigration of service heightens the obligation on the retailer to create a culture that overtly respects its staff. A company that treats its staff as disposable, and doesn't truly value them, will find in return that the staff neither respect nor value the company. Such a state of affairs is a particular problem for a retailer because his or her brand is in their hands.

John Lewis along with The Carphone Warehouse are, to my mind, amongst the few companies in the UK that truly value its staff.

'Talk to an employee of Carphone Warehouse and they will tell you that the work is hard, the hours long and that the standards are stretching and rigorously applied. They will also tell you that they enjoy it enormously. Push a little harder; ask them "Why do you enjoy it here?" A consistent story emerges: We get treated with respect; I'm trained so well that I never look stupid in front of customers; my ideas are worth something; I'm allowed – no, I'm encouraged – to use my brain; it's made clear that I can have a proper career at Carphone Warehouse if I want to.'[1]

As Richard Hammond went on to point out, The Carphone Warehouse came out of a depression in their market (one that claimed a number of their competitors) a couple of years ago all the stronger because of the bond they created with their staff. It's in adversity that a team really shows its true colours.

I can't truly remember but I think I first picked up the phrase that is the title to this chapter from Charles Dunstone, or if it wasn't him, it's certainly his philosophy. It is also the mindset of an American company, Southwest Airlines, the pioneer of budget airlines and much feted for its success in tearing up the management rulebook and doing things in its own unusual way. What struck me, as I learned the compelling account of the Southwest story (*'Nuts! Southwest Airlines' Crazy Recipe for Business and Personal Success'*), was the humanity of their approach. As Tom Peters writes in the foreword of 'Nuts',

'While most organisations are boring and rigid, Southwest is just the opposite. What I discovered is an organisation that dares to unleash the imagination of its people.'[2]

> **A question to consider** *Do you feel that your company has the confidence to unleash the imagination of you and your colleagues or does it prefer to fetter you with rules, regulations and a lack of trust? Are you made to feel important?*

Chapter nineteen of 'Nuts' is entitled, 'Customers come second' It quotes a piece that Tom Peters had written in The Reader's Digest the previous year,

> *'When Southwest Airlines CEO Herb Kelleher gives customers a terrific deal on an airline seat, he makes it clear that his employees come first – even if it means dismissing customers. But aren't customers always right? "No they are not," Kelleher snaps. "And I think that's one of the biggest betrayals of employees a boss can possibly commit. The customer is sometimes wrong. We don't carry those sorts of customers. We write to them and say 'Fly somebody else. Don't abuse our people.'"*[3]

Elsewhere in this book I laud the man, Gordon Selfridge, who coined the phrase, *'The customer is always right'.* Here I'm supporting Herb Kelleher when he says the customer is not always right. Maybe I'm showing my true colours as an adman who blows with the wind or maybe there is some truth in both apparently contradictory statements. Interestingly, Southwest Airlines has built up a reputation as one of the best customer service organisations in the world. This should come as no surprise. If you want your staff to treat your customers as adults, then you need to treat your staff as adults. Treat your staff as children and, more likely than not, they'll behave like children.

> *'At Southwest Airlines, service transcends techniques. Southwest's long-term customer satisfaction comes from service delivered from the heart, from choosing service over self-interest. Service is not the result of teaching employees to act like customers are important; it comes from employees who genuinely feel loved and who work in an environment that dignifies them by valuing their contributions.'*[2]

Some people will argue with me that airlines and coffee houses aren't proper retailers and I guess strictly speaking they're right in that retail is all about making a turn by buying something for less than you sell it. But the one thing they have in common with true retailers is that they deal directly with their end user and therefore, for all intents and purposes, are retailers in the broader sense.

Inner branding

What, you might ask, has all this stuff on staff motivation to do with a book on retail branding? If you're in the camp that thinks branding means logos (although hopefully you're now deep enough into this book to know there's more to it than that) you'll be struggling to see the relevance. If, on the other hand, you realise that true branding is an organising principle of all good retailers, you'll understand that staff motivation is the crux of retail branding.

The staff are not only the mouthpiece for any retail organisation, but they also embody what that organisation stands for. If they don't buy into what the company stands for, it's wishful thinking to suppose customers will. Retail is a people business. Retail brands are communicated through conversations between shop assistants and customers, they are brought to life through the behaviours and actions of the staff. The belief and conviction that the people who work for The Carphone Warehouse or Southwest Airlines have in their company is the bedrock of two of the strongest brands in retail.

Branding works both ways. It bonds the customer to the retailer and it bonds the employee to the company.

> 'Truly powerful brands are those where the external projection is in harmony with the internal reality.'[4]

It's a challenge for any retail organisation to communicate what the company stands for to the hundreds, sometimes thousands, of people who are charged with representing it day in and day out. Not only do the staff need to know what their company stands for, but also they need to believe in it and be able to act accordingly.

As Neill Denny, former editor of *Retail Week*, says, it's no small task to ensure that everyone is on message, pointing out that this is not a problem that manufacturer brands have to worry about.

> *'How many people work for Tesco? A quarter of a million? Even Dixon's, which isn't a particularly labour intensive retailer, probably has thirty thousand UK staff. How many people work for Mars in Britain? Probably about fifteen hundred. Retailers are much bigger entities: people are a huge part of what they do and they're a huge part of the brand because, when you go into the shop you are always interacting with someone who works for the company. If you buy a Mars bar you don't meet anyone from Mars. What this means is that the people who work for the retailer are critical towards expressing that brand in that tiny interaction that goes on at the till or whenever they make eye contact or greet someone. Whatever it might be, it's a very important part of the way that the customer thinks about that shop.'*

! **Key point** *Retail brands are communicated through the daily conversations between shop assistants and customers. They are brought to life through the behaviours and actions of the staff.*

Furthermore, the problem is exacerbated by the high turnover of staff that is prevalent in retail. This is one of the things that makes The Carphone Warehouse's commitment not to let untrained staff loose on customers so impressive, and one of the ways that they succeed in keeping everyone on message.

I mentioned earlier in this book some of the key players in the extraordinary rise of Starbucks. One of these people was Scott Bedbury who joined from Nike as Chief Marketing Executive in 1994. At Nike, he had helped create the internal brand mantra, *'Authentic athletic performance'*. These three words summed up the truth of the company and led to the famous *'Just do it'* slogan. Bedbury's contribution at Starbucks similarly was to help them articulate their brand in a simple way that everyone working for the company can understand, remember and live up to. The brand mantra, as Bedbury calls it (I would tend to call it a brand promise), that he and his team developed for Starbucks was, *'Rewarding everyday moments'*.

In a previous chapter, I compared the product-centricity of Starbucks' first sixteen years with their brand-centricity of the next sixteen. In fact, their brand-led approach can be broken down into a further three distinct phases. First there was Howard Schultz's brand vision, inspired by the Italian coffee houses. Two or three years later this was overlaid, at Howard Behar's prompting, with a new level of customer awareness. And then, six years after that, Scott Bedbury completed the brand loop by finding a way of articulating the brand. At this point, I would say that Starbucks become truly brand savvy and thereafter exploded into the stratosphere.

> *'Some of the world's most beloved brands, Starbucks among them, spend next to nothing on traditional marketing activities. Yet Starbucks employees know how to behave. Their training, their benefits, their sense of solidarity – and therefore their attitude and presentation – are consistently a cut above those employees in the restaurant-and-fast-food industry. Which is a prime example of how, if you understand your brand – its values, its mission, its reason for being – and integrate it consistently in everything you do, your entire organisation will know how to behave in virtually any and all situations. Behaviour and quality, over time, build trust.'*[5]

This is why branding is so important for retailers. It ties the organisation together. It sums the retailer up and helps the staff fully understand what their company stands for by expressing it succinctly and simply.

> **!** **Key point** *The importance of retail branding: It ties the organisation together. It sums the company up and helps the staff fully understand what their employer stands for through succinct and simple expression.*

It's not always as easy as it looks. The cynic would have a field day if he knew how much time and effort had gone into coming up with those three words, *'rewarding everyday moments'*. And similarly Nike's three words '*authentic athletic performance'*. The cynic would contend that it's obvious, claiming he could have come up with these words in a matter of minutes. Maybe he could, but the fact is that most retailers don't. More than anything else, they don't do it because they don't see the point of it. John Simmons, author of 'My Sister's a Barista', sees the point of it.

> '*The longevity of this approach was brought home to me in October 2003, eight years after The Big Dig (Scott Bedbury's brand exploration process). I visited the newly refurbished Hayward Gallery on London's South Bank to see an art exhibition. Afterwards I went into the new Starbucks located inside the gallery. It's an elegant little shop, with stylish furniture that sits with the feel of an art gallery, providing 'the finest coffee and simulating art in a space where you can be inspired, connect, escape and enjoy'. And on the chalkboard, the following words have been written by the Barista: 'Starbucks at the Hayward. Art demands time and thought. Good excuse for a muffin.*'"[6]

A Starbuck's employee six thousand miles from the company's spiritual home in Seattle, someone who has probably never met Howard Schultz or Scott Bedbury, has understood what the Starbucks brand is about sufficiently well to write a perfect encapsulation of the 'rewarding everyday moments' brand promise. I love this example – so *on* brand.

If you doubt the potency of defining what your brand stands for, just consider for a moment the success of Starbucks, and, for that matter Nike (even though not a retailer per se, unless you count the excellent Niketown outlets). Is it just coincidence that that two of the most successful companies in the world have developed a pithy expression of their brand essence on their path to glory?

Companies with soul

It has always seemed to me that the people who work in consumer goods seem to lack soul. It may be just that we speak a slightly different language and therefore never fully connect, but I think there is a fundamental difference. Marketing is, for them, more of an academic exercise; their customers are 'consumers', imaginary creatures they rarely meet; and their product is an inanimate object.

Retail is the antithesis of this. I believe that you've got to have soul in retail because it's such a people business.

I quite like the way that management guru Charles Handy describes soul.

'One of those concepts that, like beauty, evaporates when you try to define it, but like beauty it is instantly recognisable when you meet it. Organisations have a feel about them, a feel which the visitor picks up as soon as he or she enters the building, or, often, merely encounters the people who work there...there is a sense that the organisation is on some sort of crusade, not just to make money, but something grander, something worthy of one's commitment, time and skills.'[7]

This is another way of thinking about the retail brand. It is, as Charles Handy says, something of an ethereal notion. My dictionary defines soul as 'the spiritual, non-physical part of someone or something which is often regarded as the source of individuality, personality, morality, will, emotions and intellect'. This essentially is what I'm after when I want to know what a company stands for. What is the source of its individuality, personality, morality, will, emotions and intellect? The key word is 'source'. This is why all of the case studies featured in this book trace what the company stands for back to its origins and founding principles. To establish what your company stands for, where its soul lies, find out where it came from.

> **Key point** *To establish what your company stands for, where its soul lies, find out where it came from.*

I'm not quite sure if soul is quite the right word for it, but my parents' shop, Butler's Hardware Store, certainly had personality, much of it emanating from my father's sometimes-eccentric behaviours. I remember all too clearly one occasion when he went to collect the money that one of his customers owed the shop and had been slow in paying. He took me with him, I'm not too sure why, perhaps he thought his gangly teenage son could come in useful if it got nasty. Despite there being no response to the doorbell and aggressive knocking, my father was convinced his customer was in there avoiding him. To my horror he picked up a couple of dustbin lids and started clanging them together while chanting, *'this man owes us money'*.

Perhaps not the best object lesson in customer relationship management, but certainly effective as a means of debt collection. The front door sprung open and my father was paid immediately. He was also encouraged in no uncertain terms to go away. Even though my father never achieved dizzy retail heights, altercations like this seem to characterise many of today's highflying entrepreneurs. At best it's called lateral thinking and, at worst, a fear of nothing.

Sometimes I worry that an unfortunate side effect of taking branding too seriously is that it can be misinterpreted to remove the very character, personality and sense of fun that most shops could do with more of. This, I guess, is what soul is about.

There's a Thai restaurant in Battersea, Nancy Lam's, which carved an enviable reputation out of the rudeness of its proprietor. People queued to be insulted by the feisty Ms. Lam. One of my parents' customers once suggested to my mother, *'Mrs Butler, for your business to flourish I should keep your husband out of the shop'*. My mother, though, was far too canny for that. In fact, realising that many of the male customers would come in at the weekend simply because of her husband, she refused to allow him on his beloved golf course on Saturday afternoons.

Shops, like the markets that preceded them, are places where human interaction takes place. It must be celebrated.

Retailers need to play off this humanity and look to amplify those characteristics that give their organisation its personality. Describing what a retailer stands for is an exercise in defining its soul. And that soul not only comes from the founder, but also from everyone who works there.

You might like to ask whether you're made to feel an important element of the brand at the place where you work. And, if not, why not? Are you clear about what's expected from you and what you get in return? Or has the only discussion been about giving your time in return for a monthly salary?

Could it really be that the most important aspects of your work (the place where you spend the majority of your waking hours) are left unsaid and for you to guess at? You need to be emotionally engaged by the company you work for in order to help bring the brand to life. A retail brand is delivered by its people, as this comment of David Simons, now Chairman of Littlewoods Shop Direct Group, illustrates.

'I have no idea whether PC World are cheaper or more expensive than anybody else, but I go to them because my experience of the staff has been good. There's a particular individual, his name is Dennis, in the branch I go to. I always look out for him. It's trust in the experience of the individual.'

Very few retailers properly attend to their staff. Maybe it's a British thing. The stiff upper lip doesn't lend itself too easily to emotions. It's also maybe a retail thing where the inclination is to get on with it and dismiss the softer emotional side as wishy-washy claptrap. Whatever it is, in my experience too many retailers don't spend enough time thinking about their culture.

This isn't a 'How to motivate your staff' manual; there are many people far more capable and qualified to advise on this than me. But it is a book about company culture, about the soul of organisations and about the importance of having everyone singing off the same hymn sheet. However you define it, retail branding or what you stand for, is really about culture. Culture means *'the customs, ideas, values etc of a particular civilisation, society or social group'.*

This is exactly what retail branding is about. The culture of a company lives through the actions of its employees. The value of branding is that it seeks to define and articulate the company's culture so that everyone connected with that company has a clearer idea of what's expected of them.

! **Key point** *The value of branding is that it helps everyone face in the right direction. Is that true of your company? Is everyone pointing in the right direction?*

Treating staff seriously

The question for any student of retail or middle manager is how can they influence their company culture. The culture of a place is something that happens to you, but often feels too big and amorphous to be able to do anything about. Besides, isn't it the responsibility of the boss or the HR department? I would argue that culture is a matter of leadership, but that leadership shouldn't just come from the top. It's everyone's responsibility, a point that Scott Bedbury makes in his book 'A New Brand World'.

> 'Great brands have leadership at the top and in the trenches. It is everyone's job. But some brands, in particular retailers and service companies, are especially dependent on the front-line employees who come face-to-face with the customer. In companies like these, dedicated employees engender brand trust and foster brand loyalty better than any marketing programme, whereas bad employees can easily undermine a brand that took years or even decades to build.'[5]

So what can you do as a retail middle manager?

1. First of all, you can ascertain whether you work for an organisation that truly values its staff, the people who embody what the company stands for. Look at staff turnover figures. Is training taken seriously? Does the organisation operate on any written or spoken social contracts? Whenever the marketing department research new concepts, do they do conduct staff research as well as customer research? If there's a positive answer to all these questions, then you're working for an exceptional company. If it's no, then I suggest you take it upon yourself to change things or at least to get your colleagues talking about them. If you and all your colleagues sit there doing nothing and argue that it's not your job, then nothing will change and you'll end up with the kind of company you all deserve.

2. To work out what's really going on in an organisation, it's often more enlightening to listen not to management but to the shop floor. Water-cooler conversations can tell you far more than any Head Office PowerPoint presentation. Part-time staff, who are invariably neglected because they are not considered part of the company, often have particularly good insights both because they can feel less inhibited than those on the payroll and freer to speak their mind, and because they can have a more objective take on what they see. If your company has a brand vision or positioning statement, find out if people on the shop floor know it. If not, it's not brand vision it's brand hallucination.

3. Lead by example. Find out what your company stands for and then look to bring those values to life in your day-to-day work. Talk it up with your colleagues. Become an internal advocate for the brand.

4. If no articulation of what your company stands for exists, then make it your mission to impress upon the leadership of the company just how important it is. You might even want to give them a copy of this book. Help find an articulation, or brand mantra, of what the company stands for, so that it can be the touchstone for how everyone behaves. This is no simple task, but if it's done well it's one that has the potential to change the fortunes of the company.

In sum

The other day I heard an American military general defining discipline as doing the right thing even when no one else is looking. The same can be said of branding. It is the hardest thing to get right in retail. Getting an army of people, a fair proportion of whom will be transient, marching in the same direction, all to the same tune, is phenomenally difficult. It's hard enough running a team small enough to know everyone on first name terms (as is the case with my agency) let alone lead an organisation with thousands of different people spread across the country. Given all these people are going to be interpreting the brand by their every action (and when no one is looking) it really pays to keep it simple. This is why it's so important for every retail organisation to be clear about what they stand for and to articulate it so that everyone who represents it gets it, believes in it and acts upon it. If done properly, retail branding helps tie the organisation together by helping the staff fully understand what their company stands for. They, after all, are the only ones who are in a position to make it a reality.

If you only remember one thing from this chapter:

---

*If the staff don't know what you stand for
why should your customers?*

References

1. Richard Hammond, *'Smart Retail. How to turn your store into a sales phenomenon'*, Pearson Education Ltd 2003

2. 'Nuts! Southwest Airlines' Crazy Recipe for Business and Personal Success', by Kevin & Jackie Freiberg © Kevin L Freiberg & Jacqueline A Freiberg 1996

3. Tom Peters in *Reader's Digest* 1995, quoted in *'Nuts!'* by Kevin & Jackie Freiberg 1996

4. Simon Gravatt and Jane Morgan, *'Forever Young. Immortalising the Entrepreneurial Instinct'* , 2001

5. Scott Bedbury, *'A New Brand World'*, published Penguin Books 2003

6. John Simmons, *'My Sister's a Barista'* , published by Cyan Communications 2004

7. Quoted from *'The Big Idea'* Robert Jones, Harper Collins 2000 from Charles Handy, *The Hungry Spirit*, Hutchinson London 1997

8

Carphone Warehouse:
Turning Water into Wine

This case study draws from an interview with Tristia Clarke, Retail Marketing Director of The Carphone Warehouse

---

What this case study teaches us

- The Carphone Warehouse has come from nowhere to become one of the biggest and most respected retailers in Europe and made multi-millionaires out of two personable public school chums.

- Above all, The Carphone Warehouse teaches us the value of building a close-knit team of like-minded people who trust each other and get the best out of each other.

- With such a culture in place, the company has been able to be bold and opportunistic, and ride the wave of being in the right market at the right time.

- While it would be impossible to recreate the culture of The Carphone Warehouse, because like DNA, it's unique to the company and personalities involved, there are nevertheless plenty of lessons to be had about how to get the most out of people.

- The lesson of Carphone Warehouse is how to unite staff and customers behind a brand built on people skills.

Another world

As a fifty-five year old in advertising, I get used to being in a minority. As UB40 used to sing, I'm a one in ten. A reference that would mean nothing to most of my fresh-faced colleagues, drawing as it does from a twenty-four year old single from the days when music came on vinyl, telephones had dials rather than buttons and Charles Dunstone was just starting secondary school.

There are times even in my own agency when the generation gap makes it feel as if, to borrow from UB40 again, *'Nobody knows me, but I'm always there. A statistic, a reminder of a world that doesn't care'.* Truth be told, I quite like it that way. My experience does at least have some currency. Even if I may not quite have seen it all before, I do at least have a reservoir of knowledge to draw upon. Advertising may have changed in the last quarter of a century, but some of the principles and working practices have at least stood the test of time. And, although not many, there are some other survivors born before colour television to be found stalking the corridors of advertising agencies. That's if we still had corridors of course. Nowadays it's all open plan. So, although I'm in a minority of the precious few who have had to blow fifty birthday cake candles out, I'm not completely alone.

Walking into The Carphone Warehouse's Head Office in Acton, though, was altogether a different story. I felt as though I'd been beamed into another world. Even the nomenclature is out of my experience – what I would describe as a Head Office, they call a Support Centre. To describe it as an aircraft hanger would make it sound smaller than it really is. I'm not sure I've got an appropriate frame of reference that would properly explain just how big it is. Or quite how many people it contained in amongst the vast sea of youthful faces that stretched endlessly into the horizon.

The Carphone Warehouse is a young company by any definition. It trades in new technology. Mobile phones have become so common so quickly that it's hard to remember life without them, which in my case is less than seven years ago. Now a sweet sixteen, the company was born in the embers of Thatcher's reign (a product of the entrepreneurial spirit stoked up by the Conservative Government in the late eighties with Charles Dunstone choosing to re-interpret Norman Tebbit's exhortation to 'get on your bike' by focusing instead on selling something for the car). The two founders, Charles Dunstone and David Ross, are still both only just turning forty. A very large majority of its ten thousand strong workforce have not even turned thirty. Only 1% (i.e. one in a hundred) are in my age bracket, making me as obsolete as one of the cumbersome early car phones on display in reception. It's hardly surprising that it feels like a different world.

I'm almost ashamed to admit it now, but I did in fact own one of the first ever car phones in the eighties. It was a sophisticated *'press to speak, lift to listen'* model that was so heavy it almost needed two hands to hold it steady, but boy did it make me feel cool to own it.

Not only is The Carphone Warehouse very young, but it's also very big. Delivering over £40 million profit on a turnover in excess of £1.8 billion from 1,400 stores in 10 countries, it would be fair to say that the boys have done well. It is now one of the biggest retailers in the UK and, even though it may not be my kind of company, it is in my opinion, one of the best.

A number of factors could explain The Carphone Warehouse's phenomenal success. Charles Dunstone rather modestly puts it down to luck. Others have said they were in the right place at the right time to ride the telecommunications wave. Increasingly, the company line is that it's because they've always been on the side of the little guy, right from the moment when Charles Dunstone spotted the opportunity to sell mobile phones to individuals while everyone else was chasing the business customer. But, for me, the answer lies in a company culture that comes straight out of the strong team ethic of the two founding partners.

> **!** **Repeated for emphasis** *The secret of Carphone Warehouse's success lies in a company culture that comes straight out of the strong team ethic of the two founding partners.*

David Ross and Charles Dunstone met each other at Uppingham. Set on the top of a hill in a small provincial town in the heart of England, Uppingham is a solid middle-class boarding school that prides itself on providing a rounded education. Its remote location and collegiate atmosphere places particular emphasis on being a team player (not least because it can be a cold, daunting place for the loner). Charles Dunstone ascribes the benefits of teamwork and determination to his schooling.

> *'It teaches you to get on with people – you learn about human behaviour, but especially it breeds a Colditz spirit which is fantastically strong. When someone puts an obstruction in front of you, you think, no, I'm not going to take it, I'm going to find a way around.'*[1]

Charles and David form a close partnership. They also like doing business with their friends – a further six old Uppinghamiams occupy senior positions in the company. They choose to work with like-minded people and demonstrate great loyalty to those they trust. They recently bankrolled new advertising agency start-up, Clemmow Hornby Inge, by agreeing to become its first client.

> '*We were their only clients for a while, which means you get the most fantastically intensive, diligent service from amazing industry professionals. The TV ads they did for us were the first TV ads that they did for anyone – they were terribly important to us, but we were more important to them.*'[2]

As with everything else they touch, that agency has now turned to gold and is commonly recognised as one of the best in the business. The Carphone Warehouse seem to have an eye for talent.

> **!** **Questions to consider** *Is your company a close-knit team of like-minded companions or a loose association of different individuals with various motivations and all pursuing their own agendas? Has it been carefully selected or randomly thrown together? Do your colleagues number among your friends and would you trust them when it came to the crunch? Can you really call yourself a team?*

Corporate alchemists

They also know how to make that talent feel part of the team and make that a priority of the business. In my meeting with her, Retail Marketing Director Tristia Clarke explained that,

> '*Our employees are as important as our customers. Certainly the investment we make in their welfare, in making sure they have fun, is considerable. We still do the things that were done in the first two or three months of the business. For instance, every single store is given a pot of money to go out on the last Friday of every month and get drunk. There was a cafe opposite the first store and what Charles and his team did there on a Friday is still repeated across the country with every store.*'

In fact, I think she understates the underlying belief that the employees at The Carphone Warehouse are their most important customer. They don't say this in so many words, perhaps conscious that it might undermine their professed commitment to their customers, but the whole place operates as a group of close buddies having fun together. The way David Ross talks about his working relationship with Charles Dunstone makes it sound as if it comes straight from the playground.

> 'Charles and I stimulate each other. There's a degree of challenging each other the whole way – we can do this, no we can't, yes we can, let's do it. We egg each other on.'[3]

It was through this process of egging each other on that they persuaded each other to acquire the Tandy chain in 1999 when, as David Ross explains, logic may have suggested they shouldn't.

> 'Nobody should have bought Tandy. It was a basket case, but it was water into wine from our point of view. It ended up being the best deal we've ever done.'[3]

There is definitely something of the alchemist about Ross and Dunstone. They have an unerring ability to turn unexciting raw material into something special and valuable. This could be because they have the ability to rise above the detail to see the big picture.

One of my favourite gripes is that the maxim 'retail is detail' has caused untold damage to retailers by giving them permission not to look any further than the end of their nose. Retail is about a big idea (the brand) and then about making sure every little bit of the process is informed by this big idea. It's rather like those ratchet things mountain climbers have for going up a rope. They only undertake a tiny bit each time. No great leap up the rope, but rather precise small moves, each building on the previous to create a huge overall effect. The mountaineer makes each small step knowing that it will lead to his ultimate destination. All too often the retailer makes small steps with no idea where it will take him. Retail is detail only insofar as it, like mountaineering, demands absolute precision and surefootedness. Ignoring the detail is not an option. Everyone at The Carphone Warehouse, as Tristia Clarke points out, gets stuck into the smallest detail.

> *'They tend to be quite down to earth, they're not scared of rolling up their sleeves and getting on with the job. Charles, myself and one of our Managing Directors will often be found pawing over the Buyers Guide line by line. I really mean that, you have to and it's part of being in retail and it's partly being in this industry, but you have to stay on top of the precise detail of it whilst not losing the bigger view.'[4]*

It's the 'whilst not losing the bigger view' that's the key point and what separates the great retailer from the average retailer. David Ross and Charles Dunstone have had the vision to see the opportunity and the boldness to carry it through. Perhaps that's why they've been able to turn water into wine, to convert a failing chain of electrical outlets into the bedrock of their retail success, to create a company renowned for high ethical standards in a market full of sharks and dodgy dealing.

> **!** **Key learning** *You need vision to see the opportunity and boldness to grab it with both hands. If your attention to detail is to the exclusion of noticing what's going on around you, there's a fair chance that you'll miss the next big opportunity that comes your way.*

Forged on windswept rugby fields

Uppingham is a rugby-playing school. The values and camaraderie that might be found on their bleak windswept playing fields are the glue that seems to bind The Carphone Warehouse together.

> *'What's doubly curious is how those public school roots still permeate through the business...the ethos according to one who deals with them, is rather male and 'rugger-buggery'. Yet it's imperceptible to customers, as Dunstone and Ross have managed to bind together a multi-ethnic workforce of men and women from very different social backgrounds.'[4]*

This, the imperceptible binding, is what, to me, The Carphone Warehouse brand is all about and what makes it so strong. Human relationships work primarily below the surface at an unconscious level. It's said that 80% of communication is non-verbal. This is why people can be so difficult to manage. It's why the corporate world tends to struggle with the people side; it works off the erroneous assumption that employees are entirely rational and is then bemused when confronted with irrational emotional responses.

There's been a lot written in recent years about the concept of emotional intelligence. For those of you who haven't come across it, emotional intelligence like mental intelligence (IQ), is a function of the brain. IQ is made up of abilities such as mathematical calculation, memory, vocabulary, word use, etc, and involves primarily the neo-cortex or top portion of the brain. Emotional intelligence is made up of emotional drives, and behavioural tendencies that are motivated by feelings. It involves the lower and central emotional section of the brain – called the limbic system. In other words, it is concerned with people skills. It's what The Carphone Warehouse, and Charles Dunstone in particular, are so good at.

The one thing that people frequently say about Charles Dunstone is that he's a people person. His father says that he could comfortably entertain groups of adults with his stories when he was only eight. Now, thirty or so years later, he is famously open with everyone, tending to expect the good in them rather than suspect the worst. And invariably he gets the good in return. As Tristia Clarke explains,

'He's been hugely successful, but has managed to stay associated with the principles of the brand, which is about being honest and open and clear. If you're a journalist, you have Charles' mobile number; you can give him a ring and he'll always answer or will always get back, whoever you are. If you write a note to him you will always get a reply. They're basic things but they sum up the brand.'

! **Key point** *The Carphone Warehouse is, like its founder, an emotionally intelligent company with people skills at its core.*

For me then, The Carphone Warehouse brand is all about being the honest broker, about having deeper relationships with their staff, about team spirit and being a good sport. .

This is why I liked their original advertising slogan *'simple impartial advice'* so much. And, I have to say, it's why I'm not at all sure about the line they replaced it with a couple of years ago. *'Simple impartial advice'* is the benefit the customer receives from the deeper relationship that The Carphone Warehouse has with all its employees. There's an integrity about the business that comes from everyone who works there and this justifies their positioning as the honest broker. I know there are good marketing reasons to justify *'For a better mobile life'*, but I can't help feeling that it's one step too far removed from the essence of their brand.

The inimitable ingredient

The disheartening thing for other retailers hoping to copy The Carphone Warehouses formula for success is that it's not that easy. It's contained deep within the DNA of the organisation, coming both from the personalities of its founders and the behaviours they put in place right from the very first day of operation.

It's a bit like Coca-Cola, which was famously based on a secret ingredient reputedly locked away in the vaults and known only to a handful of trusted employees. When Mark Pendergrast supposedly revealed that formula in his 1993 book *'For God, Country and Coca-Cola'* it made absolutely no difference, because there's so much more to Coca-Cola than its raw materials.

Similarly, there's so much more to The Carphone Warehouse than the team spirit that's at its heart. Knowing all the moves that The Carphone Warehouse make may help you improve your own game, but you still won't be able to replicate their game. However, there still are certain lessons that every student of retail can learn from them. The first of which is to treat people with respect. A rhetorical question that Charles Dunstone poses about why you should assume the best in your customers (rather than fear the worst) applies equally to employees.

'Do we run our business for the 97% of our customers who are honest, or do we run it to protect ourselves from the 3% who aren't?'

I once heard the Chief Executive of the American mega-retailer Home Depot say the same thing and it certainly doesn't seem to have done his business any harm.

You might want to take a look at your company rules (be they written down or not). It's more than likely that you will find a set of paternalistic edicts based on the underlying principle that the employee is a like a child who needs to be told what not to do rather than what they can do. The practice that Tristia Clarke referred to of the company encouraging its staff to go out and get drunk every Friday at the end of the month is not something that many companies I know would condone, let alone subsidise.

The Carphone Warehouse operates according to five simple rules. They're not rules in terms of restrictive boundaries, and this is the second lesson, but rather a set of inspiring beliefs that all employees need to keep in mind as they go about their day-to-day business.

The five Carphone Warehouse rules

■ If we don't look after the customer, someone else will.

■ Nothing is gained by winning an argument but losing a customer.

■ Always deliver what we promise. If in doubt, under-promise and over-deliver.

■ Always treat customers as we ourselves would like to be treated.

■ The reputation of the whole company is in the reputation of every individual.

In emotional intelligence terms, these rules represent adult-to-adult communication (rather than the parent-to-child communication that all too often characterises the company-employee relationship at retail organisations). The staff are encouraged to visualise that they've got the rest of the company sitting on their shoulders whenever they talk to a customer. It's a great way of getting across a sense of responsibility and illustrating how the whole company depends on each and every conversation that every individual member of staff has with a customer.

These rules aren't tucked away in the filing cabinet of the manager's officer as can so often be the case with this sort of thing, but appear throughout the business. I like the way that they're variously printed on the back of their business cards; it exposes the expected standards to the customer. And, of course, everyone in the business knows them. It would be interesting to test what proportion of staff in every retail organisation could accurately recite the core principles of their business. I'd be willing to wager that The Carphone Warehouse would come top of such a test.

The reason I know they would come top is that they will have had the principles drilled into them through the training programme. I've always admired The Carphone Warehouse's commitment to training, the third lesson to be taken on board by any retailer who wants to be serious about service. One of the practices that really distinguishes them from most, if not all, other retailers (let alone their competitors) is their insistence that all new recruits pass a two-hour test at the end of an eighteen-day training programme. If they fail the test they don't get the job. Charles Dunstone firmly believes that they should hit the shop floor running,

> 'They are supposed to be serving the customer, not learning. If a customer comes into one of our shops looking for expert advice, he or she wants to meet someone who knows the product and can talk knowledgeably about it.'

Anyone who has, as I have, been on the other end of some incomprehensible mumblings from a pimply youth in a typical high street electrical outlet who has no idea what he is talking about, will appreciate the contrast in receiving service from someone with an intensive eighteen-day residential training programme behind them.

> 'We want to make sure that the first ever customer one of our new sales consultants deal with doesn't even suffer one or two percent from the fact they're that consultant's first ever customer.'

I once had as a client, a retailer whose CEO refused to train his staff because to do so would have meant losing 30 minutes 'selling time' a week.

Unsurprisingly, that company is now out of business. The main reason it failed can be traced to the large amount of complaints it received from customers dissatisfied with their shopping experience. I am reminded of a Mercedes-Benz TV commercial that claimed *'safety is not a luxury, it's a necessity'*; to me, retail training is not a luxury – it's a necessity.

Lesson four is that the minimum acceptable service standard at The Carphone Warehouse is 100%. To help emphasise how important this is, they print a monthly list, entitled the hall of fame and shame, of every single sales associate ranked by the average score allocated to them by their customers. They don't issue prizes or punishments for this, just publicise it for all to see.

> *'We treat our people very generously and pay them more than our rivals, but in return we expect them to meet our high standards. We invest a lot on their training from the very beginning and we will take anyone on board providing they have the right attitude.'*

The company tries hard to promote from within and so everyone knows that performance will be rewarded. It's a meritocracy. This is borne out by the example of someone like James Collins who joined as a basic sales consultant in 1995 and had risen to become Direct & Customer Contact Director nine years later.

> *'Rewards and recognition are linked directly to achievement and your contribution to the growth of the business. At The Carphone Warehouse, you see your ideas being taken seriously and you know you make a difference.'*[5]

They are also, lesson five, choosy about who they take on in the first place. You cannot for example join The Carphone Warehouse if you've worked for another mobile phone company or have worked in direct sales before. I guess the thinking is that these people are in effect damaged goods who will have been taught poor practice and bad habits. They have a clear idea of the type of person they are looking for and will list qualities such as young, friendly, enthusiastic, good learners and customer focussed. People like themselves in fact.

The Carphone Warehouse's five key lessons of exceptional employee management:

1. Treat all employees like adults. Treat them with respect.

2. Codify the core beliefs in a set of simple meaningful principles that can offer guidance to everyone as they go about their job.

3. Take training seriously. Have complete confidence that your staff are properly trained by not letting them loose on customers until they can prove that they know their stuff.

4. Demand high standards - reward high performance.

5. Recruit the right people in the first place.

But even these only scratch the surface. Replicating the close-knit culture that The Carphone Warehouse has built is an altogether harder task because it goes right into the fundamental psyche of the organisation. It's a bit like acknowledging that Nelson Mandela is a nice person, and so all you need to do is copy what he does to become what he is. For sure, behaving like Mandela would make you a better person, but it wouldn't result in worldwide respect because, however much you copy him, you could never be him. It's in the DNA of The Carphone Warehouse to be a team business and the way they do it, like any DNA, is unique to them. It's possible to learn from them and seek to apply those practices of theirs that could be integrated into your business, but perhaps The Carphone Warehouse is, most of all, an object-lesson of what can happen to a business that genuinely puts its people first.

The clever trick

This could be a case history on customer focus rather than staff. The Carphone Warehouse themselves certainly talk, with some justification it has to be said, about their brand positioning as *'the mobile phone owner's champion'*. They can point to their five rules and argue that every single one is concerned with the customer. They have a manifesto based on four customer benefits: better advice, better value, better service and better aftercare. They also say, in a little book they've produced,

'We've been the first to admit that we've been very lucky. We unwittingly stumbled upon the beginnings of the most exciting marketplace of the last twenty years. But our original business idea, and the principles that underpin it, prove you can build a great business by doing the best for your customers. It's something we're really proud of, and something you don't see every day.'

So why, you might ask, do I believe that their brand is more about their staff than their customers? It's because the essence of good branding is about finding the fundamental truth of a company. Once you've boiled everything else away, what's left? What is it that really makes the company tick and separates it from everyone else? In the case of The Carphone Warehouse, I firmly believe the essence resides in their team ethic and culture. Strip away the culture and the customer's champion feels a little flimsy, just another piece of marketing puffery. But strip away the proclaimed customer focus and you're still left with a rock solid team culture without equal. The truth is that their employees really are their most important customers.

Brands don't just radiate outwards, they also radiate inwards. This inner dimension is what gives brands their real substance. It's that indefinable quality that guides BMW to design and build their cars in the same distinctive way year after year. It's the competitive imprint that you can feel in every contact with Nike.

Truly powerful brands are those where the external projection is in harmony with the internal reality.

The clever trick I think that The Carphone Warehouse pulls off is to translate what is essentially an inner-directed brand into a compelling external focus. In others words, team spirit is welded with customer service so the two are as one. If I were to put the essence of The Carphone Warehouse brand into words I would say it stands for being *'on your side'*. It is certainly on the side of everyone who works there, they are all part of one big, close-knit team. But it's also on the side of their customer. Their little book sums this up when it says:

> *'It struck us that it was really easy to buy a phone if you were part of a large business, but really hard if you ran a small company or were self-employed. This seemed strange because mobiles were just as important to these people as they were to the large corporations. So we decided to make ourselves the champion of regular customers, trying to make sure they got the same advice and service as the big guys.'*

! **Key point** *The Carphone Warehouse brand is all about being 'on your side'. They themselves are all on the same side, supporting each other in a close-knit team. And they do everything they can to put themselves on the side of the regular customer.*

Nothing supports this more than their *'Ultimate Price Promise'*. If you buy a product from The Carphone Warehouse and if the price goes down in the following month, they'll automatically send you the difference. They don't make a big fuss about this, they just do it, because they believe in not fleecing their customers, as they like to think they're on the same side. In the past four years they've spent £22 million on it.

It should be emphasised at this point that The Carphone Warehouse is not a soft touch. Being a people company, having parties, rewarding your staff and giving generous rebates to your customers does not mean you can't be ruthless. Someone once said to me that it's 'being fair, not easy' that matters. You don't go from nowhere to become one of the biggest companies in Europe in sixteen years without a hard commercial edge. The Carphone Warehouse is highly competitive, highly price competitive. As Tristia Clarke points out, it's what their customers demand,

> *'There's a lot of customers shopping around now, so whilst the brand is hugely important and lots of them come back because of it, they still want to be reassured that they're getting the best deal. You have to specifically tell them that and prove it.'*

Over the years I've been involved in plenty of discussions with retailers who argue that they can't afford branding because they have to offer the lowest price they can. Its critics have sometimes likened branding to a tax. It can, mistakenly, be viewed as a cost or a luxury that can be cut. But this is wrong. It's not a question of brand versus price. It's both. You need to be able to offer, as The Carphone Warehouse do, the best brand reassurance at the most competitive prices.

Instinct

The Carphone Warehouse is leagues ahead of most retailers in the way they manage their brand. They're clear about their proposition (*'The opportunity to talk one-to-one with an expert sales consultant who can personally explain mobile communications and find the right phone, network and tariff for each individual customer'*), their values (*'impartiality, knowledge, simplicity, passion and fun'*); their operating principles (as expressed through the five rules) and their goal (to be a retail authority). As Charles Dunstone says:

> *'We want to be the authority that people come to trust. We're on their side, their friend. Customers look to authorities. You believe what they tell you; you believe that they have knowledge, purchasing power and will make honest recommendations in the area they work.'*

I think the secret of their success is that they manage to keep it so simple. This is one of the core values that runs through the business. It's through offering good, no-nonsense advice in the complicated jargon-ridden world of mobile phones that they believe they can really make a difference to their customers. And they apply the same principles to all their marketing activities. They keep it simple, they don't deviate from their goals, they place a lot of stock in being consistent, and they trust their instincts. As Tristia Clarke says:

> *'We don't get too worried about that sort of stuff (marketing rulebooks). I have to say lots of it is very instinctive. We've got a small marketing team, there's about twenty-six of us. Charles is very heavily involved, we all are very very actively involved in the brand. We trust our gut a lot.'*

I would also add that they get good advice. Now they are working with Clemmow Hornby Inge. In the early days they got good advice from the ex-Guinness marketer Ernest Saunders and they credit Peter Cooper from brand consultancy CRAM with making a significant contribution in helping shape the brand. The fact that they are willing to credit those who helped them over a decade ago and recognise that they made a contribution is characteristic of the value they place on people they regard as being on their side. Whichever way you cut it, the personal side of their brand and the way they do business always shines through.

In sum

The Carphone Warehouse is a close team (of five thousand people, over ten thousand across Europe) that I could never be part of. I'm too old for a start. And, if I'm honest, I operate on a slightly different plane. On a couple of occasions, I've travelled with Charles Dunstone to a retail conference in Chicago. While our relations have been perfectly cordial (it would be impossible for them not be with Charles, as he's such a consummate social animal) I think it would be fair to say that the differences in our style and personality mean that we never quite fully hit it off. But that's the thing about strong teams – the more clearly defined the team is, the easier it is to tell if you're in or out. Jose Mourinho, the new manager at Chelsea Football Club, is building a phenomenal team as much by knowing the type of player who won't fit as by having Roman Abramovitch's millions to go out and buy those who will fit. The Carphone Warehouse is a strong team because they have such a clear idea of who will fit. With this as the starting point, the rest becomes easier because at least everyone is speaking the same language and operating according to the same value system. The achievement of The Carphone Warehouse has been to keep it tight and personal as they've grown big. By staying true to their roots and their values they've created a truly exceptional company in the most unlikely of markets. They've successfully turned water into wine.

References

1. Charles Dunstone, quoted by Andrew Davidson in 'Smart Luck', Financial Times Prentice Hall 2002.
2. Charles Dunstone, quoted by Alastair Ray, Financial Times 08.04.02
3. David Ross, quoted by Simon Gravatt and Jane Morgan in 'Forever Young. Immortalising the entrepreneurial instinct', 2001
4. Andrew Davidson 'Smart Luck', Financial Times Prentice Hall 2002
5. Quoted from The Sunday Times 100 Best Companies to Work For, 07.03.04

9

The **Shop Floor** Is a Stage

What this chapter covers

- This chapter emphasises the importance of giving your customers engaging and enjoyable experiences.

- It makes the case that a retailer, in his store, potentially has a more powerful branding means than his contemporary in consumer goods.

- It emphasises how retail is the business of the real world and that retail brands are consequently grounded in reality.

- It introduces the notion of smart merchandising and the need to think about what you want to bring into focus for your customers.

- But above all else, it seeks to show how the store itself is one of the strongest statements of what a retailer stands for. It is a brand asset that should not be neglected.

The madness of the baked bean brand manager

There's a lot of nonsense in business. There's even more in marketing and, I'm afraid, even more still in my chosen profession of advertising.

In what other field of human endeavour would a bunch of highly paid executives go on a three-day retreat to define the personality of a can of baked beans? And then return, like Moses from the Mount, to triumphantly pronounce that these particular baked beans are dependable, friendly, loyal and steadfast.

Maybe I'm missing something here, but aren't they simply baked beans? Small soft vegetables swimming in glutinous tomato sauce maybe, but a loyal friend? I think not.

The practice of attributing human characteristics to inanimate objects would seem to me to be best left in the playpen or the asylum, but marketers and admen have a terrible tendency to want to bring it into the office. This fizzy drink has hidden depths, they'll tell you, ignoring that it's nothing more than a flavoured carbonate. Or they'll try to convince you that their brand of toilet roll is caring, considerate and more understanding of its users than other brands of bog paper.

It's clearly all nonsense. The ravings of people who need to 'get out more'.

One of the things I most like about working with retailers is that, on the whole, they're more down-to-earth and pragmatic. Our clients will very quickly bring us back to our senses if ever we get carried away with flights of fancy or start assuming the airs and graces of your typical adman.

On the other hand, people who work in FMCG (fast moving consumer goods, whatever that may mean) marketing tend not only to be detached from their customers, but may also spend all their working hours thinking about a single product. Hardly surprising then that over time they begin to exhibit early signs of madness, and, much like the Russell Crowe character in the film *'Beautiful Mind'* whose imaginary friend seemed all too real, begin to humanise their beloved product. Even when it is only a can of baked beans.

It's hard for a retailer to imagine the one-dimensional existence of a baked bean brand manager, because retail is so full of variety and contact with real people. For me, one of the biggest differences between FMCG branding and retail branding is that retail branding is a multi-dimensional activity. An FMCG brand exists in the mind of its customers; the primary focus of the FMCG brand manager or adman is simply to influence perceptions of his or her brand.

By comparison, a retail brand manager not only has to influence perceptions, but also has to reconcile these perceptions with the real-life experience that their customers have whenever they walk through the front door of the store. Customers physically spend time in retail brands; they experience them through their senses. A process of osmosis goes on whereby customers just take it in and will feel differently in some shops from others, without necessarily knowing why.

The baked bean consumer will see, smell, taste and maybe even (if she's in an infantile mood) feel the brand, but only after she's bought them. Prior to purchase, she has to rely on whatever memories or perceptions she has from previous experience and from branded impressions planted by the manufacturer and his advertising agency. These memories will come back to her as she sees or thinks of the can.

It's different for retailers. Their customers can't help but see, smell, feel and hear the brand before they part with any money. It's infinitely more complex, it's harder to control and it's grounded in reality.

I often think of retail theatre as occurring in the gaps between the merchandise.

> **Key point** *Consumer goods brands exist in the minds of their customers; retail brands are experienced through the senses. Retail brands are, therefore, more grounded in reality. What's the current reality of your shop? Are your gaps working for you and your brand?*

There is, though, one key similarity between FMCG branding and retail branding. It's the need to create an impression in the customers' minds that will encourage them to choose you. Although the decision is made in a different place (the baked bean customer makes it in the shopping aisle; the retail customer as she walks out of her front door) it is nevertheless the same decision.

Creative opportunities

This is a sweeping generalisation (and I accept it's much more complicated), but the primary sources of the baked bean customer's impression of her particular brand will be advertising memories and previous experience whereas for the retail customer it will mostly come from her experience of the store. One is driven by advertising; the other by environment. As Neill Denny, former editor of Retail Week said:

> 'Retailers don't need to advertise in the same way, a lot of what they do is about making the store a living embodiment of the brand. That's the ad. It's the store, the staff, the mentality behind the staff, all the little touches in the store, the architecture, the floor, lighting. These things are important for retailers. They really care about lighting, flooring, signage, and the door handles. All sorts of detail, that you

> wouldn't really notice, have all been thought about and aren't just
> there randomly. If you look at different shops, they are different, so
> there's obviously thought processes going on about why a certain
> look and feel is better than another one. The temperature of the store,
> the ventilation – it's those little things, not always apparent, that make
> the store an advertisement for the brand.'

Although my Dad ended up as a shopkeeper, he started his working life as a designer. He was consequently always drawn to any creative opportunities at the shop.

This once got him into trouble at his local golf club when he decided to sponsor one of the holes on the course. All the other sponsors erected small formal signs announcing that they sponsored that particular hole. Such discretion was not in my father's nature. He produced a twenty-foot hand painted sign that he curved around the edge of one of the sand traps with the immortal slogan, *'You might be bunkered here, but you won't be bunkered at Butlers'*. It was a cleverly targeted work of art, but was unfortunately unappreciated by the committee, who had for a number of years previously resisted my father's application for membership on the grounds that 'we don't have shop-keepers as members.' Dad's first foray into billboard advertising probably confirmed every petty prejudice that existed in that committee room.

Perhaps more productively, he used his creative talents in the shop as well; on one occasion winning Ever Ready Battery's Best Shop Window in the Country competition, which netted him £1,000 (quite a sum in those days).

My parents also claim to be pioneers of retail traffic flow. They expanded their store, buying the two neighbouring shops and knocking them all together to create what, although not a superstore by today's standards, significantly expanded the scale of their operation. Blocking up the door in the middle, they designated one door as the entrance and the other, which was nearer to the till, to be the exit.

Unfortunately the experiment failed because their customers persisted in coming in through the out door. It has to be said that a lot of people liked it because they could easily exit through the entrance without paying. The true sign of a creative genius is a willingness to try something and get it spectacularly wrong.

I'm sure my father's sense of creatively using space must have rubbed off in some way as I'm interested in the physicality of a shop and I'm doubly interested in what that says the retailer stands for. The store itself seems to be a medium that's growing in significance.

Blowing away the bookseller's cobwebs

The Internet may still only account for a small proportion of retail sales, but is growing exponentially and undoubtedly has had an impact on how retailers think about their stores.

No more so than booksellers who have had to adjust to the considerable threat posed by Amazon by leveraging their competitive asset – their bricks and mortar – to their advantage.

Bookshops used to be dull, functional places, a maze of bookshelves where you could spend hours without seeing another living soul; apart, perhaps, from some old ex-librarian wheeling around a trolley of books and glaring at you if you so much as coughed.

This all changed when they woke up to the new competitive threat posed by Amazon offering a huge selection at the click of a switch. Those book retailers, such as Waterstone's and Borders, who reacted quickest to the changing market conditions by turning their stores into places where people could comfortably while away the hours, created a new retail brand experience.

Nowadays, you can use your bookstore like a library. No-one is going to try and hurry you out of the shop if you sit down to read the book there and then rather than buy it; in fact they now have comfortable armchairs, coffee concessions, welcoming staff, book events all designed to encourage you to stay as long as possible.

In truth, Tim Waterstone had started to change the face of book retailing when he opened the first store to carry his name back in 1982. He is credited with changing the face of British bookselling by introducing bigger stocks, later openings and more knowledgeable and friendly staff. Although he has since left the business twice (selling it to WH Smith in 1993 and returning to buy it for the HMV Group five years later before resigning again in 2001) he laid the foundations for a brand that could evolve into a new kind of bookstore, a place where book-lovers can happily spend as much of their time as they can spare.

Retail Week's editor, Tim Danaher, enthuses,

'Waterstone's use their store environment particularly well. They've got a very classic brand and communicate it well. Their store in Piccadilly, the old Simpson's store, articulates an atmosphere of relaxed learning. It's very spacious and encourages you to spend time there to browse. It actually makes you feel a good person for looking at books rather than wasting time in a pub. You can sit on a sofa and browse through a book for an hour or so while waiting for your girlfriend. That's not an hour killed, that's an hour really well spent and hopefully you'll buy something at the end of it.'

Digressing a little, it's interesting to note how the Waterstone's brand still retains something of the original character of its founder even though he is no longer involved. I feel there's a difference between someone who shops in Borders and the Waterstone's equivalent. Waterstone's is an English literary customer, whereas Borders feels more transatlantic. It's quite a subtle distinction perhaps, but one that's reflected in the staff and that's bought out through their respective physical environments. The layout, colours and the general ambiance are strong signals for what a retailer stands for.

Questions to consider *How different is the interior architecture of your shop from your competitors? Does the layout, colour and ambience of your store properly separate you from your competitors by creating a different impression?*

Theatrical experiences

Tim Waterstone, currently running the Daisy & Tom and Early Learning Centre retail brands, underlines how retail is all about creating a sense of theatre.

'I saw Kate Swann, chief executive of WH Smith, the other day doing her 'retail is detail' act. People love that phrase, I think because it rhymes. It doesn't mean a thing. What retail is about is creating theatrical experiences for people.' [1]

The Daisy & Tom children stores are keen exponents of providing theatrical experiences for their very young audience. Disneyland-like appearances from children's characters come to life along with various in-store activities; competitions and story-telling regularly entertain their customers.

A word of caution though comes from the fact, as rumour has it, Daisy & Tom don't appear yet to have found a way to make their formula profitable enough. It's easy for retail commentators and ad people like myself to get excited by theatrical retail concepts and neglect the bottom-line imperative. No business can afford to attract people who never buy anything: that's a recipe for failure if ever there was. The two most important considerations for any in-store creativity are, does it build the brand and does it build the business? An example that succeeds in spades on both counts comes from across the Atlantic.

Catering for a similar children's market as Daisy & Tom (if not a little bit older), the American Girl stores in New York and Chicago takes it to another level. Selling a range of expensive dolls to middle-class American girls by wrapping them in a historical-educational context, these huge stores offer their eight-year old customers a proper hairdressing boutique where they can get their doll a new hairstyle, a personal shopper where they can do serious damage to their parents' credit cards, an in-store theatre with daily shows featuring plays based on the dolls' characters and, the coup-de-grace, a cafeteria with specially designed seats so your doll can share afternoon tea with you (with, of course, her own doll-sized teacup). There is currently a six-month waiting list for reservations at this much-loved cafeteria. A visit to American Girl sticks in the memory, it's so much more than a shop to buy a doll. I have to say that it's a little American (and, it has to be said, a bit too girly) for my taste, but their sense of retail theatre has to be admired even if it might need to be toned down for the UK.

Garden Centres get it right. People used to go to church on a Sunday morning before Garden Centres came along. Now they spend their pastoral time wandering around Garden Centres, enjoying the experience, being tempted, savouring the outdoors (they've even got slides and coffee bars now) and, most importantly, they're buying. That's a good mix of retail experience and commerciality. On the back of this, Garden Centres have grown to become a near £5 billion market.

As Steven Sharp, Marketing Director at Marks and Spencer, says, it's important that the experience is appropriate to the place.

> 'You can go to a market stall selling apples in Soho's Berwick Street
> and see well presented fruit. That's theatre, no question about it.
> Alternatively you can visit the Apple Store in Regent Street and see the
> latest state-of-the-art store and, boy, that's theatre as well. At one the
> apples are simply thrown on a bench; at the other the Apple computers are
> gently polished and carefully placed. Two very different pieces of retail
> theatre. Both work because each is appropriate to their particular
> environment and each re-enforces the desired brand impression.'

Knowing what you stand for informs the style and nature of the presentation. Only if you know and understand your brand can you bring it to life in an appropriate manner.

> **Key point** *In-store creativity and retail theatre are increasingly important weapons in the retailer's armoury, if deployed with common sense. Always ask these three questions. Is it appropriate? Does it build the brand? Will it build the business?*

Smart Merchandising

One of the masters of delivering retail experience is Selfridges (analysed in greater depth in the case study that follows this chapter). After all, there aren't too many English department stores where you can stumble across 600 naked people going up and down the escalators as Selfridges did for their Body Craze promotion. But it's more than just events that deliver the experience. Richard Hammond explains some of the architectural features that give Selfridges its unique character and atmosphere.

> 'Quite simply the best merchandised store in the world. Imaginative
> ranging and promotional techniques play an important role in this eclectic
> retail palace but critical is the way in which the store has been laid out.
> Every floor feels different. Music and lighting is cleverly used to enhance
> a space or delineate a boundary. Take a moment too to check out the
> sightlines; at every important junction, customers can see an uncluttered
> path to a selection of different but complementary store sections.'[2]

Debenhams, like Selfridges, experienced something of a renaissance in the nineties. In part, this transformation came about from smart merchandising. Terry Green, who was at the helm at the time talks about what he did with the blouse department by way of explanation.

> 'We eliminated overlap in the ranges. Previously, customers had been confronted with a sea of merchandise on racks all at the same height. You would come in and see, say, a thousand blouses that you could walk past in about five strides. If I'd interviewed you and said what do you think of the blouse department, you probably would have said 'What blouse department?' So we eliminated the overlap in the merchandise, rationalised the offer, and created space. In the example of the blouses, we concentrated on the five key shapes coming through that season. We highlighted every one of them, talked about them, the features and benefits of those blouses. We would have a big visual of a woman wearing them and place that visual so that it could be seen from a distance, right from the back of the shop. As I'm walking towards it, I can see one, two, three, four, five images of blouses and I can see that they're all different and I can see that they're all exciting. Now when you ask a customer out of the blouse department, they are more likely to respond with, "Oh yes, I've seen a couple of things there that I might like to buy."

When Terry Green took over as CEO in 1991, Debenhams were making profits of £28m. Nine years later he recounts profits were up to £150m, and Debenhams had been transformed from a tired old retailer into one that could legitimately claim to be 'Britain's favourite department store' (as they described themselves in their advertising tagline).

> 'I used to call it bringing into focus more real choice. As a customer, you start to see an awful lot more. Suddenly the back wall has become as important as the mat. The visuals increased sales, not only of the merchandise featured on the back wall, but also (and we tested this) on other items. It generated traffic flow and traffic flow is what generates sales everywhere.'[3]

Like Selfridges, they embraced the notion of branding, unlike Selfridges they chose to enhance their own brand by creating a lot of their own fashion designer brands. By doing so, Debenhams became a more desirable destination and a stronger identity. Terry Green was surprised to see how competitors such as Burtons wrongly assumed that Debenhams' success was simply down to rationalising their offer.

> *'We brought into focus more real choice, not less real choice. Back then, they (Burtons) brought into focus less real choice. I was bringing into focus more real choice, because I was developing brands in the gaps that I had created behind rationalising the rest of the offer. We were attracting more and more customers with a wider and wider offer, they were attracting less and less customers with fewer offers.'*

At one level this is simply good merchandising and good retailing. At another it creates the canvas that brings the retail brand to life. In Debenhams case, it enabled Terry Green to sex up a mid-market department store.

> **!** **Questions to consider** *Does your store overwhelm your customers or is it presented in a way that brings the right things into focus? Less is more. People can only absorb so much in one go. How much are you asking them to take in?*

The retailer's medium

In the case of Starbucks, the store itself represents a conscious attempt to re-enforce the brand's positioning as the 'third place'.

> *'I think that Starbucks has become the 'third place' in all the communities in which we do business. And what I mean by that is the place between home and work. We have delivered something to the customer that's very important in their lives, and that is a great cup of coffee. We've also become an extension of people's front porch in the way they use our stores.'*

The notion of the 'third place' is by definition a physical concept. Every Starbucks store is required to follow a well-defined set of guidelines concerning colour schemes, graphic treatments, aroma, style of furniture and layout. The principle is that every Starbucks has its own individual stamp and at the same time is recognisably part of the Starbucks family. Each store needs to be a 'third place' for its customers and create an atmosphere that is capable of delivering the brand's core proposition of 'rewarding everyday moments'.

It's often said that the store is the retailer's billboard. Any retailer needs to be confident that his or her shop gives the right message about what they stand for. It's a good exercise to walk down the high street or through a shopping mall going into every shop that you pass and asking, 'What does this store say that this retailer stands for?' You should also interrogate what your own store says about you. In advertising the communication is often summarised with a tagline. It can be instructive to consider what tagline a shop might have if shops were indeed billboards with taglines.

Bloomingdales in New York have a tagline, *'like no other store in the world'*, that suggests exclusivity. This is consistent with the impression created by their Manhattan store.

> 'The original Manhattan branch of this superb department store lives up to its grand billing as one of the world's best retail spaces. Many of its finest qualities are similar to those of Selfridges although it could be argued that this is a less funky atmosphere. More luxury than cool. That is probably appropriate since Bloomingdales appears to cater for a slightly more mature and certainly more conservative audience.' [4]

Provocation *If your store was a billboard, what would it say? In other words, try to sum up in seven words or less what message is projected by your store. How would someone sum up the overall impression if they were standing right in the middle of your shop?*

Innovative cosmetics retailer, Sephora, is another good example of a retail brand clearly defined by its physical space. The layout, colours and overall atmosphere of their stores are carefully choreographed to create a distinctive and memorable impression.

> 'They sell well-known brands from couturiers like Armani, Chanel and Dolce & Gabbana, but in such a convincing manner that instead of buying Armani or Chanel, you're buying Armani or Chanel from Sephora. Their presentation, their service, the clothing the staff wear, their packaging and the authority of their knowledge and assortment are so convincing and overwhelming that this brand surpasses the strongest of product brands.'[4]

With this observation about Sephora, Michel Van Tongeren shows that retail brands have much greater potential power than FMCG brands. My colleague Mark Taylor talks about retail brands as having a bigger paint box to play with. With less opportunity to influence consumer perception (i.e. a small paint box), FMCG brands are inevitably less colourful, have less texture, less depth, less contrast and less perspective than retail brands.

I find it strange when I come to think of it that consumer products have tended to set and dominate the branding agenda. Say the word brand and people will tend to think of Coca-Cola or Persil rather than Tesco or John Lewis. That retail brands are largely defined by their physicality, that they are tangible and that they work as much on a sensory level as at an imagined level should mean that they are capable of making a deeper impression.

The tide may be turning though. Books like this, the growing realisation that retail concepts like Starbucks are in fact brand concepts and the increasing necessity for all retailers to assume more of a branding mentality, all these things, I hope, herald a golden age where branding increasingly becomes the province of retailers.

Branding will then become a tool of the real world rather than some flighty nonsense dreamt up in the ivory towers of advertising agencies.

Taking to the stage

I would encourage any student of retail to consider the following seven thoughts about their store.

1. In your store, you have a three-dimensional branding device. Use it to its full capacity. Lay it out, decorate it and plan it carefully so that

every little detail is a positive re-enforcement of what you stand for. Just walk into the shop and ask, what does it say to you? How does it make you feel?

2. The retail brand is grounded in reality because the main archetype for the brand is a physical place. This has implications for communication and can inhibit the opportunities to suspend disbelief in the way the brand is presented through its advertising. As a general rule (although by no means a hard and fast rule), the most effective retail advertising is closely aligned to the store. GAP may currently be a little out of favour, but for many years they effectively created a seamless bond between their ads and the outlets.

3. Think of your shop floor as a stage where you can bring your brand to life and deliver theatrical experiences to impress your customers. What else can you do to entertain your customers and make your store a vibrant gathering place that brings your brand to life? Our local bakery shop pours its freshly baked croissants on to a wonderful old wooden Provencal platter that's cracked with age and riveted with authenticity. I defy anyone to resist one of the croissants in that platter.

4. Think of your shop as a medium. Marshall McLuhen famously said, 'The medium is the message.' For the retailer, 'the store is the message.' [5]

5. Remember that more often than not it's those little touches that create the biggest impression. 'A brand is a living entity, and is enriched or undermined cumulatively over time, the product of a thousand small gestures.' [6]

6. The notion 'retail is detail' is only any good if that detail is informed by an idea, a brand idea.

7. Each and every employee in each and every one of your stores needs to understand and 'get' your brand. Keep it simple.

In sum

I'm reminded of the quote *'Don't tell my mother I'm in advertising, she thinks I'm a piano player in a whorehouse'*. Perhaps the retail equivalent could be, *'Don't tell my mother I'm a retailer, she thinks I'm on the stage.'*

The serious point I'm making, though, is that many of the best retailers have the flair and flamboyance of a theatrical director. It will be to your benefit if at times you can see your shop through the eyes of a theatrical director.

Consider what opportunities may exist to bring your brand to life through presentation. It doesn't have to be grand gestures, it may come from the simplest little touch, but the lesson, I think, is, be aware of the space and dimension of your shop and the impression it creates.

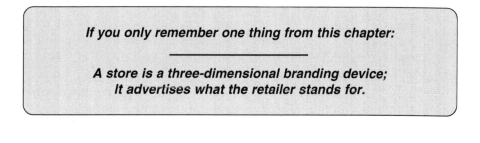

If you only remember one thing from this chapter:

A store is a three-dimensional branding device; It advertises what the retailer stands for.

References

1. Tim Waterstone quoted in *Director* magazine, June 2004

2. Richard Hammond, *'Smart Retail. How to turn your store into a sales phenomenon'*, Pearson Education Ltd 2003

3. Howard Schultz, quoted from *'The Future of Brands'*, Interbrand 2000, Macmillan press

4. Michel Van Tongeren, *'Retail Branding. From stopping power to shopping power'*, BIS publishers Amsterdam

5. Marshall McLuhen, *'Understanding Media'*, 1964

6. Michael Eisner quoted in *'A brand new world'*, Scott Bedbury, Penguin Books 2003

10

Selfridges: Theatre of Dreams

This case study draws from an interview with Peter Williams, Chief Executive Officer of Selfridges until he resigned in 2004

What this case study teaches us

■ Gordon Selfridge knew that his first task was to make his store an attractive destination in the same way that this book argues that the first task of any retailer is to build a desirable brand.

■ This case study teaches us that any good retailer needs to rent space in the mind of its customers, so that they will think of the store even when they're not there. Out of mind, out of business.

■ Selfridges forces itself into the minds of its customers by creating an impression through a memorable shopping experience in an unforgettable location.

■ If nothing else, we learn from Gordon Selfridge and his recently revived legacy that in retail fortune favours the bold.

Towards the end of 2004, a ninety-five year old department store was voted the hippest brand in the UK by a panel of style gurus. From a field of 1,300 recognised 'cool brands', Selfridges came first.

Department stores aren't supposed to be cool by any stretch of the imagination. The words 'cool' and 'department store' occupy different universes.

And, according to this book, retailers aren't supposed to be very good at branding. So what's going on? How can a retailer, and a department store at that, receive the ultimate brand accolade from a panel of cool connoisseurs?

One of the panel, Martin Raymond (of trend consultancy The Future Laboratory), said it was because *'Selfridges has turned around British retailing'.*[1] This seems a bit of a grandiose claim given that retail spending as a proportion of GDP has declined over the past two decades. Or perhaps Mr Raymond has seen into a future of a Selfridges-inspired retailing renaissance. After all, it is his job, as Future Director of The Future Laboratory, to do such a thing.

I'm being flip. I guess that Mr Raymond was referring as much as anything else to the stunning new building where Selfridges have set up shop in Birmingham. While, in fact, there is plenty more reason for Selfridges to be described as the coolest brand in Britain – that I'll come on to later in this chapter – it is the architecture of their Birmingham store that has really caught the imagination. Before it even opened, *The Observer* previewed it as one of the five most important cultural events in 2003. When it did open, *The Guardian's* architecture correspondent, Jonathan Glancey, among many others, eulogised about it:

> 'Four stories high, and wrapped in a sinuous, seamless outer skin decorated with 15,000 spun aluminium discs painted blue, like some XXXL dress by Paco Rabanne, Selfridges is a truly audacious achievement. Designed by Future Systems, architects of the Space-Age press pavilion at Lord's cricket ground in St John's Wood, it has about it, from the outside at least, not just something of a Pop era frock, but something of the sea and even the ocean depths – something, too, of outer space exploration. All this, believe it or not, is to its credit. Seen from almost any nook and corner viewpoint in central Birmingham, this unexpected building – unclassifiable in neat, art-historical terms – is all but guaranteed to raise a smile.' [2]

Shortly after it opened Giorgio Armani arrived at the Selfridges London store clutching a torn out page from an Italian magazine that featured a picture of the building. Unfortunately Mr Armani had come to wrong place, but it must say something when a department store building in Birmingham appears in a Milanese design magazine and tickles the fancy of one of the world's top fashion designers.

Brave new world

Echoing Martin Raymond's prophecy, *The Guardian* review from which Jonathan Glancey's quote is taken is subtitled, *'The astonishing new £40m*

Selfridges building in Birmingham is the shape of things to come.'

So what, one wonders, might the brave new world of retailing be that Selfidges is signifying?

Perhaps it's that shopping (as opposed to simply buying) is fun. That it's a cultural experience. Something, first and foremost, to be enjoyed; a stimulating activity and a source of inspiration.

Perhaps it's that the responsibility of retailers is to entertain: to deliver shopping as a leisure activity rather than a functional task. Maybe the example of the new Selfridges building is that retailers, more than anyone else, have the opportunity to shape the landscape we live in. Selfridges doing for Birmingham what The Guggenheim did for Bilbao is a refreshing counterpoint to the mind-numbing banality of featureless shopping malls that have become a depressing part of our lives.

It certainly opens the mind to the possibilities of a retailer. Why make do with a bog-standard layout when you can create your own little theatre of dreams? Why place the emphasis on easy and convenient when fun is, well, so much more fun? Why be the same as every other shop on the high street when you can be radically different? I think these may be some of the lessons to be had from that brave new building in Birmingham's Bull Ring.

> **(!)** **A challenge** *Does your shop have a positive impact on the local landscape? Does your building or facia in any way cause people to stop, look and maybe even smile? Is it memorable? What could you do to it to make it so? Think about your windows, do they make your street more interesting?*

Funnily enough, this is a lesson from the past as much as it is a lesson for the future. In my studies for this book, I have found time after time that the answers for the future lie in the past. Selfridges are the most overt example of this, because in 1991 the management deliberately went back to the core principles, that the company had lost sight of over the years, in order to define their new strategy. As Peter Williams the former Chief Executive Officer says:

> *'History, especially in retail, is quite fascinating. It's always interesting to find out why that business was successful when it was successful and*

why it was created in the first place. This doesn't necessarily mean that you solemnly follow what was done in the past, but what we did with Selfridges was pick out (from the archives, the external architecture, the use of the theatre, the use of events, and the notion that everyone is welcome) the original values and beliefs of Gordon Selfridge.'

Everything that Selfridges have done to dramatically overhaul their business over the past fourteen years has been inspired by their founder. It's to the credit of the management of this time – Peter Williams, Vittorio Radice and others – that they looked back in order to see forwards.

Nothing it seems is new in retailing. Perhaps the secret of success is to become a retail archaeologist and unearth all those good ideas from the past.

Selfridges was the brainchild of Harry Gordon Selfridge (a true retail giant) flourishing from its inception in 1909 up until the Second World War. Thereafter it survived as a steady retail enterprise under various different ownerships and management, but without the inspiration of its founder who had left his company in 1941 and died in relative poverty in 1947.

When Peter Williams arrived as Finance Director in 1991, the store was under the disinterested ownership of the Sears Group and was suffering from a lack of attention.

'Sears, frankly, didn't do much with it and didn't invest in the interior. The inside of this fantastic, wonderful building was slowly crumbling away. The escalators were about 30 years old and desperately needed to be replaced. There was no air conditioning. A lot of the brands that we take for granted today, like Ralph Lauren and Calvin Klein, wouldn't supply Selfridges in 1991, because they said the interior was too poor. At that time Harrods and Harvey Nichols had invested in their stores and were looking much better. We came a very poor third to both of those stores.'

Thirteen years later, when Peter Williams left his position as Chief Executive, Selfridges was the coolest brand in Britain.

To effect such a transformation, the new management started literally and figuratively with the foundations of the place. As Vittorio Radice, Chief Executive from 1996 to 2003, said,

> *'You have to define the foundation to begin with. You clean up the
> rubble, get the foundation right and then you can build.'* [3]

Stairways to heaven

The master plan that was drawn up in the early nineties, and completed in
1999, concentrated in the first instance, on the physical space. The first step
they took was to put a set of escalators in the eastern side of the building,
where there hadn't previously been any, but where, they had noticed, most
people tend to enter the store. Sales immediately went up 25% in the area
around the new escalator, compared with 5% elsewhere in the store. This
gave grist to the new management team's argument that the store would
benefit from investment, and confidence to Sears that such investment
would pay back. (However, despite funding much of the change,
Sears' heart was never in the store and five years later, in 1998, Selfridges
de-merged to become an independent company. Five years further on, the
business sold its independence to Canadian billionaire Galen Weston for
£680m. This was the cue for Peter Williams, who had fronted a competitive
management buy-out team, to leave).

One of Gordon Selfridge's principles had been accessibility (immortalised
in his slogans *'Everyone's welcome'* and *'Selfridges is for everyone'*) and so
it was appropriate for the revitalisation to begin by putting in escalators in key
places. In retrospect it seems an obvious move, but at the time it was
considered highly risky. In his book, *'Smart Retail'*, Richard Hammond wrote:

> *'Retail analysts began to get seriously cold feet when Vittorio Radice
> and his team invested millions in ripping out and renovating the store's
> central escalators. They were shocked that the store would lose so
> much vital square footage for so long.'* [3]

One of the things that bedevil retailers is the unrelenting pressure to
deliver sales today. Tomorrow doesn't exist, only today matters. I know this
only too well as an adman. Good advertising doesn't always pay back
immediately. Advertising is an investment in the future, it can take time to
influence customers to change their behaviour. All too often my retail clients
will consider an advertising campaign a failure if it hasn't produced a

sales uplift within twenty-four hours of being aired. So Selfridges sacrificing sales today as part of an eight-year plan to overhaul the building was hard for the so-called experts and analysts to understand. If the team ever doubted the wisdom of their plan they could always remind themselves that Gordon Selfridge had taken sixteen years to complete the original building.

They could also take confidence in that they knew what they were doing and where they were headed. They were simply executing Gordon Selfridge's principle to structure shop floors so that goods were more accessible to his customers. As Peter Williams describes it:

> *'We took out some selling space on every floor – a brave move – to give the whole building a centre of reference. We wanted people to know that once they get to the main atrium, they're in the centre of the building. One of the things that puts people off from going into department stores is the sense that they'll get lost. They want to be able to get in and out; so one of the things we did throughout the whole master plan project is put escalators in very obvious positions.'*

Points to consider *Is the layout of your shop optimally designed for the benefit of your customers? If you had the opportunity (at no extra cost or lost time) to start from scratch and redesign the space, would you take it? Are you making do with a less than perfect layout? Is there really nothing you can do to make it better for your customers? Is it perfect? If not, why not?*

In another demonstration of his commitment to accessibility, Gordon Selfridge pioneered the change in the way items for sale were displayed. He moved them from behind counters to place them on display in front of customers. Nowadays this is common practice, but at the time it was a radical move.

A Cuban heeled Wisconsinite

Harry Gordon Selfridge may have a blue English Heritage plaque commemorating his achievements, but I believe he is an unsung hero.

No one understood the theatre of retailing more than Gordon Selfridge, who himself dramatically rose from humble origins in Wisconsin to become one of the most influential retailers the world has ever seen. He showed an early appreciation of the importance of creating an impression by taking to wearing Cuban heels after suffering rejection from the US Navy for being too short. The Navy's loss became retail's gain when he joined a twelve-year old establishment in Chicago called Field, Leiter & Co. in 1879 as a stock boy.

Eight years later, and only thirty years old, he became General Manager of the Retail Division of the now renamed, and soon to become great, Marshall Fields store.

English history books, and even the Selfridges website, rather underplay his achievements in his homeland, saying simply he was a junior partner at Marshall Fields when he left in 1906. In fact, he was a driving force behind building, in Marshall Fields, one of the great American retail brands.

He came up with a whole raft of innovative ideas such as creating a bargain basement; putting a tearoom in the store and advertising not just the merchandise but the entire institution, its competitive performance, buildings and service.

> 'Marshall Field and his partners recognised the importance of building a credible, engaging brand for their company – one that wholesale and especially retail customers associated with the store's name, merchandise, and service. Field and, later, Harry Selfridge...did not use this terminology however. The language of branding, like the emergence of corporate mergers, was a twentieth-century innovation.' [4]

Interestingly, Selfridge left America as Harry and arrived in England as Gordon. He left in the year that Marshall Field died, ostensibly over differences in opinion over strategy, but, I suspect, it was more down to a reluctance to play second fiddle to anyone else. As well as his new name, he also came to these shores with a considerable personal fortune that he had amassed from his twenty-five years with Marshall Fields.

Unimpressed with the quality of British shops, he invested £400,000 in building his own department store in what was then the unfashionable west end of Oxford Street. It was to become the first and only department store to have been conceived as such right from the beginning rather than growing into one, like nearby drapers outfit John Lewis. Commissioning the same Chicago architect, Louie Sullivan, who gave the Marshall Fields store its iconic crimping columns and big brass plaques, Selfridge was unashamedly bringing the best of American retail to London. And, by doing so, his aim was to create the *'third biggest attraction for sightseers in London'*, second only to Buckingham Palace and the Tower of London.

Promotional literature from the local Georgian House Hotel evokes a sense of the world that Selfridge was operating in and that he was intuitively in touch with.

> *'The London stores disappointed him and he saw them as 'formless and inefficient.' He wanted a unified and luxurious store that encouraged browsing and fantasizing. Selfridge envisioned the store as a safe, paternalistic, and all-caring mansion, in which he temporarily replaced the husband, father, or brother as protector. Women were encouraged to shop there with the slogan 'Why Not Spend the Day at Selfridges?' Women were only beginning to walk alone, without the necessary gentleman escorts, and were enjoying their freedom. Selfridges encouraged this freedom by stressing shopping as a fun activity, not work. Customers didn't come to buy what they needed; they came to spend the day. There was a library and a silence room for reflection (with the polite instruction, 'ladies will refrain from conversation'), comfortable seating, sophisticated restaurants with reasonable prices and appointed reception rooms for French, American and German customers. By providing a large selection of merchandise, much of it not available at other shops, and all under one roof, the focus was on providing the greatest convenience for the customer.'*

Selfridge was a champion of women's emancipation. The housewife in one of his advertisements is pictured saying, *'I was lonely, so I went to Selfridges ... one of the biggest and brightest places I could think of.'* [5]

After his wife died in 1918 (an event that appears to have precipitated his subsequent decline) he showed a different side of his interest in women by taking up with the Dolly sisters, twins who inspired the subsequent expression *'Dolly Bird'*.

A theatrical experience

English Heritage commemorated Gordon Selfridge because, they say, he set new standards in retailing based on his belief that a great modern store should be as important to public life as great landmarks. They also added, *'it is largely thanks to Selfridge that Oxford Street remains the commercial heart of the West End'*, which may seem something of a dubious honour to anyone who has tried to struggle through the waves of shoppers there on a Saturday afternoon. The man himself though would be pleased, particularly given his stated ambition:

> *'To make my shop a civic centre, where friends can meet and buying is only a secondary consideration.'*

Shops as social centres where people can pass away the time of day without feeling obliged to buy anything. This is an enlightened view even by today's retailing standards. Few retailers have the confidence to assert that the merchandise and the transaction is less important that the atmosphere of the place. This is, of course, a different way of expressing the argument that this book makes – that people buy what you stand for rather than what you sell. Gordon Selfridge knew that his first task was to make his store an attractive destination in the same way that I am arguing the first task of any retailer is to build a desirable brand.

Selfridge's store itself – the iconic landmark building, the dramatic architecture, the sense of theatre and the buzz that this was a happening place – was at the heart of his brand. As the company's current website describes it,

> *'Gordon Selfridge was a showman and innovator who viewed the store as a theatre.'*

The promise of a theatre is to put on a show, to give its audience an experience. This is what Selfridges is about. It seeks to deliver a retail experience like no other. If I were to sum up the Selfridge's brand, the word I would use would be 'enriching'.

From the minute you walk in through the doors, (and even before, as you first spot the building, be it in London or Birmingham) your senses are prepared for a treat. The entrance, as Peter Williams says, has all the drama of the grand Victorian Railway stations.

> *'The floor ceiling heights in Selfridges are very high, which is fantastic because you walk through the door and you've suddenly got this grand feeling of fantastic space and grandeur and generosity. Like the grand railway station, it's the sense of arrival.'*

It's hard not to feel awe when you first walk in (I have a similar reaction in New York's marble Grand Central Station). I'm made to feel different by the sheer grandeur of the place. It's the ultimate brand immersion and, I'm sure, must work in the same way on the staff who are constantly reminded what the Selfridges brand stands for by the majesty of their workplace. The store, in the words of Richard Hammond,

> *'Buzzes with the energy and excitement of a Turkish bazaar while at the same time retaining the chic and style of an exclusive Bond Street boutique.'*[3]

Selfridges describe their current marketing strategy as 'exposure to the new', which echoes the role of a theatre in bringing new ideas and interpretations to the stage.

Although Selfridges is now plugged into the energy source of what it originally stood for, it was a million miles away from it in 1991. Peter Williams describes an atmosphere more akin to the Grace Brothers in *'Are You Being Served?'* than the coolest brand in Britain. It was a formal and deferential place where everyone called him Mr Williams, a company so lacking in confidence that its identity was defined by its competitors rather than on its own merit.

> *'In 1991 when we first started all this off, Selfridges did not have a proper definition. We were almost apologetic about it, describing Selfridges in relation to other people. We used to say we're more fashion orientated than John Lewis, we're not as expensive as Harrods.'*

This is a sure sign of what, in marketing terms, is described as a 'me-too' brand. An imitator with no sense its own identity, usually under insecure and unimaginative management and probably not long for this world.

> **Questions to ask yourself** *Does your company define itself in relation to its competitors or has it got a sense of its own of identity, of what makes it special in its own right? A self-referencing retail brand that knows what it stands for shouldn't have to refer to its competitors.*

With the benefit of hindsight, it seems extraordinary that a company such as Selfridges, with – in the genius and legacy of its founder – so much raw material to play with, should suffer an identity crisis. But it happens time and time again that management neglect the underlying truth that differentiates and drives the company in favour of a misguided strategy to be like everyone else.

It takes instinct and bravery to plough your own furrow and not worry about anyone else. In his excellent book *'Eating the Big Fish'*, Adam Morgan talks about lighthouse brands that stand as a beacon for people to navigate themselves around and contrasts them with second-rank brands that fail to establish their own identity.

'Reebok is a second-rank brand that has continually failed to define who it really believes itself to be, and thus poses a weak challenge to Nike's dominance of the footwear market. Instead of accepting that Nike has appropriated the high ground of athletic performance (and has more claim to it anyway, given the origins of the Nike brand in college sports versus Reebok's origins in aerobics fashion) and uncovering another, genuinely differentiating place for itself to live, Reebok has spent the last few years as a weak Nike wannabe. It is a brand that lacks an identity, lacks self-belief in who it is or can be and it shows.' [6]

The Selfridges management team regained the initiative for their brand by returning to what it originally stood for. Vittorio Radice was an inspired appointment as Chief Executive in 1996. He had successfully converted a £7 million loss into a £14 million profit in his previous four years at Habitat, demonstrating at the same time the branding skills, style and design sense that Selfridges needed. (Interestingly, whether due to lack of time or fit, he was unable to weave the same magic with his Life Store project at Marks and Spencer, for whom he forsook Selfridges in 2003). Richard Hammond describes how he literally re-energised Selfridges.

> 'While the press and analysts were nervously watching, Radice was also looking to the store fundamentals: fixing basic product mix issues, taking the dust off the merchandising, engaging the marketing team to reclaim the reputation of Selfridges as a 'house of brands'. He had the team creating a place to go for a treat – exciting, stylish, competitive retail therapy for customers. A new energy swept through the store. The combination of new image, shocking and innovative ranges catering all the way through and beyond value, and a physically upgraded store space, all contributed. But for my money, above all else, the most effective element of Vittorio Radice's Selfridge's transformation was the re-introduction of surprise. Customers were once again surprised, shaken even, challenged and delighted. After ten drab years, an inspired Selfridges became a place to visit just for a treat, a nice place to browse, just for the hell of it and 'oh and what if I happen to come away with a nice designer shirt?" [3]

The Selfridges that Radice and Williams re-created was in the image of its original incarnation. It is all about providing an enriching experience that rises above the mundane. Radice, in a 2002 interview, talked about merchandising tomatoes as if he were a theatrical director looking to heighten the audience experience through an extra-ordinary interpretation of the ordinary.

> 'Sometimes I get frustrated because I go down to the food hall and see we have a stock of tomatoes. What are we going to do with it? Let's make it the item to have today. Let's make it that you'll die if you don't buy one of these.'

If Selfridges can raise the level of excitement to such a degree that you'll die for a tomato, just think what it must be like to buy an Armani suit there. Peter Williams explains Selfridges' role as provider of the experience.

> 'Selfridges is the theatre, Selfridges the brand editor, Selfridges the content provider. We used the theme, internally, of 'exposure to the new.'

Putting on a show

Nothing better illustrates Selfridges' showmanship than their events.

> 'Selfridges sets itself as something of a retail theme-park. It stages
> 'events' to encourage people to visit and, as Mr Radice puts it, to buy a
> souvenir. This year the store staged an art exhibit called Body Craze, an
> 'uninhibited celebration of the human form' in which 600 naked people
> rode up and down its escalators in full view of press photographers.' [8]

While it's hard to imagine that the sensibilities of his time would have permitted Gordon Selfridge to have 600 naked people parading around his shop, you just know that he will be dancing rather than turning in his grave at the thought of it. This is the man, after all, who, when Louis Bleriot became the first aviator to fly across the English Channel on July 25th 1909, drove down to Kent to pick up the crash-landed Bleriot XI and hire it for display in his newly opened department store. It was irrelevant to Selfridge that he didn't sell aeroplanes, he simply wanted to stage an event that would catch the imagination of the time and attract people into his store. And, with 150,000 people queuing to see the wreckage, the event certainly got Selfridges off to a flying start.

Selfridges still has that keen sense of the dramatic. During the renovations, rather than the standard drab tarpaulin that is used to cover building works, they wrapped the building with an image from leading photographer Sam Taylor-Wood. It was the biggest photograph ever taken.

Selfridges describe it all as 'Shopping Entertainment'. It's certainly in line with Gordon Selfridge's original vision,

> 'We strive to create excitement within our customers, delighting them
> with an unrivalled shopping experience.'

The philosophy is based on the idea that if you succeed in generating footfall and then provide an enriching experience, people will be in the mood to buy. With 60% of every one of the twenty-one million people that pass through the store each year making at least one purchase, it seems to be a strategy that's working.

Selling the experience

Selfridges' sell over 3,000 different brands. Over half the floor space is occupied by concessions. And unlike most other department stores, each vendor is encouraged to be creative and individualistic in the way they present their wares. This mindset applies to the staff who, irrespective of whether they're employed by Selfridges or the individual brand company, all go through a Selfridges training programme that emphasises the values of the company. One of the core values they're taught is to practice a relaxed and relevant selling approach, emanating from Gordon Selfridge's belief that staff should essentially be on hand to assist rather than sell. As Vittorio Radice describes it, the emphasis is on delivering an experience that is relevant to the product being sold. That is the Selfridges way.

'Whatever brand the staff work for, they work for one company: Selfridges. For the customer, your contact is with Selfridges, the receipt is Selfridges, the smile is Selfridges, and the yellow bag is Selfridges. But the experience is very particular to what you are buying. If you work in books, you should know everything about books. It is not important if your sense of style is not correct because that is not what the customer wants. They are not there to buy a wonderful fitted pair of jeans. They are there to buy a book. Provided the staff give fantastic advice on books, they're my hero. Even if they wear ripped-off jeans. If, however, you are selling suits, we expect you to look immaculate, to know about suits and to have a sense of style.' [7]

Peter Williams describes the importance of good empathetic service that Selfridges strive for.

'You know yourself you can go into a really crappy store, but if the sales assistant is a decent person and really helps you, you think positively about it. Alternatively you go into a store that is bloody marvellous in terms of the product, but you've got some snobby sales assistant and it puts you off. We wanted people not to be overly familiar with the customers, but to acknowledge them, not to be pushy with them and basically give the message that 'I appreciate that you want to browse – just give me a shout if you need any help.'

While this selling approach may not necessarily be right for all retail scenarios, it is certainly 'on-brand' and completely empathetic with what Selfridges stands for and applies to everyone, not just the front of house staff. Peter Williams said that while they were overhauling the building in the early nineties they were also overhauling the staff.

'We deliberately loosened it up, to make the staff feel more comfortable and more relaxed and to use their own initiative more, not to feel that they have to follow a rule book. We took people from the leisure industry rather than from retail, because we were trying to make the whole thing more of an experience.'

This inevitably meant parting company with those who were more comfortable with the traditional command and control mode of retail management.

'We ended up replacing the whole buying team because a lot of them were of the old school and could not make the transition into this new world that we were entering.'

A revealing example offered by Peter Williams is of a member of the old buying team who had turned down a new product line from Fendi because she insisted that her customers were not going to like it,

'Who the hell was she to question the fact that Fendi decided they were going to go big time on this bag? They were going to give it to every Super Model who turned up at the fashion show; they were giving it to all the fashion editors and they were promoting the hell out of it. They were putting this wall of investment behind it that eventually got through and made it hugely successful. But we didn't initially have it because our buyer thought she knew best. When she said this is not what my customer wants, she meant I don't like it. The traditional department store buyer can be the block between the bag and the customer.'

The subtext to this story is Selfridge's apparent, and surprising, deference to the brand owner, in this case Fendi. In today's age of relative retail power the relationship between the retailer and brand owner often resembles a parent-child relationship, with the retailer calling all the shots.

The ethos of Selfridges eschews that kind of relationship (the Ricky Gervais school of management), favouring instead to do business on an adult-to-adult basis, as one of Gordon Selfridge's most famous quotes illustrates.

> 'A boss creates fear, a leader confidence. A boss fixes blame, a leader corrects mistakes. A boss knows all, a leader asks questions. A boss makes work drudgery, a leader makes it interesting. A boss is interested in himself or herself, a leader is interested in the group.'

This is the kind of dialogue that Selfridges aim for with their staff, their suppliers and their customers. Anyone they do business with in fact.

House of brands

Selfridges have enormous respect for the brands they stock. It's an intrinsic part of their proposition to encourage individual expression that enhances the experience. The experience of shopping at Selfridges is often described as being like a bazaar, a description that evokes a sense of colour and activity and buzz.

> 'Allowing the individual brands to create their own displays in their different ways breaks up the space because they are all fiercely trying to differentiate themselves from their competitors. It makes the store look and feel more like a bazaar by loosening up the space. It makes us a house of brands.'

A true bazaar is an enriching experience. In Selfridges, the individual brands are like different traders in a Persian market. Peter Williams goes on to explain the benefits of giving the brands greater freedom of expression than they might have in other department stores.

'Letting the brands portray themselves in their own image makes it easier and more interesting for the shopper. By contrast, for example, John Lewis might put all the cosmetics brands in identical wooden counters, and by doing so they waste all the brand identity that the cosmetics companies have spent millions of pounds on over the years and are absolutely manic about. Our view was to let the likes of Clarins have their own area and design the space as they felt fit. They're the experts after all. If you go into the fashion department in Marks and Spencer in Marble Arch, what catches your eye is not a product, which it should, but the bloody fixtures because you see all this wood.'

This approach will naturally attract a different kind of shopper than one who is drawn to the order of a John Lewis or a Marks and Spencer. I don't have the different profiles of the customers of the competing department stores, but it's a fair bet that Selfridges attract a younger, more style conscious and more brand aware individual than their rivals.

'We try to have a younger centre of gravity because department stores are often viewed as places where older people go to shop. We were at pains to make both the perception and reality of Selfridges more contemporary than its competitors.'

It all adds up to a young, energetic and creative place full of interesting things.

'It's about getting the message across that if it's cool and it's new and it's interesting, Selfridges will have it.'

Peter Williams might as well have added *'...because Selfridges is cool, new and interesting.'*

In Sum

For the first thirty years of its life, Selfridges, inspired by the vision and energy of its founder, cut a swathe through the British retail scene bringing many new revolutionary ideas that are common practice today. It was a brand way before the expression had been invented. Through the next fifty years, without the guiding hand of Gordon Selfridge, it begun to lose its distinctions, its excitement and its identity. Increasingly it became a department store like any other. Then it was rescued by a visionary and energetic management team who had the wisdom to refer back to the founder for their inspiration.

They redesigned the physical space mindful of Gordon's Selfridge's belief that retail space is a stage for creating an experience; they re-positioned themselves as a house of brands as a way of bringing back the colour and excitement that had been part of the original vision, and they introduced the idea of 'exposure to the new' to regain its spirit of innovation. And within fourteen years, Selfridges was, once again, the coolest brand in Britain.

References

1. Martin Raymond, quoted in *'How to be cool (or which brands buy status)'*, *The Guardian* 29.09.04

2. Jonathan Glancey, *'Top of the blobs'*, *The Guardian* 1.09.03

3. Richard Hammond, *'Smart Retail. How to turn your store into a sales phenomenon'*, Pearson Education Ltd 2003

4. Nancy F. Koehn, *'Brand New'. How Entrepreneurs Earned Consumers' Trust from Wedgwood to Dell'*, Harvard Business School Publishing Corporation 2001

5. Quoted from an essay by Elaine Showalter, *Emile Zola, Au Bonheur Des Dames* (The Ladies Paradise), 2004 Penguin Group (USA) Inc.

6. Adam Morgan, *'Eating the Big Fish. How challenger brands can compete against brand leaders'*, 1999 John Wiley & Son's Inc.

7. Judie Lannon, *'Welcome to the Brand Bazaar'*, World Advertising Research Centre Ltd and The Marketing Society

8. *'Reinventing the store – the future of retailing'* *The Economist* 22.11.03

11

The Value Equation

What this chapter covers

- This chapter will explain how Tesco transformed themselves while remaining true to their roots as a competitively priced retailer.

- It will show how a price-only strategy encourages least loyal shopper behaviour.

- It will highlight the fallibility of building your business on the basis of price alone, introducing the concept of the value equation as a new way of thinking about price.

- It will conclude by hypothesising that today's preoccupation with price will evolve into a much healthier dialogue about value as branding becomes an increasingly important strategic tool for retailers.

An oxymoron

In the 1970s, a popular playground taunt went,

> 'Let's all go to Tesco's where (add name of disliked pupil) buys his/her best clothes.'

In other words, Tesco was perceived to be cheap with a capital 'C'.

Always a pioneer, it was one of the first discount retailers. 'Slasher' Jack Cohen built his reputation by piling it high and selling it cheap. And yet today, Tesco is lauded as one of the most respected brands in the country.

How can this have happened? There's always been some tug and pull between pricing and branding: common wisdom dictates that it costs money to build a brand, money that tends to be passed on to the customer in higher prices. How could a company with such a deeply engrained price-cutting culture as Tesco possibly have built such a strong brand? I think that's what they call oxymoronic.

Probably as much has been written about Tesco's rise as about Marks & Spencer's decline, but what is indisputable is that Tesco have built a powerful brand. Anyone who needs convincing should consider this. Tesco doubled sales in ten former Safeway stores they acquired last year. One minute those ten shops are chugging along as Safeway stores, the next minute they're attracting 70,000 more customers every week simply as a result of being re-branded as Tesco stores and doing things the Tesco way.

There are many reasons why Tesco have become so successful. Their portfolio of stores, their loyalty card, their customer focus, the quality of their management, the list goes on. Without doubt their success is down to all of these and more, but from a branding perspective, there's a simple explanation. Their towering achievement has been to evolve their price-based proposition into a brand idea that touches every corner of the organisation. *'Every little helps'* turns the mentality that counts pennies into a state of mind that everyone can understand.

A poster in the staff lavatory sums it up. *'A dripping tap can waste 41 litres of water a day. This could cost your store £350 a year'*. One might be inclined to think that £350 a year isn't very much in a store with an annual turnover of £70 million, until you remember that *'every little counts.'*

Former Chairman, Lord MacLaurin, observed, in a video interview with us, that,

> *Tesco have always been known as a very good value retailer from Jack Cohen's era – sell it cheap, Slasher Jack, the cheapest in the marketplace – and Tesco are amongst the cheapest in the marketplace. We've always been able to maintain that. We've added to that huge value.'*

Tesco have built a brand out of their price competitiveness by translating it into an added-value proposition. The fact they've been able to do this while also keeping prices low may help debunk the notion that price competitiveness and brand building are somehow conflicting strategies. The truth is that it needn't necessarily cost money to build a retail brand (unlike an FMCG brand which will tend to rely more heavily on advertising investment) because retail brands tend to be built on behaviours more than promises.

The genius of Tesco has been the way they've re-interpreted their essence beyond a basic price proposition that could never set their business apart from others, into an emotionally based territory that they can own. 'Selling it cheap', as Jack Cohen did, is difficult to sustain in the long-term because it can always be bettered and because it's very one-dimensional. On the other hand, as Jim Hytner wrote in *The Guardian*:

> 'Every little helps' has just helped Tesco through the £2bn profit mark, and it sums up not their rational offering, but their attitude. What you offer as a brand evolves and can nearly always be challenged, but who you are and what you stand for is like a DNA that simply can't be copied. No retailer in their right mind would challenge Tesco on their brand territory now, but could the same be said for the more rationally based retailer brands?'[1]

! **Key learning** *Tesco translated their rational price proposition 'sell it cheap' into 'every little helps', an emotionally based brand positioning. Is your business overly dependent on basic price propositions or is there more to your brand?*

Retail suicide

The fallibility of building a brand on price alone is illustrated by Richard Hammond who shares an experience he had when working for Comet.

> 'We offered a 14" portable colour TV at £99 when the previous entry price-point for this product was £109. All our competitors were at the £109 price when Comet introduced the category-killing £99 TV set. For how long do you suppose that competitive advantage lasted? A year? A season? Well Dixons, Currys and Argos cut their price point to match ours within weeks. All that happened was the whole sector now made £10 less profit for every one of those 14" televisions sold. That's £10 lost out of gross margin don't forget.'[2]

Presumably, all these retailers believed that their customers would not stay with them if they were a little more expensive. They must have assumed that their customers didn't factor in service, advice, after-sales or any emotional connection, and that all they stood for in their customers' eyes was price. In such markets, where retailers only compete on price, customers will inevitably shop around not only for cheap but for the cheapest, and migrate accordingly.

These types of customer are the least loyal and hard to sustain a profitable business on. This example serves as a warning of the dangers of building your brand on price alone.

Hammond goes on to say:

> 'Their current strapline is 'Home of Low Prices, Look no Further.' Actually if you do look further then you can sometimes find products on Comet's own website for sale at a lower cost than in store.'[2]

As Paul Edwards, then Managing Director of The Henley Centre, said of Wal-Mart's imminent arrival to these shores five or so years ago,

> 'I think the danger is that Wal-Mart is going to introduce rather more suicide amongst retailers than murder.'

I love this thought, although it was unfashionable at the time.

We've seen a number of discounters fail in this country because the only thing they offered was cheap goods. The best retailers deliver value for money. Price is an intrinsic part of value, but not the be all and end all.

Oscar Wilde defined a cynic as *'a man who knows the price of everything and the value of nothing'*[3]. There are times when I feel retailers spend too much time thinking about price and not enough on how to deliver value.

A question to consider *Does your company spend more time talking about price than it does about value? Try reframing some of those conversations from 'how can we give our customers the lowest price' to 'how can we give them the best value?'*

People go to Amazon not because it's the cheapest, it isn't; people go to Amazon because it's a good experience. Amazon first broke into the book-selling market with an aggressive price platform (underpinned by the logic that without the overhead burden of the bricks and mortars of traditional retailers, they were free to offer more competitive prices), but has since evolved to compete as much on service as on price.

Price, price, price, where's the value in that?

Philip Green (owner of BHS, Topshop and seemingly half the high street) is a ruthlessly successful retailer who initially made his mark, his reputation and his millions through a keen eye for a bargain and clever trading in companies. I had expected him to contend that retail turned on price. Instead he told me:

> 'I think a bit too much of it is all price, price, price', gesticulating towards a bottle of mineral water, he continued, 'I would rather buy, say, the best bottle I can at a price I think is competitive rather than buy some cheap horrible bottle. It's all about trying to buy and offer the best you can in the marketplace you're in. Therefore it's not just about price. I guess within that there are certain things that are commodity-driven and are price-led. Tesco or whoever have a different rationale for selling jeans at £3 in their stores. It seems to me that food retailers are starting to treat some of their clothing as if they were baked beans. That's certainly not what we're about; we look to give our customers a different aspiration.'

We are becoming a more affluent society. Our parents' generation (or rather my parents, your grandparents), conditioned by the rationing of the war years, were much more frugal in their buying behaviour. By comparison, today's shopper is more liberated, more image conscious (the pressure to conform has been replaced by a more narcissistic urge for self-expression. Ironically though, this in itself is a form of conformity, which is why I so much liked The Gap's positioning of 'The uniform of the individual') and more brand savvy. There's more to shopping than getting a good price. What the shop says about its customers weighs heavily on their decision of whether or not to shop there. It's important, as Philip Green says, to be in tune with your customers' aspirations.

> **!**
>
> **Key point** *Make sure you are in tune with your customers'
> aspirations. Offering good competitive prices is one thing, but if it
> increasingly means that you're only selling cheap goods you may soon
> find that you're out of kilter with your customers' aspirations.*

There is a place for retailers who trade on price alone, but it's not, as
Philip Green points out, a particularly comfortable position. It means your
whole raison d'etre is based on something that be can bettered almost
overnight.

*'If we want to sell a cheap product – I use the word cheap with a big C –
in our business, we would be out of business very quickly. I always
think quality, value, as opposed to cheap. If you've got a brand with a
perception of cheap, a la Primark, that sells cheap, then that's okay. It's
what it stands for, what it wants to stand for, its whole mission and it
does a fantastic job in that particular market. But I don't want to be in
that business, I've been there and done that. "Cheap" is just not a place
where I want to be. I want to be able to offer great products in the best
environment and, hopefully, give outstanding value, whatever the
definition of value is.'*

So, what is value?

Traditionally, value has been thought of as a pretty simple formula:

$$\text{Value} = \frac{\text{Quality}}{\text{Price}}$$

I was inspired by the following re-interpretation of the value equation at
a retail conference in Chicago.

$$\text{Value} = \frac{\text{What I Get}}{\text{What I Pay}}$$

… where 'What I get' is all about quality, quantity and the overall experience (the emotional benefit of what I'm getting); and 'What I pay' being obviously about price, but also including a component for time and emotional commitment.

Some things that don't cost very much give enormous satisfaction. The clever development in some supermarkets of turning the shopping trolley into a vehicle for kids delivers a huge emotional benefit for the young mother who has to manage her child while also doing her weekly shop. It costs her nothing, but will improve her shopping experience and is therefore of value. Thinking of value in this wider sense emphasises important considerations that may not come into a retailer's thinking if he or she is stuck with the traditional definition.

This new value equation takes into account the various considerations that customers will weigh up in their minds when choosing to shop in one place rather than the other. Some people, for example, might decide to pay a little more because they can save time by shopping just around the corner at their local petrol station. In that instance, the perceived value comes from the convenience. The old way of thinking would have you believe that just because the same item is priced less somewhere else, that it has to be better value there. But this isn't necessarily the case. It may actually be more valuable to a customer for whom time is a premium, even though she's paying a higher price.

One can think of many examples of contentedly paying more for something because of pleasant surroundings and impeccable service. Take, for example, a traditional breakfast in a greasy spoon café versus a top hotel: I know where I would rather negotiate a delicate deal with a city banker and where I would go on my own. The eggs, bacon and mushrooms cost both establishments the same, but that's where the similarities end.

> **Key point** *Think of value in terms of what your customers get from what they have to pay. Think beyond the transaction itself. Consider the emotional benefit and emotional cost. Have your customers been rewarded with good experiences for the time they gave up to come to your shop?*

In a service economy, expectations of service are raised. Arguably there are greater opportunities for retailers to differentiate themselves and to stand out from the crowd through delivering a better, more tailored service than by offering the cheapest price. As Maureen Johnson of The Store says,

'You can't have the service element with the very lowest price. Something has to give.'

Many retailers, Tesco included, endeavour to try to marginalise or even neutralise price as an issue by focusing attention on other aspects of their brand (while still cleverly offering highly competitive prices). By now, Tesco's customers know they can trust their store to deliver on price, but, even in this highly commodity-driven sector, they are still given a myriad of other reasons to choose Tesco over their competition.

I wouldn't mind betting they pay more for certain items without knowing and would probably continue to do so if the other elements of the experience were sufficiently compelling.

What is truly great about Tesco's transformation and brand evolution is that now I suspect people don't think of them as being cheap and cheerful, but rather more as the smart place to shop. A not dissimilar role being played by the likes of EasyJet.

Steven Sharp, Marketing Director at Marks and Spencer, points to the fading relevance of John Lewis's *'Never Knowingly Undersold'* statement,

'I think the importance of never knowingly undersold has diminished. It's not really true anymore, well it is true and they still say it, but it isn't why you go there anymore. I think the motivation to shop at John Lewis is more about trust, safety and expertise. I last went there for a vacuum cleaner or a child's safety seat and I went because there's an expert who could tell me every little detail, advise me on the best one to get, who's really knowledgeable and who won't have been moved around from department to department. The chances are you'll be served by the same lady who served you the year before.'

A few years ago, I was completely blown away by this quote from John Brady, retail specialist at McKinsey. Not only does it sum up everything in a single sentence, but he said it in such an off-the-cuff manner. A powerful insight, simply expressed.

> 'It seems to me that price is always an underlying issue and it bubbles
> to the surface when everything else is on parity, but that doesn't
> mean that you can't charge a premium for a distinctive and valued
> customer experience.'

If you remember nothing else about pricing, please don't lose this thought.

The death of distance

One strength of the Internet is that it kills distance. There are advantages and disadvantages of this for the retailer. It's an advantage when you want to sell in far flung places without having to set up shop, and a disadvantage because of the ease with which it enables your customers to compare your prices with competitors near and far. With greater transparency of prices, retailers need to be able to offer, if not the best price, then certainly a price that doesn't rip their customers off. Customers need to know they can trust their retailer not to take advantage of them. As Charles Dunstone says:

> 'It's very difficult to gauge how important price is to people. If you sit
> them in a focus group, they will say it's not important, because they're
> worried about what their peers might think about them. And yet there are
> certain hot products, and I'm sure this is true of every category, where
> people are highly sensitive about price, where if Dixon's drop the price
> on that particular item, we will react instantly, because we know that
> people will have a look at all the different stores and the prices.'

Price is perhaps the one area where research respondents feel the need to be economical with the truth. If you took at face value what people said about price in focus groups, you would conclude that no one ever bought on price, whereas in fact almost everyone does. One of the things that most irritates me about the retail trade is how some unscrupulous retailers manipulate peoples' price sensitivity by introducing an item at an inflated price simply so that they can claim a few weeks later that it's 70% off.

The furniture retailers are particularly naughty in this respect. Unfortunately it works. Even though most people know that the beautiful leather sofas with vertically challenged models (to make the merchandise look bigger) aren't really 70% off, they still allow it to help make their mind up. I've seen it time after time, and even, to my horror, find myself saying I had better buy it now because of the discount, until I remember that it's not true and I'm simply being conned.

The reason it annoys me so much is that it abuses a customer weakness. It hits below the belt. I feel it demeans the retailer, which in turn demeans retail. By all means sell at a discount, but don't inflate your prices one week simply so you can claim to be offering a bigger discount the next.

I can't help but believe, and hope, that this must be counterproductive in the long-term.

I'm not knocking discounting per se, simply putting a plea for retailers to be – to borrow the old Advertising Standards Authority line – 'legal decent, honest and truthful' about it. I'm all in favour of price competitiveness and am full of admiration for the way the budget airlines have exploded their sector by having some fun with prices.

I know a family of five who went to Milan with Ryanair for 5p (plus airport taxes). That's a penny for a return flight to Milan. You can't help but smile at that. David Simons, previously my client at Somerfield, now Chairman at Littlewoods Shop Direct Group told me:

> *'Most of us are bargain hunters in some categories, but not others.*
> *When I buy wine in a restaurant, I'm buying on price and I'm certainly*
> *not looking for the cheapest bottle, and yet with an airline ticket, I find*
> *myself shopping around to find the best bargain.*
> *Invariably I'll end up with flying in the middle of the night because it only*
> *costs £10 compared to £50 the following morning. And I'll conveniently*
> *forget about the £40 taxi fare that I need to pay for arriving at such an*
> *antisocial hour. We are so inconsistent.'*

Playful pricing I'm all in favour of, because it says something positive about the retailer. It's also a good way of engaging your customers.

The truth is that price is critically important in retail. I hope that more and more it will come to be used as a positive attribute of the retail brand rather than a slightly underhand means of conning your customers.

Tesco have built their brand out of their low price heritage; B&Q use their buying muscle to make previously unaffordable luxuries within reach of their customers; John Lewis use their price reassurance *'Never knowingly undersold'* to re-enforce their underlying trustworthiness; and their sister company Waitrose cleverly support a premium price positioning with their wonderful advertising slogan, *'Quality food honestly priced'*.

As Tim Danaher, editor of *Retail Week*, quite rightly says:

> *'The really interesting retailers are those, like Waitrose, who are able to establish a premium price positioning that not only doesn't affect them, but can also be seen as an attribute. I went into The Body Shop the other day, having failed to find a shampoo I wanted in Boots and ended up spending £4.50 on a shampoo that probably would have cost £1.50 in Boots. And yet there's something wholesome about The Body Shop that made me feel the shampoo was probably going to do something wonderful for my hair.'*

This is a measure of a strong brand. Not only can it charge a premium, but also its customers feel better and somehow reassured by having paid more. This is because it creates a virtuous circle that delivers a better experience, reassurance of quality and a set of beliefs that their customers can identify with and are prepared to pay for.

> **!** **Provocation** *Are you stuck in a vicious circle of cheap prices, poor service and questionable quality, or does your store stand for something that your customers are prepared to pay for?*

In sum

I don't profess to be a pricing expert or to understand the finer points of price architecture. It's a specialist skill that's fundamentally important in retail. Because pricing is so fundamental it has an impact on branding. Any retailer that stands for anything needs to know where they stand on price. But as branding becomes increasingly important, I envisage that today's preoccupation about price will evolve into a much healthier dialogue about value. Branding is all about building value into a business.

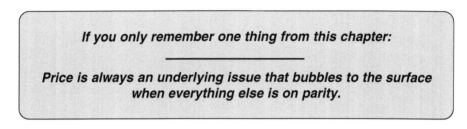

If you only remember one thing from this chapter:

Price is always an underlying issue that bubbles to the surface when everything else is on parity.

References

1. Nicholas Hytner, *'When the message doesn't get through' The Guardian*, 18.04.05

2. Richard Hammond, *'Smart Retail. How to turn your store into a sales phenomenon'*, Pearson Education Ltd 2003

3. Oscar Wilde, *'Lady Windermere's Fan'* 1892

12

B&Q: Beyond Nuts and Bolts

This case study draws from an interview with David Roth, Marketing Director at B&Q

What this case study teaches us

- This is a story of an entrepreneurially minded company that has grown to become one of the UK's biggest retailers by staying true to its core belief of 'you can do it'.

- B&Q teach us the importance of refusing to accept the status quo, of always living in a state of restless dissatisfaction, of always wanting to be better.

- B&Q stand for 'affordable improvement', for bringing the promise of a better home within reach.

- To deliver this promise B&Q use price as a strategic tool. B&Q don't simply look to offer the best price, they try to find ways of changing the market dynamics by bringing items that were previously unaffordable within reach of the mass-market.

- The primary lesson, therefore, of this case study is how to build a strong coherent retail brand that turns on price without being cheap.

Tools of success

As son and heir to a hardware store that did little more than make a modest living, I have followed the meteoric rise of B&Q with a certain degree of interest. What is it that distinguishes the phenomenal retail success stories from the also-rans that populate our high streets and struggle on a daily basis to make their books balance?

My parents had a ten-year head start on Mr Block and Mr Quayle. In fact they had grown to become a three-store empire by the time the two brothers-in-law first started their business in Southampton. Mind you, eleven years after opening those South Coast doors, Richard Block and David Quayle had twenty-six stores and had sold out. Both men subsequently lost their fortunes; and, famously, only one of them – David Quayle – regained it.

So what makes the difference? My parents set up shop in the same line of business as Block & Quayle. They were both there at the right time to benefit from the cultural factors that were behind the booming do-it-yourself market – increased home ownership, increased pride in the home, increased disposable incomes, and increased leisure time. So why, I wonder, has Butler's Hardware Store been consigned to the fading memories of a few ageing residents of Strawberry Hill, while Block & Quayle has gone on to become a billion pound enterprise called B&Q?

Without wishing to denigrate my father who did, in fact, run a moderately successful business that supported his family and met the hardware needs of a small corner of Middlesex, I think the difference in outcome between Butlers' and B&Q is down to ambition, vision and an idea.

My parents were ambitious for a better life. The shop gave them a good lifestyle, tied them into their local community, enabled my father to escape from his job as a design draughtsman and freed him up to play lots of golf. However, they didn't have the same scale of ambition as David Quayle, who left his senior management position at flooring company, Marley Tile, to start his new venture. Although he could never have envisaged that the company he was launching would, thirty-five years later, employ a 39,500 strong workforce turning over £3.9bn in 337 branches across the UK and stretch across Europe all the way to China, it's fair to suppose that his sights were raised higher than my parents right from the outset. They were shopkeepers; he was an entrepreneur.

David Quayle also had a vision. While my parents weren't looking far beyond earning a crust in Strawberry Hill, David Quayle had been inspired by a new retailing concept that he had come across in the recently established Benelux region of Europe. A handful of companies in Belgium in the sixties had opened a new kind of store – a 'hypermarket' – that included self-service departments selling home improvement products.

David Quayle saw the future and when he couldn't sell it to his employers (who were wedded to counter sales help and a tightly prescribed product mix) he chose to launch the self-service home centre concept in the UK himself.

> *'It was totally unheard of in the United Kingdom then. Based on what I saw in Brussels, I knew what Marley was doing was all wrong.'*[1]

Companies with vision tend to do better than those without. A vision is a guiding light. It means that the business is founded on a point of view and has a sense of purpose. It has something more to prove than turning in a profit on each day's trading. In terms of the argument proposed by this book, it shows that the retailer stands for something.

Questions to consider *Is your company determined by a vision? Is it sparked by the opportunity to do things in a different and better way? Or does it, like every other company in its sector, simply recycle old ideas and formulas?*

David Quayle, together with his brother-in-law Richard Block, translated this vision into an idea for their business.

> *'We started off with quite a good idea: supply what people need for the home, car and garden at a good price and a good value.'*[1]

Hardly rocket-science, but it contains a number of important elements. Firstly, it comes from the perspective of the customer. Nine out of ten shops are set up and defined by what the shopkeeper has to sell rather than what the customer wants to buy. Good marketing is all about putting yourself in your customer's shoes, which is a lot easier than it sounds. As the old native Indian American saying goes about never judging a man until you've walked a mile in his moccasins; well, I would encourage anyone thinking of setting up a shop to don their customer's moccasins, so to speak, for a good few miles. I don't know, but I suspect my parents started with the idea of setting up a hardware shop rather than by imagining what the residents of Strawberry Hill might need in their home over the next ten years. It's a subtle difference, but if you start from the premise of offering what your customer needs, now and in the future, rather than simply selling what you've got, you will be in a stronger position.

As I have said, the word 'retail' is derived from the French word 'retailler' which means to cut off, in other words, to take a cut. This shows that retailing comes from a different place from marketing. The etymological origins of retail lie in reselling goods for a margin; its start point is the goods, the product that needs to be sold. By comparison, marketing is implicitly concerned with the market for those goods; its start point is the buyer of the goods that need to be sold. This is an important distinction and fundamental to the argument proposed by this book.

The natural inclination of retailers is, rightly, to focus on what they have to sell. I say rightly because the table-stake of being a retailer is being able to make a turn by selling something. It's the basic talent of any good retailer. If you don't have this quality or instinct, then you're in the wrong job. It would be like a professional footballer that couldn't kick a ball. However, it's not enough.

The great retailers (the ones who get past one or two shops) do much more than just think about how they're going to make a good turn on what they've got to sell. They see the bigger picture; they understand what their customers want now; they anticipate what they will need in the future and they appreciate the importance of differentiating their offer from that of their competitors. To pull this off requires a level of customer knowledge that can only come from adopting the customer's position, by standing in their shoes. Quayle and Block, or should I say Block and Quayle as that is how they first named their business, understood this as shown from the way they phrase their initial idea – *'what people need'*.

Key point *One of the things that separate a great retailer from a mediocre retailer is the ability to 'walk in the moccasins' of their customers, and to see the world not from a seller's perspective, but through the eyes of their buyers. Do you wear your customers' moccasins?*

The other important elements in the original idea of B&Q *'supply what people need for the home, car and garden at a good price and a good value'* are that it clearly defines the scope of business (a scope that has tightened in its focus on home improvements to the exclusion of the car), and that it specifies the two defining benefits of the business today – range and price. The statement implicitly offers a full range in setting out to *'supply what people need for...'* And price is given double emphasis through *'at a good price and good value'.*

It's these three ingredients (tools of success, if you like) – ambition, vision, and an idea – that have helped elevate B&Q beyond their humble origins in Southampton to become not only Europe's largest home improvement retailer but also a pioneering force in changing the way we shop and the way we all feather our nests. Interestingly, these elements were there at the outset, spelt out in the initial vision and idea, indicating that in retail you make your own success; it's not something that simply happens to you.

One of the advantages of retail is that you know immediately if something is right or wrong, if a new idea is going to work or not. You don't have to wait for tracking studies, or other delayed performance indicators, as you might if you were a manufacturer. Instead you get feedback right from the moment you first open your doors. This helps in controlling your own destiny because it gives you the opportunity to act on the information.

Self-improvement

B&Q's business has been built on the insatiable appetite of the British public to continuously improve their homes. As any home-owner knows, the opportunity for improvement is endless, whether it involves repairing and replacing parts that have run their course, making substantial alterations such as loft extensions to upgrade the property, simple tinkering in a quest for perfection to make those small details better or just changing for change's sake. There's a quality in human nature that strives to better itself all the time. This appetite for improvement that B&Q have been able to take advantage of is also a quality that the company itself possesses.

David Roth, Marketing Director at B&Q, describes the organisation as having a self-critical state of mind and, like any good DIY enthusiast, is always looking for a better way of doing things.

'There's a tremendous restlessness in the organisation.'

This sense that there's always a better way did, after all, inspire David Quayle to set the company up in the first place and it has led B&Q to becoming one of the major innovators in retailing.

The first shops – with their large range and self-service style – were substantially different from anything else on the high street at the time.

Right from the outset, B&Q involved *'everyone, even at the lowest levels'* (to quote David Quayle) in merchandising. Staff involvement, unusual for any retailer then and arguably even now not practiced to the extent that it should be, soon became a B&Q trademark. After first buying up disused old cinema sites in an attempt to get more floor space and sufficient parking, B&Q pioneered the growth of out-of-town shopping centres. At a time when 10,000 square feet was considered a reasonably large store (and still today would constitute a decent sized shop) they started developing 35,000 square feet outlets (then the largest retail space in the UK) before moving to 90,000 and then 130,000 square feet. This year they opened a new 170,000 square foot store in Trafford Park Manchester. Today B&Q has over twenty million square feet of retailing space in the UK, operating from ninety-one mammoth Warehouse stores and two hundred and thirty-eight Supercentres.

The company is always on the move and receptive to new ideas. Four years ago, B&Q set up in China (in itself a pioneering move) and is now finding, as Marketing Director David Roth points out, that it's able to learn from its Asian experience.

'We've learnt a lot from our stores in China where our stores don't carry any of the baggage of the brand that they do in the UK. The advantage of this is that customers don't dispute our authority to sell sofas and soft furnishing elements, which they might in the UK where we are sometimes regarded as more of a nuts and bolt merchant. Our Chinese stores have a ground floor level much as you would find here in the UK, but they also have an upstairs floor containing furniture, room sets, kitchens, bathrooms, displays and a huge installation service where you bring in the plans of your apartment and we do the rest. We design and work with you to give you a look and a feel; produce drawings to get a three-dimensional view and then convert those drawings to reality.'

There aren't that many companies that would be so keen to learn from what might be viewed as a less mature market. By having open eyes on the experience and by regarding everything that they do as an opportunity to do better next time, they may well find that the answer to unlock the next phase of their UK development lies in China. In which case, a very English company would have initially been inspired from something in Belgium and then thirty years later from China.

Surviving like a shark

> **Consider:** *Which of these two philosophies will serve you better? 'Change before you have to' or 'If it ain't broke, don't fix it.'*

In doing the interviews for this book, and getting under the skin of leading retail organisations, I've noticed how all of them have commented how they're currently at a key moment in their evolution and development.

Now, either there's something in the retail zeitgeist at the moment, or, as I suspect, there's a characteristic of retailers that gives them an inflated sense of importance of the here and now. The present moment is always a critical moment for the retailer. The past is history, it's gone, and the future, well, we don't need to worry about that yet, at least not until we've dealt with the present. This tendency of retailers to live in the moment is both their major strength and their Achilles' heel. It's a strength, because the moment matters, particularly in retail where everything is so immediate. But it's also a weakness when it diminishes the inclination toward long-term strategic thinking.

Whilst 'resting' between jobs, Stuart Rose told me over a glass of wine something like, if you're in step with your customer you are in fact behind them. But, if you're one step ahead of them, you may well lose them. You must develop the skill of being half a step ahead. Though simply expressed, it's a great mind-set to adopt and keeps a necessary view on developments. The more you think about it the deeper it's meaning, I like it a lot!

Everyone I spoke to felt that his or her company/brand was at a critical point. For David Roth, it was that B&Q has to find a way of evolving from its functional brand position to occupy a more emotionally based territory if it is going to keep up with its customers.

> *'We're seeing a huge shift in the way in which people relate to their homes, their families and their lives. If we want to be as relevant to them in going forwards over the next thirty-five years as we have been for the past thirty-five, then the brand has to change, the product ranges that we sell have to change, the way in which we do things has to change.'*

This is not an admission of failure – far from it. It's an acknowledgement that the company needs to keep moving as it always has done in order to survive. It's said that if a shark stops moving it will die; the same is true for retail companies. The moment when businesses start to feel complacent, and confident that they know best, is when their death-knell begins to sound. It's arguably the state that Marks & Spencer reached in the late nineties, a position that they've been desperately trying to recover from ever since. Because they know that they need to change, B&Q are attuned to what's happening around them.

> 'Customers have had their eyes opened, a bit by us and a lot by home improvement programmes such as Changing Rooms. The fashionisation of everything that you buy nowadays has replaced the permanency of everything twenty years ago. You don't now buy a kitchen to last twenty years and you don't paint a room to last for twenty years. Functionally a room might be fine, but emotionally it has to change.'

This represents a significant shift in customer attitude and behaviour of which B&Q need to be cognisant. The fundamental premise that B&Q built their business on is changing.

> 'B&Q started from the notion that it could be a lot faster, a lot quicker and a lot cheaper to do it yourself, rather than employ a tradesman. And you probably had the skills in those days to do it, either learnt from your parents or from school. Now we're moving to an environment where people have a reasonable amount of money; they don't actually have the basic skills anymore (because they've stopped watching their parents do things and schools aren't spending a great deal of time on general craft skills). They also don't want to spend all their weekends doing it, because they've worked really hard during the week and want to go out and enjoy themselves. So what is B&Q's role for those people?'

It can be difficult for big companies to change course. They're like super-tankers who take time to alter direction. The potential disadvantage of having a strong brand with a well-established position is that when the market dynamics fundamentally change, that position of strength can quickly seem entrenched and become a hindrance. B&Q is known as the place to go for the basic DIY items such as nuts and bolts.

> *'If your tap was leaking, and you needed to replace it, you would go to one of our stores for a new washer or a new tap. Now what's happening is the tap is functioning fine, but it's not stylish anymore or you've changed something else in your bathroom and perhaps the tap doesn't match anymore. It becomes a more emotional proposition.'*

Would B&Q, a place where you would go for washers and expect to see lots of hairy-armed tradesmen, be the natural choice for advice on the aesthetics of your bathroom? How does B&Q evolve to become a credible choice in the softer 'finishing-off' end of the home improvement market, without losing its roots as the best place to go for the basic items? If it doesn't evolve in this way, it's as likely to die as a static shark. If it moves too suddenly or too far from its roots or too early into a territory where it hasn't sufficient credibility, it risks cutting off the oxygen that has sustained it for the past thirty-five years. And if it tries to keep feet in both camps, it may appear schizophrenic and end up diluting the potency of its proposition. This is where the significance of B&Q's learning in China could come in, because it enables to company to experiment in a market where it isn't hindered by preconception.

These are tough branding challenges. As David Roth admits, they create tensions in the business that protect it against complacency.

> *'There are tensions within the way in which the brand is seen and the way in which we want the brand to be seen, the way in which the market is going and the way the stores are. The challenge of retailing is actually how do you manage all those tensions all of the time and get them into some sort of equilibrium where it works for the retailer as well as it works for the customer.'*

As Jack Welch, the charismatic leader of General Electric used to say, *'Change before you have to.'* This is perhaps the hardest thing to pull off in business. Humans tend to be creatures of habit and tend to repeat learnt behaviours and patterns. The same is true of companies. When you have something that works, particularly when it works as well as the B&Q formula, the inclination is to continue doing it until it stops working. The motto, *'If it ain't broke, don't fix it'* is tremendously comforting, but in the ever-changing world of retail, it's just plain wrong.

Businesses that succeed over time fix things before they're broke and change before they have to. Innovative American multinational, 3M, for example insist, as policy, that 40% of their profits must come from products that weren't invented three years ago. B&Q have that same instinct (the instinct of never resting, of always wanting to do better) to keep moving. It should serve them well.

> **Point to consider** *Do you work for a company that is comfortably complacent or do you work for a company that always knows it can do better and believes in re-inventing itself to stay ahead of the game?*

It all turns on price

In their receptiveness to new ideas and their state of constant restlessness, B&Q have shown that they have the mind-set to overcome changes in their market.

> *'This is the law of the Yukon, that only the strong shall thrive; that surely the weak shall perish, and only the fit survive.'*[2]

From a branding perspective, the secret of successful evolution lies in thinking about what you sell not simply in terms of the physical product, but in terms of the benefits it brings. I've always liked the quote of an old marketing manager at Dulux, Anne Ferguson, who said, *'we're not selling chemicals in a can, we're selling the transformation of rooms'.* A classic marketing article, *'Marketing Myopia'* by Theodore Levitt, argued that the demise of the US railroad barons at the turn of the century came about because they were unable to see outside their own world. They thought they were in the railway business, but Levitt suggested they might have done better if they had seen that they were, in fact, in the transportation business.

If B&Q defined their business as selling hardware items, such as nuts and bolts, they would have little scope for development. This trap of not seeing beyond the product bedevils many shops; my parents' hardware store, I'm sure, included. To be fair, B&Q have always seen beyond hardware and have tended to describe themselves as a DIY retailer. The shift they will probably need to effect over the next decade is to define the scope of their business as home improvement. David Roth describes the benefit that B&Q offer as 'better homes',

'Helping people make their homes better, which is a much more emotive proposition and a much higher level position in the DIY market.'

David Roth went on to say that he felt the biggest threat to B&Q is *'to think we operate in a DIY marketplace and believing our competitors are in the DIY shed.'*

Key point *See the bigger picture and look to define your business in terms of the benefit you are offering rather than the product you are selling. B&Q don't just sell nuts and bolts - they're selling the promise of a better home.*

The B&Q brand is, therefore, rooted in the promise of *'improvement'*. The source of its competitive strength is, I believe, price and value. The underlying promise of the B&Q brand, therefore, becomes 'affordable improvement'. It's all about 'can do', which is why their advertising slogan *'you can do it when you B&Q it'* is so strong. It expresses the essence of the brand in a motivating way.

B&Q provide a good object lesson in using price as a fundamental platform of their brand. One of the key benefits of the scale and self-service nature of their original concept was that B&Q could offer very competitive prices. The bigger space, larger stock and more efficient staffing costs helped minimise the overhead contribution on each individual item. Thus the two brothers-in-law were able to realise their founding vision of *'a good price and a good value'*. As the company grew, taking even larger retail spaces and strengthening its bargaining position with suppliers, this cost-benefit equation became more and more favourable. It's this that has enabled B&Q to use price as part of their strategic armoury.

'Five years ago, pressure washers were something that only the trade bought. They were phenomenally expensive, so, unless you had a need to use one regularly, it was uneconomical. We felt there was an opportunity to take that pressure washer for £500 and bring it in at £99. To do that takes sourcing skill, specification skill (to know how to de-spec it from a top end professional to a mass-market product), buying power and entrepreneurialism (taking the risk on buying a large volume on the unproven belief that the market would be there if we did). This is exactly what we did. We sold them at £99 and, by doing so, brought pressure washers within reach for people who couldn't otherwise have afforded one. Now you can get one for just £20.'

David Roth speculates that by applying this model to the fashion end of home improvement, the market that B&Q want to start competing in, they would have a reason to be there, a purpose.

'Why are stylish things expensive? They're only expensive because people get away with charging large premiums. We could go to a top designer and get them to design a really stylish kitchen. Then we could approach the best manufacturer and spec it out. And as a result, because we sell in such huge volumes, we are able to offer a designer look at a mass market price.'

It's the same economic engine and idea that drives Wal-Mart. They use their immense buying power to fulfil the promise within Sam Walton's vision 'to give ordinary folk the chance to buy the same things as rich people.' B&Q are poised to do something similar in home improvement.

The underlying philosophy is something along the lines of B&Q continuously striving to bring everything that anyone could ever need to make their home a better place within reach of everyone. Their stated mission is to keep home improvement affordable and to help you make your home better in every way. With echoes not only of Wal-Mart's vision, but also Coke's *'a Coke on every street corner of the world'* or Microsoft's *'in every computer, on every desk, in every home'*, perhaps B&Q's rallying call could be *'better homes for all'*.

David Roth refers to it as democratisation.

> *If we lose the good value, down-to-earth, basic (and don't mean that in a pejorative sense) aspect of our business – what I used to describe as democratisation to people around the board table – accessibility... if we lose that bit, we're dead. That is our psychological contact with the consumer.'*

Key point *Price competitiveness is the flywheel of B&Q. The ability to increase the opportunities for their customers to be able to afford to better their homes and to continue to bring new possibilities for improvement within reach, is fundamental to the B&Q brand.*

David Roth is quite intense, a deep thinker; not necessarily the kind of character you might expect at a roll-up-the-sleeves retailer like B&Q. There's something a little incongruous when he says 'we tend to not over-intellectualise things', because he clearly has devoted a considerable amount of thought to his brand. Maybe this is because his background was in advertising rather than retailing. He used to be the strategic planner at B&Q's advertising agency before being persuaded to cross the divide and become their Marketing Director, a poacher turned gamekeeper. I like David, I like him a lot, I have been to retail conferences with him and I was surprised by the move but it certainly explains why B&Q seem more comfortable with the notion of branding than many other retailers. They talk the language, they understand the importance of clearly setting out what you stand for and they place great stock in staying true and consistent to the core idea.

> *'All the DIY players were positioned in the 'do-it' end of the market place. When we moved into larger stores, our sheer range dominance at the 'do-it' end of the marketplace forced our competitors to set their*

> differentiation around B&Q, which is great. With the exception of Wickes, most have exited what we would call the origins of B&Q – the nuts, bolts, screws, and the widgets, the component elements that you need in order to do a project. Nine times out of ten, they're not seen in the end project, but you can't do a project without them, and for us that's an integral part of the brand. We have to retain that earthiness; so if you want a widget you know you can get it at B&Q.'

It'll be interesting to see how B&Q succeed in transforming themselves over the next ten years. I've no doubt that they'll pull it off because of their strength, their vision and their can-do attitude, but it's a tough challenge. Offering service at the finishing end of home improvement leads to quite a different customer relationship from that required to sell a widget. As David Roth points out, you don't go to Tesco and say to a member of staff '*I'm thinking of making a soufflé, please tell me what I'm going to need, give me the recipe for it, tell me how long I need to cook it'*. You're more likely to ask at a DIY store how to put up a shelf, but wouldn't necessarily expect that advice to go beyond functional suggestions concerned with the task in hand. But you're not yet going to turn to B&Q for opinions on wallpaper patterns and whether your sofa fabric might clash with your favourite dress.

But if anyone can do it, B&Q can do it.

Doing it

If ever an advertising line bridged the gap between a company's proposition to its customers and an encapsulation of its culture, then *'you can do it when you B&Q it'* is surely it.

> '*It's not just a tripsy line that a well-paid advertising company came up with; it's now ingrained in the culture of how we perceive ourselves.'*

It's a line that cleverly captures the generic benefit of the DIY category for B&Q, positioning it as a positive and empowering thought. It diverts attention away from the lost weekends of home improvement on to the possibilities that open up when you take control of your own destiny. Similarly, it talks to everyone who works at B&Q and instils a spirit of self-determinism. A critical aspect of branding is coherence. It has been said that advertising will help a bad product fail more quickly because it will persuade more people to try the product, thus more people will find out for themselves that it is bad and never buy it again. Effective advertising will amplify a truth about a product or company, and if it's good it will make the truth interesting. Poor advertising will distort and misrepresent that truth. The way in which a brand projects itself externally needs to be consistent with its internal reality. It would be no good B&Q proclaiming that 'you can do it when you B&Q it' if the customer experienced a slovenly and slothful attitude on the shop floor. B&Q are all about doing. To use an over-hyped word, B&Q are about empowerment.

> 'We're much better at the doing bit. We have an idea and we're so keen to go and do it.'

B&Q go even further towards closing the gap between external projection and internal reality by featuring their staff in their advertising. In itself, this it nothing new: recently The Halifax have made a media celebrity out of Howard, one of their more shy and retiring members of staff, by having him front some big budget commercials. Retail organisations will often use this tactic (of featuring staff in their advertising) because the staff of any retail organisation do literally personify the brand. In B&Q's case the advertising works because it successfully conveys the down-to-earth integrity of the place. The branded B&Q aprons provide a clear visual link to the store and help the viewers suspend disbelief and imagine themselves in direct dialogue with the member of staff. Equally important is the halo effect that the advertising has among the staff themselves. David Roth makes this point by comparing B&Q's advertising with an earlier campaign from a now deceased competitor that featured a hammed-up fictional character with an unreasonably deep voice, Texas Tom, who was intended as a metaphor to emphasis size, scale, approachability and advice.

> 'Did any of the store staff aspire to be Texas Tom? Absolutely not – they actually felt very embarrassed about it all. Our staff are proud to be in the advertising. They enjoy doing it and they're proud to be representing B&Q, being the spokesman for B&Q, and being part of B&Q.'

This is the kind of virtuous circle that any retailer should be looking to create. Staff who, because they're proud to be representing the company, represent it all the more effectively, leading to a more successful operation, which gives them all the more reason to be proud. B&Q's triumph has been to pull this off in a sector that's traditionally associated with poor quality, and demotivated and unhelpful staff.

> *'People in the DIY market were the weakest link in the chain. I remember the perception that DIY stores were all staffed by YTS trainees who had never put up a picture hook, let alone shelves, and were incapable of giving advice. We have found a way of unifying large and small stores and starting to create involvement with the staff, so that even if they can't provide expert advice they can at least give a friendly feeling.'*

B&Q's staff are one of their greatest assets because they are involved in the company. This practice has been there from the beginning when David Quayle involved everyone in merchandising and now, three successful decades later, they're involved in the advertising.

> **Points to consider** *By being involved and empowered, B&Q staff embody the spirit of their company. Are the staff at your company right at the centre of what your company stand for?*

B&Q bolster the service provided by their staff with a DIY bible, entitled, unsurprisingly, *'You Can Do It'*. Now a best-selling and much acclaimed book in its own right, it supports the staff by giving them an additional reference point. It also means that the B&Q brand, philosophy and service ethic travels beyond the store and into the home. A customer review on Amazon illustrates how effectively the core B&Q message has been taken on board.

> *'This is an indispensable guide to the terrifying tasks a new home contains, and fills even the most bumbling fool with the confidence to have a go. You might not be ready to convert your attic after a flick through it, but even relatively major problems will suddenly seem surmountable.'*[3]

David Quayle and Richard Block received an early indication of the potential gains of delegating power, responsibility and reward. Having initially opened new units where they could find adequate space and parking, they changed their growth plan to more of a franchising model after seeing how successful their friend Roger Hemmingway had been when incentivised by a 40% stake in a new store in Kent. *'Within a year,'* remembers David Quayle, 'Roger had three stores opened, and our theory became why not grow by *'giving away' the rest of England.'* Jim Hodkinson, who ended up staying twenty-six years, rising to become Chief Executive Officer of B&Q, was hired to open the company's fourth store after being the only person to respond to an ad that B&Q had run in the Daily Telegraph soliciting responses for *'the most exciting job in retailing'.*

In sum

There are so many angles to the B&Q story that it's hard to pick the main learning point. The case history features, in particular, evidence of entrepreneurialism, continuous and relentless evolution, and coherence between internal reality and external projection. But for the purpose of this book, I think the key point concerns the essential role of price.

Retailing is all about competitive pricing: any retailer worth his salt will try to persuade his customers that he's offering the best price, or if not the best price at least the best value. Most of the billions of pounds that are spent every year on retail advertising go on price promotion messages. It's the retail battleground. But what distinguishes price in the B&Q story is how it is used as a strategic tool rather than just a tactical tool.

B&Q don't simply look to offer the best price, they try to find ways of changing the market dynamics by bringing items that were previously unaffordable within reach of the mass-market. They are the Robin Hood of home improvement. They really do enable their customers to do it. This is an intrinsic part of the B&Q brand DNA and is what makes them such a formidable competitor. I would like to say if B&Q can do it, you can do it, but it's not that simple.

References

1. Quoted from an article about B&Q in *National Home Centre News* by John Caulfield (March 22 1999)

2. Robert W Service, *Songs of a Sourdough* (1907)

3. Customer review on Amazon.co.uk

13

Breaking Free from the Crowd

What this chapter covers

■ This chapter is about standing out and standing up for what you stand for.

■ It explains why differentiation is at the heart of branding and why it is important to separate yourself from your competitors.

■ It shows how buyer behaviour is largely determined by the customer beliefs and so emphasises the need for retailers to give their customers something to believe in.

■ It illustrates the power of differentiation through the case of IKEA and bemoans the tendency of retailers to hide their light and their individuality under a bushel.

■ It concludes that customers need to know what shops stand for in order to determine whether or not those shops are for them.

A fable about parrots

I remember being told about a consignment of white teeshirts that weren't selling. An enterprising fashion guru apparently offered the following suggestion,

> *'Stamp an effing parrot on the front of them or a cabbage. Give 'em added value.'*

Absolutely right. If you're selling white teeshirts then, in order to attract attention, you've got to do something like sell three for a fiver. The trouble with that is that someone down the road will soon be selling four for a fiver, and then someone else two for £2. There are a number of different ways of dressing up the offer, but whichever way you cut it, once you're locked in a price war, you're stuck in a downward spiral.

But the minute you stamp a parrot on the front of that teeshirt you've not only added value, but you've changed the rules of the game. Suddenly you're selling something different and can charge £10 for it. If, however, you've put a can of beans on it that no one wants to wear, then you've buggered up a sure sale at £1 a teeshirt. That's the risk. It's all about understanding the market. Some intuitively do, others don't. Or, as my best mate and best man Jimmy McHale (a chartered accountant who has held my hand through more mergers and acquisitions than I care to mention) always says, profit is the reward of risk.

This is what branding is all about. To extend the example, imagine a handful of teeshirt stalls in a street market all selling plain white teeshirts. They're all desperately competing with each other, but find that all they've got to attract customers to their stall is their own vocal volume, personal salesmanship and clever price promotions. This is a commodity market.

One day, one of them breaks away and starts selling red and blue teeshirts. It's an immediate success; suddenly people have more of a reason to visit that particular stall. The other stall owners notice and quickly follow suit. Now they all offer colour teeshirts and, although there's greater opportunity for a little more variety from one stall to the other, the colour teeshirt has become the commodity. For a brief period of time, when the world was still in its white teeshirt phase, the colour teeshirt offered a point of difference, but because the differentiation came from the merchandise, it was purely functional and wasn't sustainable.

Then someone starts overprinting his teeshirts with parrots, which is harder (although not impossible) to copy. Not only that but he also charges three times as much. And people buy them. Because he's making more on each individual sale, he doesn't need to sell as many as his competitors to make more money. He can afford to reduce his stock and create more space. He might decide to branch out by also selling teeshirts with cabbage motifs or he may decide to stick with parrots as his specialism. He might change the stall's name to something like 'Pretty Polly' or 'Squawk'. He might invest in a real life parrot, teach it to say 'Pretty Polly' and hang its cage at the front of the stall. He might then start selling different types of parrot teeshirts like the cockatoo range.

The teeshirt vendor will have repositioned his stall around a brand idea. He's taking a risk because he's putting all his (parrot?) eggs in one basket.

If the parrot theme proves unpopular, then he's in trouble, but Lacoste have done well out of crocodiles, Ralph has scored with his polo ponies and so one would imagine that he'll be okay with his parrots. He might even emphasise his parrot theme by donating 1% of his takings to the parrot preservation society. The point is that he now stands for something.

In a row of similar teeshirt shops, Pretty Polly stands out. It's different. People have more reason to go there from the squawking parrot at the front, the cleverly themed and attractive teeshirts and the reassurance that it's going to a good cause. They may even, in some small way, be emotionally engaging with the brand. And that's not easy to copy.

A word of advice *Always look to add value and to separate your shop and its offer from the crowd. Ask yourself if you are giving your customers enough of a reason to give you their custom rather than take it elsewhere.*

Stand for something, rather than nothing

Differentiation is at the heart of branding. As Richard Hyman from Verdict said,

> *'Retail branding is fundamental. It's about differentiating one retail brand from another.'*

To choose to stand for something by definition involves deciding not to stand for something else. The risk with branding is that you back the wrong horse. John Williamson of brand consultancy Wolff Olins feels that Marks and Spencer's problems stem from the fact that they stand for something that no longer exists,

> *It used to represent middle-class Britain but who wants to be middle class anymore? None of us. We all want to be estuary, ethnic or some other category. What Marks & Spencer lost was the notion of middle class and it needs to replace it with an equally compelling idea to become more attractive.'*[1]

I disagree with John Williamson if he is advocating that Marks and Spencer should pluck a brand idea out of thin air, although I'm sure that's not what he would advise. Their challenge is to find a way of shifting their fundamental positioning and presentation to make it relevant again. As Tim Danaher, editor at Retail Week, says,

> *'The previous management had been trying to turn M&S into something it wasn't. The brand has particular associations and values that make it difficult to change. It's hard to make M&S fashionable because M&S is reliable, solid, and consistent. Stuart Rose has recognised that he is the guardian of that brand. It's a fantastic inheritance. He should manage and treasure it, not try to turn it into something it isn't.'*

It's not easy. In fact it's probably the hardest thing in business to reframe a deeply entrenched brand. Philip Green, who could himself have been wrestling with the Marks & Spencer conundrum had his take-over bid succeeded, commented how difficult it has been to shift perceptions of BHS.

> *BHS have got a loyal tried and tested customer base, many of whom have been shopping there for twenty-five years and like the sandwiches or whatever. People have a very fixed view of what that brand stands for, which has pluses and minuses. Every time I take people there they say to me, "I didn't know they had changed", and you're banging your head against the wall thinking, 'how do I change the perception of what the brand stands for?'*

When it comes to branding, people suffer cognitive dissonance, in other words they will ignore evidence that contradicts their own beliefs. It's a hugely difficult task to change someone's beliefs, which shows just how important it is to give your customers a reason to believe in you in the first place. Beliefs are powerful and play a significant part in buying behaviour.

There's an amusing anecdote from my parent's hardware shop that proves this. Because the shop was located near Shepperton Studios, my parents were frequently asked for permission to feature the shop in various TV shoots. They always said 'yes' despite the disruption it sometimes involved and never received any payment for it. Once the shop appeared in an episode of a popular series of that time called 'Doomwatch'. The scene involved a baby being snatched from its pram immediately outside the shop. For months afterwards, customers avoided coming near the shop and would certainly never leave an unattended pram out the front, despite all my parents' protestations that the event was nothing more than dramatic fiction. The experience showed me just how powerful TV can be, but it also illustrated how, once people have a fixed belief in their mind, they can resist any persuasion that counters that belief.

But the risk of getting it wrong is not a valid argument for avoiding differentiation. John F Kennedy once said:

'There are risks and costs to a programme of action, but they are far less than the long-range risks and cost of comfortable inaction.'

Unless you stand for something, you stand for nothing. And if you stand for nothing, how can you possibly expect anyone to give you the time of day. But, as Philip Green said earlier, it's incredibly difficult to change what you stand for. With BHS, he doesn't need to, he was simply frustrated that the dramatic improvements at BHS continue to surprise people. The point is that if you do need to change, your actions need to be bold, deep and meaningful. Cosmetic change will not shift perception one iota.

Successful repositioning is only achieved when the retailer gives his or her customers substantial reason and permission to reappraise their brand.

Tesco pulled it off, by changing from the inside. Those of you who remember Hepworths the tailors will know they changed everything, their chief executive, their merchandise and even their name. It was a brave decision, but with George Davis choosing the merchandise with true fashion prescience, it wasn't long before this retailer was leading the high street. Its new name summed everything up: Next.

Obviously change, true change, is a big subject, but touching on it here, I hope, demonstrates the difficulty of getting people to change their mind once they've settled on an initial opinion. I've had several clients who wanted to change customer perception and thought they could so by simply changing the logo. Enough said.

> **!**
>
> **Key point** *Customer beliefs influence buying behaviour. Be sure to give your customer something to believe in. If you want to change what they believe in, give them permission to do so.*

A love hate relationship

Possibly the best example of a truly differentiated retail brand comes from Almhult in Scandinavia. IKEA is something of an oddity. It's a series of paradoxes: a global giant from Sweden; a place where customers fall over themselves for an experience they profess to hate; a proselytising founder with a few skeletons in his own flat-packed wardrobe; a company that has succeeded by making its customers do most of the work.

Anyone who has battled through an IKEA store to first unlock the indecipherable product code system and then find what they were looking for thirty feet up one of its vast warehouse storage racks, fought off the crushing sense of boredom that accompanies the interminable wait at the painfully slow and chaotic tills and then, against all odds, managed to assemble their furniture (occasionally without all the requisite parts and always without comprehensible instruction); anyone who has been through all this will know that IKEA take their philosophy of encouraging the customer to do the work very seriously indeed.

IKEA, without any sense of irony, proclaim in their philosophy (somewhat grandiosely entitled *'The Testament of a Furniture Dealer'*) *'the feeling of having completed something is an effective sleeping pill. A person who retires feeling he has done his bit will quickly wither away.'* This perhaps explains why their furniture can be so hard to assemble and they always leave out the essential screw. They don't want their customers to ever complete anything because they believe it is bad for the soul to stop working!

> *'IKEA's moral crusade extends uncompromisingly to the customer. Whether you like it or not, it intends to teach you the value of good, honest, simple hard work. Self-assembly, viewed from this perspective, is more than a cost-cutting measure: it's a tool of evangelism, designed to make you sweat for your edification.'*[2]

I don't seriously knock IKEA. It is the perfect exemplar of what this book preaches. It is radically different from its competitors; it has built its business around a defining set of beliefs and has been phenomenally successful as a consequence. Oliver Burkeman wrote of IKEA in *The Guardian*,

> 'It is frequently observed that, for a broad swathe of Britain, IKEA has designed our lives; it is almost as frequently noted that its customer service sucks, that the traffic jams outside its stores are intolerable, and its assembly instructions indecipherable. We love it and hate it, rely on it and satirise it, often simultaneously – as if it were not a shop at all, really, but something far more emotively substantial'[2]

Earlier I've written that brands establish an emotional engagement with their customers. They rise above the rational considerations of buying behaviour and strike a chord to become part of their customers' lives. IKEA definitely succeeds in striking an emotional chord. People feel strongly about it, not always positively, and they go there in droves.

IKEA shows how the power of differentiation can rise above things like a pleasurable shopping experience.

Clearly its success is down to more than just the fact that it's different: the product it sells is in tune with current fashion, it offers incredibly good prices and its scale provides a range of options sufficiently large to furnish your home several times over.

But product, price and range alone do not explain the success that has reputedly made its founder Ingvar Kamprad the richest man in the world with a personal fortune, I read, of £32bn.

Of course, no one can be quite sure if indeed he has overtaken Bill Gates because both the man and his company are famously secretive.

Provocation *The success of IKEA suggests that it's more important to stand for something and be different, even if that means some people won't like you, than to be anodyne and anonymous. Are you prepared to take the risk of not being liked by everyone to secure the emotional commitment of those customers that really matter?*

Spot the difference

It's surprisingly difficult to think of many retail brands as radically different in their sector as IKEA is. In making the following observation, John Brady of McKinsey's points to the fact that in an undifferentiated world, price competitiveness assumes a greater degree of prominence.

> *'In many different sectors now you could argue that the retail experience is not very different across different retail players. I suspect if a man came down from Mars and walked into a few of the big grocers, he would find it hard to tell you which one he was in. In that world, it should be no surprise that price is relatively important.'*

While I agree wholeheartedly with John Brady that a Martian would struggle to distinguish one supermarket from another, I think it's interesting to observe how every company tends to be subtly differentiated. Neill Denny, the former editor of *Retail Week*, talked about differentiation as something that tends to be more apparent to the insider.

> *'Someone moving jobs from the BBC to ITV would probably be confronted with a raft of cultural differences that weren't apparent to an outsider and that the two organisations use to define each other. And while I don't think it's as strong in supermarkets, I bet there's still a sense among Tesco people of, "oh, I couldn't work for Sainsbury, they're so stuffy". They would say, "all that hideous bureaucracy … I couldn't bear to work there." Sainsbury's people, on the other hand, would probably think, "I'm not sure I could ever work up in Cheshunt. Tesco are still really the same underneath you know, even their head office is like a shed on an industrial estate."'*

If you look hard enough, subtle differences in character and nature tend to reveal themselves. The shame of it is that most retailers are drawn into a herd mentality where they feel they have to disguise their true nature in order to be like everyone else.

It's often said that the middle of the road is a dangerous place to be because you end up getting squashed. Much better to be on the edge, to stand for something.

Terry Green, former CEO at Debenhams makes this very point.

'The middle market is under severe and increasing pressure from the discounters at the bottom end and the brands at the top end. Unless middle market retailers develop what I call a "premium value" offer, they will disappear. A good example of premium value is the "Designers at Debenhams" range I developed in the nineties whilst CEO. We signed up more than 25 designers and took the concept from a department taking nothing to an entire division taking more than £100 million when I left in 2000. Today that figure is over £200 million.'[3]

My job as a retail brand adviser and the message of this book is to bring retailers out of themselves more; to encourage them to be themselves, to strongly stand for something rather than copy everyone else; to give their customers more of a choice and more of a reason to visit their store.

I passionately believe that as a retailer you shouldn't hide your light under a bushel.

A retailer that I've long admired has been The Gap. I know they've stumbled in recent years and consequently parted company with their driving force and creative inspiration, Mickey Drexler, but they grew to a position of strength from unpromising beginnings precisely because they had a clear vision of what they stood for, were prepared to make bold, brave decisions to achieve it and very cleverly succeeded in projecting a coherent identity across everything they did.

'Part of the reason The Gap has succeeded as well as it has is that for every aggressive fashion statement it makes, it also strives for timelessness, for classicism, and avoids being too trendy or fashionable. This sort of stability provides consumers some degree of comfort in a world otherwise swept by often-disconcerting change. Sure The Gap is not perfect. It may stumble, but over the years it has done an amazing job of honouring its core brand values of simplicity and affordable style.'

Take a standard pair of Chinos, made in some Far Eastern company and sold by Burtons. Take the same pair of Chinos sold by The Gap. In the main, previously people would feel a good deal happier about buying those Chinos from The Gap than from Burtons. They would have exactly the same product, but it would have a different label stitched into the back. They would feel more positively about their Gap Chinos than if they had bought them from Burtons and, because of that, The Gap may have been able to charge a premium.

Tim Danaher, editor at Retail Week, points out the role that the customer's self-image has to play in this.

> 'What's in a brand? And this is the point about the difference between The Gap and Burtons – it's "What does that shop say about me? Is it a shop I'm happy for my mates to see me walking out of?"

The lesson of branding is that you can't be all things to all men. In order to appeal to your core franchise of customers, you need to be prepared to sacrifice all those that fall outside those boundaries.

Provocation *What does your shop say about your customers? If it says nothing, you should be worried. What do your customers think their friends would say about them as a result of their shopping in your shop? Do your customers freely tell their friends they shop at your shop or do they keep quiet about it?*

People shop at places they identify with. We are, all of us, a bundle of insecurities who need continual affirmation of who we are and where we fit in. A retailer needs to clearly flag up what her shop stands for in order to give her customers the opportunity to decide whether or not it's their kind of place. Is it somewhere they can identify with? Is it somewhere that will in its own little way enhance their own feeling of self-worth? Retailers who stick their head above the parapet will find they are chosen. Those who meekly refuse to assert their individuality will quickly find themselves, like the kid who is the last one chosen for the playground football teams, out of favour.

In sum

Every retail organisation is different. Every one is individual in its own way. Branding is the art of bringing these differences to the fore and leveraging them for the benefit of the business. Doing so, gives customers something they can identify with. At a rational level it gives people a reason to choose one store over another. At an emotional level it allows customers to connect with their shop and feel part of the group, or tribe, that it represents. Don't be shy of telling your customers what you stand for. Or who you are.

> *If you only remember one thing from this chapter:*
> _____
>
> *If you don't stand for something, you stand for nothing; and if you stand for nothing, why on earth should anyone choose you?*

References

1. John Williamson, *'Brand New World'* Wolf Olins website

2. Oliver Burkeman, *'The miracle of Almhult'*, *The Guardian* 17 June 2004

3. Scott Bedbury, *'A New Brand World'*, published Penguin Books 2003

14

HMV: Eternal Impressions in an Ignorant Mind

This case study draws on an interview with John Taylor, Marketing Director, and Gennaro Castaldo, Head of Press and PR, at HMV.

What this chapter covers

- This is a story of how a music company inspired by an oil painting of a dog has ridden the storms of change and competition by sticking to what it knows best.

- HMV show the ability of brands to penetrate the subconscious with associations and memories powerful enough to influence even the occasional customer.

- HMV highlight how the specialist retailer can play off its authority in its fight against generalist retailers encroaching on its turf.

- The primary lesson of HMV is how to exaggerate and amplify the advantage of a specialist.

Although not into music, I find myself in HMV's Oxford Street flagship store every December buying Christmas presents. I've no idea why I always go there: the Virgin Store in Piccadilly is nearer, Amazon is probably even more convenient, and my local Tesco even cheaper, but something draws me to HMV year after year. Perhaps it's that I'm always able to find what I'm looking for and that I'm never shown up for my ignorance in matters musical.

Thinking about it, I do remember going into Virgin once and feeling overwhelmed. HMV seems to have a sense of order that helps me find whatever it is I'm looking for, as well as throwing up other good ideas. I feel comfortable there, even though, as a non-muso, I know I've strayed into alien territory.

Funnily enough, despite drowning in the sounds of discordant rock hits and teeming in sartorial inelegance, it always gives me the impression of being a serious place. It's serious about music. Its greys and pinks are sober in comparison to the vibrant bright colours of Virgin or Tower Records. Perhaps that's why I gravitate there in my hour of need; I'm unconsciously looking for the reassurance of an expert.

I find it difficult to imagine buying my Christmas CDs from Tesco despite knowing that they cater for people like myself by selling the popular titles that I only ever buy. I'm sure they're cheaper as well, but somehow, although an Elton John Greatest Hits CD is going to be exactly the same item irrespective of whether it comes from Tesco or HMV, buying from an expert bestows the item with that little added extra value.

Two questions that have been troubling me

1. Why am I prepared to knowingly pay more, walk a little further and put myself out a bit more to buy something that I'm not particularly interested in?

2. And how come, given my lack of knowledge, I find I've got a reasonably clear impression of different music retailers?

The two questions in this box were why I wanted to feature the HMV case study in this book. I wanted to understand how a retail brand is able to achieve such impact with a light user such as myself. I understand Oddbins because I'm passionate about wine, but HMV is different for me because I don't care much for music, and yet the two retail brands are similarly rooted in specialist expertise.

From Elgar to the Kings of Leon

Delving into the story of HMV, I find everything about it reinforces its status as the authoritative music retailer.

In the week I meet them, HMV are hosting a personal appearance in Oxford Street from one of the big names in rock, Kings of Leon. Eighty-four years earlier their doors were officially opened by one of the then big names in music, Sir Edward Elgar. HMV claim that Elgar's was one of the world's first in-store personal appearances. Nowadays they put on a good three hundred a year throughout the country, knowing they bring kudos and excitement to the brand and traffic to the store.

Presaging Coca-Cola's global mission some sixty years later to put a bottle of Coca-Cola within arm's reach on every street corner in the world, Sir Edward Elgar used the opportunity of his speech, at HMV's brand new shop at 363 Oxford Street, to campaign *'for a gramophone with a first-class selection of records to be placed in every school in the country'*. Were he to see that the means for listening to music has gone far beyond schools to every home and increasingly to every individual through Walkmans and MP3 players, he would probably feel quietly satisfied that his plea had been heard. But I hate to think what he would have made of the Kings of Leon. Had he had any premonition as to where the popularisation of music might lead, I suspect he would have politely declined the invitation to endorse HMV.

HMV have arguably done as much as anyone to democratise music. When they opened their Oxford Street shop in 1921 they were a manufacturer called The Gramophone Company. Gennaro Castaldo, Head of Press, describes an atmosphere far removed from today's set-up.

'The store was a relatively elitist operation for wealthy people who could afford gramophones. You would make an appointment, be greeted by a uniformed commissionaire; the manager would sit you down in a lounge environment and bring the catalogue along for you to see what had been released. It certainly wasn't the mass market operation it became in the fifties and sixties.'

Twenty-one years before opening their first shop, The Gramophone Company had acquired the rights to a painting entitled *'His Master's Voice'*, by artist Francis Barraud of his dog, Nipper, listening to a gramophone. The original painting featured a phonographic cylinder machine. Had they continued the precedent of re-painting in each and every development in music playing machines, Nipper would now have an iPod. While the image of the dog and the gramophone have gone on to become one of the world's most enduring brand icons, the painting also ended up lending its title to the company in the abbreviated form of HMV. The £100 paid for the painting and reproduction rights looks a pretty good deal when you throw in a company name as well.

The famous image depicting a scene, very much of its particular age, is a reminder of just how long HMV have been around.

As Gennaro Castaldo points out:

'We are probably the only organization that has sold every format of music over the last eighty-two years. Clearly we were there at the advent of the gramophone and then 45s and 7" singles – I don't think any other retailer in the world can match us. It's one of the things that sets us apart and underpins a lot of our values and heritage.'

Today the music industry is experiencing a maelstrom of change with on-line music available in a very different digital format from the albums we've become used to over the past forty years. HMV are sanguine about these developments, seeing them simply as a part of the evolving industry they've been at the forefront of for many years. HMV themselves have evolved from a manufacturer to a retailer, from gramophone machines to vinyl to CDs, from selling music to selling home entertainment. They've come a long way, but their origins remain the root of their authority. 99% of their customers, probably more, don't know or care about HMV's history, but they'll have a sense that it's a leading player in music. As Marketing Director John Taylor says,

'The brand has come to represent authority and heritage. It's associated with music in a very definitive way. It's all about authority and expertise Whether it comes from the staff, how we communicate to the public, advertising, on-line or in our e-mails, it's got to ooze authority.'

HMV's authority is critical for their continued success. The relentless march of supermarkets has taken them beyond simply selling food into clothing, electrical goods, household goods; you name it. And now they're encroaching on HMV's turf.

'Supermarket growth into non-foods has far-reaching implications for the whole retail industry, especially specialists and generalists as they are caught in the cross-fire of competitive pricing used by grocers to win share in what to them are new market opportunities.' (Mintel Retail Review 2004)

To ward off this threat, HMV need to be able to leverage their specialist credentials to the benefit of their customers. They need to continue to assert their status as the definitive music and home entertainment retailer and translate it into the kind of customer value that the likes of Tesco can't offer.

The four primary sources of HMV's authority that give it, as a specialist, a competitive edge over a generalist competitor are; heritage, endorsement, range and staff.

HMV's source of authority

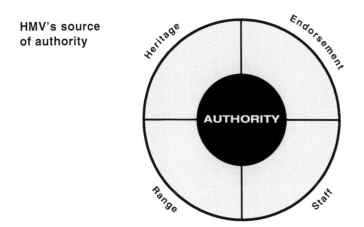

Heritage: Part of the landscape

In itself, HMV's heritage doesn't count for much. After all, it operates in an industry that is openly disdainful of the old and the old-fashioned. But its heritage underpins everything. It means that all its customers will know that HMV have been selling music for as long as they remember. At a subliminal level they will know that the HMV brand and its iconic trademark have been part of the landscape ever since they first started buying music. It means the brand will be firmly embedded in their minds as one of the places to go for music.

So long as HMV can keep it fresh and contemporary, their longevity is an asset that allows them to legitimately claim to know more about music than the likes of Tesco. As Gennaro Castaldo points out:

> 'If we make a recommendation to our customers about something they should listen to or watch, they will be inclined to trust us and believe us because we have built up that trust over time.'

The same recommendation from Sainsbury's, for example, wouldn't carry the same weight because Sainsbury's haven't proved to anyone that they know enough about music. They don't have the same track record.

HMV's advertising slogan, *'top dog for music, dvd, games'*, is a competitive claim that re-enforces the retailer's authority. The reason they can make such a claim comes in part from their eighty-four year track record at the forefront of the industry.

The Times identified HMV's history as a critical component of the brand in a feature on the company a couple of years ago.

> *The music industry has always lived in "interesting times" and is not for the faint-hearted. Given the scale of the HMV operation, the sums committed to "getting it right" in response to changing products and changing retail patterns are enormous. A long history does have advantages; in changing times, having a positive brand identity not only gives HMV an important competitive advantage over its rivals, it also helps create the basis of continued growth in the future.'*[1]

Endorsement: The place where people in the know go

HMV's heritage also works at a celebrity level. The movers and shakers in the music industry will have grown up with HMV. Spend any time in HMV's Oxford Street shop and you are likely to brush shoulders with any one of a number of leading musicians stocking up on the latest CDs. John Lennon was a frequent customer, Michael Jackson also (before his passport was temporarily taken from him), Robert Plant had a basketful of CDs in there the other week and a whole host of personalities, who I wouldn't recognise, apparently shop there.

> *'In a way, I owe my career to the HMV store in Oxford Street. In early 1958, I made a demo disc there with the Drifters...it led to our contract with EMI.' (Cliff Richard)*
>
> *'The HMV logo has always appealed to me, even as a kid. It is to me the tradition of music and record stores.' (Phil Collins)*

People who know about music shopping there and eulogising about the place sends out a powerful message to anyone interested in music. Apart from the occasional pop song about life as a checkout girl by a band like The Streets, it's hard to imagine a supermarket being credited as an inspiration by a leading player in the music industry.

Personal appearances are all part of this. Over the years, HMV have hosted appearances by artists such as Paul McCartney, Robbie Williams, Kylie Minogue, Coldplay and David Bowie to name but a few. As John Taylor explains:

> 'Personal appearances by artists is something that we do a great deal of, I think about three hundred a year at the moment. They're very good: they manifest what the brand is about and give people access to something that's very exciting. Often they help break new acts, which is good for us to be associated with.'

It would be interesting to know how many of the once-a-year CD shoppers like myself are aware that HMV do all this. I suspect it's an extremely small proportion. Were it not for my interest in retail, the celebrity personal appearances at HMV would have passed me by. But what I do notice when I'm there is that it's full of people who appear to be into their music. The place reeks of music expertise and that gives me reassurance that I've come to the right place. It's a reassurance that's worth paying a little more for.

In the war between specialists (like HMV) and generalists (like Tesco), it's imperative for the specialist to continue to attract the custom of heavy-users in their category, the customers who are in the know.

! **Points to consider** *Do 'people in the know' shop in your shop? What can you do to attract them and build authority in your marketplace?*

HMV focus much of their marketing effort at music enthusiasts. Their recent advertisement in Mojo magazine for example recommends two fairly obscure albums, one by a band of *'Minnesotan post rockers'* and another that is described as *'uneasy listening from a mercurial underground guitar hero'.* This ad is clearly not talking to me, it might as well be in Japanese as far as I'm concerned, but where it works for me is that by attracting music buffs, it re-enforces the store's credentials as the place where experts go.

The sponsorship programme is similarly designed to position HMV as a brand in the know for people in the know.

> 'We've done things with MTV, EMAP, Virgin Radio, and have sponsorship deals with the likes of The Mean Fiddler, places where again we can get the authority across.'

Range: "Have you got 'In The Aeroplane Over The Sea' by Neutral Milk Hotel?"

Depth of range is a particularly important weapon against the generalist. Generalists, by definition, stock a small amount of everything. John Taylor makes the point that this is an Achilles' heel that inhibits their capacity to compete with the specialist.

> 'The supermarkets will bang on about selling CDs, but you might get there and find that number 36 or number 31 are actually out of stock.'

A key requirement for HMV is that they stock a broad and deep range. There is no greater sin for a retailer than being unable to meet the needs of your loyal and regular customers. As John Taylor says, they might forgive you once, but not twice.

> 'Very simply, a lot of it is down to having exactly what our customers want 99% of the time. I've bought music my whole life and if I went to buy an unusual CD, which I have many a time, I wouldn't go back to the same place if they couldn't help me on two separate occasions.'

Customer loyalty can be hard earned, but easily lost. Buyers of music can be demanding customers. It's not simply enough to stock the right CD, but the merchandising needs to work in a way that easily navigates people to their own particular area of interest and displayed in a way that introduces the customer to other music that he or she may like.

'The further you get in to the store, the more you find yourself in your own little area and your own little heaven of products. You are then into a little specialist world finding what you want and discovering new things.'

This isn't simply a question of making additional sales; it's part of providing an enriching and, in music terms, educational experience.

John Taylor emphasises the importance of getting the merchandising right by saying that he felt the old Tower store on Piccadilly Circus tended to present *'the music to gratify themselves'* rather than think about making it easy and enticing for their customers.

'We would like to think that we merchandise better than anybody else. If you go in our Oxford Circus store you can easily find what's going off in America for example, and you'll come across various different features presented in the store every week, as opposed to just racks of CDs which I think has had its day. Expecting everybody to wade through rows of CDs just doesn't happen anymore.'

As well as catering for the enthusiast, HMV have also to make it easy for the likes of me.

'The entrance to any store is basically full of all the new products and things that people expect to buy. That is just for the casual buyer and we do pretty well on that stuff, because it's there, well merchandised, and easy to get quickly. That's all some people want out of their shopping.'

It appears that they deliberately keep me at the front of the store, which, as well as satisfying my own needs to get in and out relatively easily, stops me bumbling around the inner sanctum of true enthusiasts.

I was struck when interviewing John and Gennaro at just what a broad church of customers HMV needs to satisfy.

> 'We've got a big share of the singles market, which is very, very young.
> Young teenagers, most of it. We've also got a big share of the classical
> market, which goes up to 60-70 year olds. It's a huge age range.'

Few other non-staple retailers I can think of cover such a wide spectrum.

Staff: Punk marketing

I've yet to come across a great retail brand with only adequate staff. It's
simply not possible. The staff are both the embodiment and the
manifestation of the brand. If the staff are mediocre and indistinguishable
from any other shop assistant, there is effectively no brand. I always advise
my clients to treat their staff as if they were their most important customers.
HMV are naturals in this respect because they recruit only from amongst
their most enthusiastic customers. When John Taylor, now their Marketing
Director, says he used to be a punk I believe him. HMV have an advantage
in that music tends to attract people who live and breathe it.

> 'We wouldn't take on anyone to serve behind the counter who had no
> interest in what we sell. We take on people who are passionate about
> what we sell, they love it, that's what they want to do.'

There is though a balance to be achieved between passion for the
product and good service. John Taylor's comment reminds me of the scene
in *High Fidelity* where the Jack Black character berates a hapless customer
for his poor taste in music.

> 'The last thing you want is a member of our staff expressing their opinions
> on what people are buying. There are no rights or wrongs with the music
> and films, it's all subjective. However if a customer asks them for an
> opinion and advice on what they should buy, fantastic, they're away as
> that's what they know about.'
>
> 'It's passion. Everyone who works here is passionate about the brand, the
> business, and the products they sell. That's what brings the brand to life;
> it's presented to the public through passion.'

Passion for the product is something supermarkets would struggle to compete with.

Serious entertainment

HMV stand for *'serious entertainment'*. This is the brand idea that gives them their authority in the marketplace. It's underpinned by their heritage, which gives their customers permission to trust them; the endorsement of 'people in the know', which provides reassurance; their depth and breadth of range, which leads to confidence that the customers' needs will be met; and their enthusiastic staff, who deliver knowledgeable and enthusiastic service.

HMV's brand authority

As with almost every other retailer I've talked to, HMV haven't articulated or written down what they stand for. It tends to be a feeling that exists in the ether. As Gennaro Castaldo explains, people know it but they can't describe it.

> *'A lot of people who come to work in Head Office come from the stores, so they have an appreciation of the culture. We all have a sense that we're guardians of the brand and what HMV stands for. We can't always define it, but we feel it.'*

I think this will change over the next few years as the contribution of branding to retail is recognised. It's important to recognise, though, that the proper process of defining what you stand for comes after, not before, the development of the retail brand. The trap that many fall into is to describe an idealised brand that they aspire to, but bears no resemblance to the reality of their operation. Retail branding is more like an archaeological pursuit, in that the archaeologist can only explain what's already there rather than conjure up what's not there.

In sum

I opened this case history by posing two questions that have troubled me.

1. Why am I prepared to knowingly pay more, walk a little further and put myself out a bit more to buy something that I'm not particularly interested in?

2. And how come, given my lack of knowledge, I find I've got a reasonably clear impression of different music retailers?

In this case study, I have primarily considered HMV in relation to the supermarkets that are increasingly encroaching on their turf. It's a story of the specialist against the generalist. And it's a story that reveals how the specialist can offer more experience, more knowledge, better choice, a fuller selection, more excitement, better service and more involved staff. It tells me what I'm paying more for when I go to HMV and I'm left feeling that it's probably worth it.

It has also illustrated to me how the best brands succeed in imprinting themselves on public consciousness simply by doing what they do in a consistent and coherent manner year in, year out. I'm not a music lover, but I do occasionally buy music. This means my mind needs to store some simple information about where to go, for those moments when I do eventually need to go. So, even though I don't think much about it, I do hold some impressions in my head on different music retailers and what they stand for. This is what branding is all about – leaving impressions in your customer's minds. The thing I've found from getting deeper into HMV is just how robust and accurate my low-level impressions were, which is testament to the strength of the HMV brand.

Reference

1. *'Building on a brand' The Times*, 13.01.03

15

Why Retail?

What this chapter covers

■ This final chapter doesn't talk about retail branding. If you're not converted to my argument about the power of the brand by now, you probably never will be.

■ Instead it takes the opportunity to advocate a career in retail. I honestly can't think of a better place to start a career and end a book.

A recent advertising campaign for The Metropolitan Police featured a number of exceptional people admitting that they weren't sure if they had it in them to deal with the kind of problems thrown at policemen in their line of duty.

Without wishing to denigrate the important recruitment of our future law-enforcers (clearly a higher calling than a career in commerce), I would, as one who started off as a police recruit, nevertheless like to put forward the case for a career in retail.

The first thing to say is that, like the police force, it's not for everyone.

Not everyone has it in them to keep their enthusiasm up when standing alone on an empty shop floor on a cold wet Tuesday afternoon, or to remain cordial when confronted with an abusive and unreasonable customer, or to have to work when most of their mates are out enjoying themselves.

But for those who have it in them; who don't mind working while others play; who can cope equally well with the painfully slow lost hours of no custom as well as handle the madness of being overrun by swarms of hurried and harassed shoppers; who feel more at home on their feet than sitting behind a desk; who can't resist the challenge of making a sale; and who are restless to get on with their life; for these people there's little better. You've got to enjoy being judged at the end of every single day and be the sort where getting something done tomorrow is not soon enough.

To get to the top in retail, you have to have a uniquely strange skill set. It's all about an obsessive attention to detail and a huge visionary self-belief that you know what your customers want before they do. Most people who are good at detail don't usually have the creative flair to see the bigger picture.

A disadvantage of being a son of a couple of shopkeepers was that I couldn't see beyond the till. It never occurred to me that such great career opportunities existed in retail, that you could join the likes of Marks & Spencer and get a good grounding in retail as well as being catapulted into the stratosphere of running some of the most important businesses in the country like Stuart Rose has.

The same age as me, Stuart, the son of a civil servant, joined Marks & Spencer in his early twenties. Since then he has headed up Burton Menswear, Evans, Dorothy Perkins, Principles, Argos, Booker, and Arcadia before returning to run M&S.

Similarly, Terry Leahy, the son of a Liverpudlian ship's carpenter turned greyhound trainer, joined Tesco as a twenty-three year old marketing executive in 1979. Eighteen years later he was appointed Chief Executive. He has since been knighted, earns a basic salary of over £955,000, made over £3.4 million in bonuses last year, and is one of the most respected businessmen in the country. For all his talents, I doubt he would have made such an impact if he had joined one of the FMCG giants such as Unilever or Procter and Gamble.

The flowering of retail in the twentieth-first century means that the opportunities are even greater today than they ever were. It really is a great business to get into, you don't stay on the floor for long (if you don't want to); it's all very fast moving. The big FMCG brands used to be the places to go for great training. Now it's Tesco or John Lewis, who offer the same grounding only more so because it's the real world. As with the police force, where recruits always start on the beat, the great thing about retail is you learn literally from the shop floor upwards.

Historically, most retailers have been weak on providing good well-rounded training and development, perhaps relying too much on experience picked up on the job over providing a more structured commercial grounding and skill-set. Consequently it hasn't always attracted the best talent. The changing commercial realities of the current retail marketplace demand smarter retailing: the major retailers are now waking up to the need to attract and properly develop the best talent. It is undoubtedly a better career option than it ever has been.

One of the most exciting developments in this respect is the imminent launch of Philip Green's Retail Academy. As with many of the great social innovations, it has taken a philanthropic individual from the private sector to address the need for world-class retail grounding. Philip Green explains his motivation:

> 'One of the reasons I want to start this Academy is that I feel a lot of the people I've come into contact with are wholly unrounded, they're simply one track. Somebody who's streetwise may not necessarily be commercial. I always say you can teach a lot of the base case things: you can always get a guy to operate a computer for you, you can find a shop-fitter, but you've still got to know yourself what's right. Does it look right? For example, most people will tell you black with brown won't work, but it can be made to work. One of my ambitions is to inform people about all the elements you need to understand and learn in retail, so they're able to walk into a store and immediately see if, say, a cupboard's in the wrong place. Equally people need to understand and be involved in the whole process: how the goods are made, how you get them to market, to understand the logistics, to know how the whole thing works. This more rounded training is essential if you want to be in the retail business.'

I would certainly start in retail if I had my time again. I love it because it answers a lot of the issues that are naturally in me. I'm interested in buying and selling. I'm interested in experiential and spatial issues. And I like the science of semiotics and what makes people buy. Being an inherently impatient person, I'm passionate about change and even more passionate about speed of change, which is just as well, because this is at the heart of the constant search to keep your customers interested in what you stand for.

Retail requires a good degree of intellect, but not so much that you need to lock yourself in a cold dark room to draft a contract like a lawyer, or an accountant, who really needs to close himself away to think hard about something. It's savvy, streetwise, commercial intelligence rather than academic intellect. There are no absolute answers in retail, just degrees of getting millions of things right or wrong.

It also demands considerable organisational ability. I can't think of many other organisations that are as good as supermarkets at getting the right thing to the right people at the right time. In my household, we can't stop fresh fruit from going off in the week we bought it. I know supermarkets have science on their side, but how do they buy, pick, transport and sell all those exotic fruits without having to throw half the soggy ones away before the shop opens. Retail is a huge logistical exercise. Several retailers have cited poor logistics, or even something as prosaic as warehousing, as the root cause of poor profits. You have to be good at organisation in retail and, if you are, you'll get the opportunity to learn from the true masters once you're in there.

Retail is not for the work-shy. It favours the hard working. Perhaps the biggest thing my parents gave me was a strong work ethic. They always used to tell me, *'You'll get nothing unless you work for it.'* They also ensured I got this message, by sending me to work as soon as got back from school, delivering goods to our customers (all part of the service) and worst of all delivering paraffin in five-gallon drums. I remember often not getting back until eight o'clock on cold winter evenings and only then sitting down to do my homework with paraffin fumes emanating from my hands. There were times when I felt hard done by, but the work ethic I picked up has sustained me through my career. Retail is not for the fainthearted.

I asked some of the retailers and retail gurus that I interviewed for this book for advice to anyone embarking on a career in retail or thinking of doing so.

This is what they had to say.

'Retail is not to be undertaken lightly – to be good at it you've got to be passionate about it. It's not just a job you drift into. You've got to really think about it because it's a great career. People I've talked to and met say it's transformed their lives and the way they think about themselves. It takes a certain sort of energy to get to the top in the retail business. You clearly have to be very good with people. If you're running even a medium sized supermarket you've probably got two or three hundred people working for you, and so how you get on with your team of people is critically important. The same is true of higher up the business; a good retail board is a good team. It is a people business.'
(Neill Denny, former editor of Retail Week)

'Retail is a fantastic business. When I was growing up, retailing was quintessentially the small business, but now it's completely different. It's very, very challenging. It's a mixture of art and science. Art because you can't run a retail business out of a theoretical book. Retail will always be about judgement, and a lot of judgement is intuitive. The science of it is going to get bigger, because in making those judgements you need intuition, but more and more you're going to need to validate it. The margin for error is narrowing. For bright people, it's a fantastic area to go into. It's an area where the rewards are going to get better and better, because the differences between mediocre management and really good management are fundamental. Retail needs desperately better quality people, better quality management, more objectivity and more science to go with the vital merchanting skills.' (Richard Hyman, Managing Director, Verdict)

'It's a fantastic job. Retail is often slightly looked down on as a career path, but people need to look beyond that and see what being involved in retail means. I can't think of any other job where you get as much flexibility in such a breadth of functions and so much contact with your own customers. I would find it very difficult to head up marketing for a packaged goods company, where my customers were owned by the retailer, meaning that I would have to rely on focus groups and research to tell me what was going on as opposed to being able to walk round the shop and have a look.' (Andrew Woodward, Marketing Director, John Lewis)

'The one thing that strikes me above all else about the most successful retailers is how obsessed they are with detail and the in-store experience. I love the fact that you can never set up a meeting with a retailer on a Friday because they're all in the stores. They will turn down invitations to events on Thursday night in London, because they need to be in a store in Scotland the next morning. It's that commitment, attention to detail, paranoia and always putting themselves in their customer's position, that's the mark of every successful retailer.' (Tim Danaher, Editor, Retail Week)

'It's a fulfilling career, certainly at HMV. The options of working in a record store have changed. You can now manage so many diverse functions: people, customers, developments in IT, finance, accounting – it is very multi-talented and multi-tasked.' (John Taylor, Marketing Director, HMV)

'We spend so much of our time at work or on our way to work or thinking about work that not to enjoy it is, to me, a catastrophe. Retail connects with everybody at some level. It's one of the few industries that touches everyone. There's something in it for everyone.' (Peter Williams, former CEO, Selfridges)

"Retailers don't need reports, they want answers on a page. They need to react to situations very quickly. They make mistakes, but learn from those mistakes. Never make those mistakes twice, but be prepared to make mistakes rather than do nothing. If you walk the stores enough and if you watch your competition enough you know instinctively what to do. The good retailers are instinctive. You've got to trust your gut and go for it.' (Maureen Johnson, Managing Director, The Store)

It's fun and you can move very quickly in it, but there is an awful lot of detail. You have to be passionate and care about what your customer wants down to the minutest possible detail. Listening to Tim Mason (Marketing Director at Tesco) talking about his finest range of lasagne the other day really brought home just how much you have to care about it.' (Tristia Clarke, Marketing Director, Carphone Warehouse)

It's the most enjoyable industry I've ever been involved in. You've got to love being competitive. Every day is a race to beat the other guy, more than in any other job I can think of.' (David Simons, Chairman, Littlewoods Shop Direct Group)

Philip Green, owner of Arcadia Group, BHS et al, said:

'If you like meeting people...

If you like change...

If you like speed...

If you like being on a regular rollercoaster...

If you like the adrenalin pump...

If you like any of these things, then you should be in this business, because every day there is something great happening or you've got to make it happen.'

Picking up on this, and with due respect to Rudyard Kipling -

If you can grasp the commercial fundamentals: 'that what you buy something for' and 'what you sell it for' is what it's all about...

If, especially having read this book, you know the art of adding value...

If you enjoy people, and enjoy being part of a team. You can't be a one-man retailer; if you're going to be successful, you've got to have other people doing it for you...

If you're intuitive and learn to trust your gut reaction...

If you can find your way around obstacles with solutions that answer the problem and also leave enough leeway for others to use their own initiative...

If you can continue to learn everyday and retain your restlessness to always make things better...

If you can do all these things and many more, then, my son, you'll be a great retailer.

Nowadays the rewards are great.

They weren't, but they are now.

Look at America where, over the past fifteen years, retail has grown to become a real driving force.

That's what's happening over here now.

A retailer, Wal-Mart, is now the biggest company in the world.

The retailer is king. And the brand is his crown.

Index: Names, Brands & Highlights

Selected highlights

If you only remember one thing

People buy	28
Integrity	62
Great retailers	99
Staff	131
Branding Device	162
Price	192
Standing for something	221

Key observation

Great retailers	105

Key point

People buy	16
Add value	23
Brand essence	33
First impressions	41
Reassurance	51
Trust to dust	56
Belief	58
Essential truth	67
Conviction	70
Learning	89
Championing	106
Behaviours	124
Understanding	125
Stands for	127
Right direction	129
People skills	139
On side	146
Reality	151
Retailer's armoury	156
Customer aspirations	186
Value	187

Seeing the world	196
The benefit	203
New possibilities	205
Permission to believe	216

Key question

Customer turning	19

Learning tip

Company history	30
Giving confidence	50,
Listen with intelligence	95
Your buyers	110

Points to consider

Company's name	31
Carrier bags	35
Keeping promises	43
Creative messaging	72
Recruiting to fit	74
Doing things	79
Perfect layouts	168
Staff centric	208
Building authority	229

Provocation

Real people	103
Overall impression	159
Vicious circle	191

Questions to consider

Staying fresh	47
Talked about	113
Like-minded	136,
Different impressions	154
Less is more	158
Different and better	195

Bibliography and further reading

Barker, Paul . The New Statesman 15.11.99

Bedbury, Scott. 'A brand new world', Penguin Books 2003

Burkeman, Oliver. 'The miracle of Almhult', The Guardian 17.06.04

Burney, Ellen. 'Topshop's lofty status', WWD (Feb 2003)
article from Thomson Gale

Caulfield, John. National Home Centre News, (March 22 1999)

Clark, Emma. 'A woman's touch for Peter Jones', BBC News 29.08.04

Conti, Samantha & Burney, Ellen. 'Catering to the masses',
WWD (Jan 2004) article from Thomson Gale

Davidson, Andrew. 'Smart Luck', Financial Times Prentice Hall 2002

Forbes.com, 'No follower of fashion' 25.11.02

Freeman, Hadley. 'Riding the retail revolution',
The Guardian Weekend 23.10.04

Freiberg, Kevin & Jackie 'Nuts!' Texere Publishing 2001

Glancey, Jonathan. Top of the blobs', The Guardian 1.09.03

Gravatt, Simon and Morgan, Jane. 'Forever Young.
Immortalising the Entrepreneurial Instinct', 2001

Hall, Amanda. Real Business, June 2001

Hammond, Richard. 'Smart Retail. How to turn your store into
a sales phenomenon', Pearson Education Ltd 2003

Handy, Charles. 'The Hungry Spirit', Hutchinson London 1997

Horyn, Cathryn. 'She's a Topshop Girl', New York Times 11.07.04

Hyman, Richard. 'The Retail roller-coaster: Message from the high street', Market Leader, Summer 2002

Hytner, Nicholas. 'When the message doesn't get through' The Guardian, 18.04.05

Interbrand 2000. The Future of Brands, Macmillan press

Jones, Robert. 'The Big Idea', Harper Collins 2000

Koehn, Nancy F. 'Brand New'. How Entrepreneurs Earned Consumers' Trust from Wedgwood to Dell', Harvard Business School Publishing Corporation 2001

Krass, Peter. 'The Best Way to Build a brand', 1997, appearing in 'The Book of Entrepreneurs Wisdom', published by John Wiley & Sons Inc, 1999

Lannon, Judie 'Welcome to the Brand Bazaar', World Advertising Research Centre Ltd and The Marketing Society

McLuhen, Marshall. 'Understanding Media' 1964

Morgan, Adam. 'Eating the Big Fish. How challenger brands can compete against brand leaders', 1999 John Wiley & Son's Inc.

Olins, Wally 'On Brand', Thames & Hudson, 2003

Pascal, Blaise. Lettres Provinciales (1657)

Peters, Tom. Reader's Digest 1995

Ray, Alastair. Financial Times 08.04.02

Richer, Julian. The Richer Way, Richer Publishing, 2001

Schickel, Richard. The Disney Version, Simon & Schuster 1968

Service, Robert W. Songs of a Sourdough (1907)

Showalter, Elaine. Emile Zola, Au Bonheur Des Dames (The Ladies Paradise), 2004 Penguin Group (USA) Inc.

Simmons, John. 'My Sister's a Barista', Cyan Communications, 2004

Smith, Shaun. 'Experiencing the brand and branding the experience', Admap article reprinted from WARC

The Constitution of the John Lewis partnership, ninth edition reprinted April 2004, original version 1929

The Economist, 'Reinventing the store – the future of retailing' 22.11.03

The Guardian 'How to be cool (or which brands buy status)', 29.09.04

The Guardian, 14.06.04

The New Statesman, 'Not knowingly undersold – employee partnership in business' 15.11.99

The Sunday Times 100 Best Companies to Work For, 07.03.04

The Times. 'Building on a brand' 13.01.03

Trout, Jack 'The Power of Simplicity: A Management Guide to Cutting Through the Nonsense and Doing Things Right'

Van Tongeren, Michel. 'Retail Branding. From stopping power to shopping power', BIS publishers Amsterdam

Vincent, Sally. 'How I Did It', The Guardian Weekend, 23.10.04

Waterstone, Tim. Director magazine, June 2004

Wilde, Oscar. Lady Windermere's Fan 1892

Williamson, John. 'Brand New World' Wolf Olins website